The Bilingual Revolution Series

A BILINGUAL REVOLUTION FOR AFRICA

Ayé Clarisse Hager-M'Boua and Fabrice Jaumont
(Editors)

CALEC - TBR Books

New York - Paris

Copyright © 2023 by Ayé Clarisse Hager-M'Boua and Fabrice Jaumont

All rights reserved. No part of this publication may be reproduced, distributed, or transmitted in any form or by any means, without prior written permission.

TBR Books is a program of the Center for the Advancement of Languages, Education, and Communities. We publish researchers and practitioners who seek to engage diverse communities on topics related to education, languages, cultural history, and social initiatives.

CALEC - TBR Books
750 Lexington Avenue, 9thfloor
New York, NY 10022
USA
www.calec.org | contact@calec.org
www.tbr-books.org | contact@tbr-books.org

ISBN 978-1-63607-376-7 (Hardback)
ISBN 978-1-63607-220-3 (Paperback)
ISBN 978-1-63607-377-4 (eBook)

Library of Congress Control Number: 2022922354

Cover photo © Annie Spratt, School children in Sierra Leone, following the Ebola outbreak.

Cover Design © Nathalie Charles

TABLE OF CONTENTS

Praises i

Acknowledgment vii

Preface by *Yao Ydo, Director of UNESCO International Bureau of Education* 1

Introduction. *Ayé Clarisse Hager-M'Boua & Fabrice Jaumont* 5

I. LANGUAGE AND CULTURAL IDENTITY

1. Creating space for students' linguistic and cultural heritage in the French classroom: The example of the FHLP in the United States. *Agnès Ndiaye Tounkara* 13

2. Assets and advantages of bilingualism: The acquisition of French as a foreign language. *Ayé C. Hager-M'Boua, Ama E. Flora M'Baye & Pascaline A. Kouamé* 23

3. Bilingual revolution in sub-Saharan Africa. Particularities, scope, limits and perspectives. *Mbacké Diagne* 37

4. Mother, teach me: On the importance and possibility of decolonial multilingual education through African mother tongues. *Djeneba D. Bagayoko* 48

II. BI-CULTURALISM: AFRICAN CULTURE AND EUROPEAN CULTURE

5. The place of heritage languages in the Cameroonian and Ontario school systems: the current state and a prospective view. *Carole Fleuret & Julia E. Ndibnu-Messina* 63

6. Our languages in school, that's like a bar of African gold': Parents' and teachers' visions for multilingual education in Côte d'Ivoire. *Michelle L. Solorio* 79

7. Translanguaging in indigenous Kenyan languages: Include all learners no silencing. *Brenda A. Wawire* 92

8. Improving the quality of education in Africa using African languages for teaching. *Maria J. Aaron* 102

III. MULTILINGUALISM / LANGUAGE EQUITY

9. The urgent need for reorientation with regards to multilingual education advocacy in Africa. *Daniel N. Obah* 115

10. Multilingual teachers for the multilingual classroom. *Pierre de Galbert & Cornelius Wambi Gulere* 122

11. Multilingual glossaries for teaching and learning: an initiative at the University of South Africa. *Feziwe Shoba & Koliswa Moropa* 132

12. Multilingual education for improved foreign language acquisition: The importance of using students' native languages for learning foreign languages. *Tony V. Muzau* 150

IV. BILINGUAL EDUCATION: MOTHER TONGUE / FRENCH; MOTHER TONGUE / ENGLISH

13. The need for bilingual education for the promotion of regional integration of communities in the eastern part of the Democratic Republic of Congo. *Félicien M. Maisha* 169

14. Tips from the hen: Bilingual school as a social project. *Thomas Bearth et al.* 180

15. The power of multiliteracy in The Gambia and Ghana. *Ari Sherris & Joy K. Peyton* 193

16. The challenges and relevance of tone didactics. *Venance Tokpa* 214

17. Fulfulde-French bilingual education: Advantages and solutions to the difficulties encountered. *Djibrila Tetereou* 224

Conclusion *Ayé Clarisse Hager-M'Boua & Fabrice Jaumont* 238

About the authors 245

References 251

Index 273

About TBR Books 285

About CALEC 287

Praises

The International Organization of La Francophonie (OIF) has been involved in bilingual education for more than 20 years, notably with its "École et Langues Nationales en Afrique" (ELAN), in English "School and National Languages in Africa" program which involves more than 7 million students.

This book illustrates the strength of this approach in different linguistic contexts, particularly in French-speaking Africa where multilingualism is a daily reality in which the French language contributes to the dynamic synergy for the development of quality education and the promotion of cultural and linguistic diversity. Two pillars of sustainable development and peace.

— Zahra Kamil Ali, Permanent Representative of the International Organization of La Francophonie for the Americas.

This book is a welcome addition to the Bilingual Revolution series. It problematizes how the robust individual multilingualism so prevalent throughout the African continent often conflicts with the monolingual language ideologies that form the basis of most educational practices. The various chapters emphatically and convincingly argue for prioritizing the lived experiences of multilingual students and for valorizing their impressive linguistic repertoires in academic settings and in society in general. These case studies not only elucidate important phenomena in various African countries, but also offer valuable models to the rest of the world.

— Maya Angela Smith, Associate Professor, University of Washington, Seattle, WA, USA. Author of *Senegal Abroad* (2019) and *Sénégalais de l'étranger* (2022)

This book not only stands out as a call for promoting bi/multilingualism in education but also offers great insights into the importance of languages in the education we offer our children. The chapters in the book provide evidence that children underperform in schools not because they do not have the ability to learn, but because they struggle with the languages used in school. The numerous case studies presented in the book emphasize the success of code-switching, particularly in early grades, for quality teaching and learning.

The book serves as a reminder that languages are vehicles for culture, and if we do not include the learners' languages in the code-switching education we offer them, then we are dismissing their culture, treating it as non-existent. In addition, the book presents great examples of how multilingualism is used in different contexts where Africa's many languages co-exist with the colonial languages that dominate education systems. It is my hope that policymakers will take note and use this information to inform and shape policies that promote, encourage, and provide space for bi/multilingualism in their education systems.

— Teboho Moja, Professor, New York University, USA and University of the Western Cape, South Africa

A Bilingual Revolution for Africa is a groundbreaking book that delves into the fundamental role of language in shaping our social world and our sense of identity. The authors expertly demonstrate the innate ability of human beings to learn language and the crucial role that the native or first language plays in child development, particularly in multilingual environments such as Africa. They highlight the link between our thoughts and the use of our native language and show how the historical and cultural knowledge and know-how of different communities shape the way in which individuals understand and interpret the world around them.

The book also offers a fresh perspective on the importance of education programs, language policies, and multilingualism, and provides a blueprint for creating more inclusive and empowering educational environments that promote multilingualism as a valuable asset. A must-read for anyone interested in the power of language and its impact on human development.

> — Jane Ross, International Educator and Author of *Two Centuries of French Education in New York* (2020) and *Deux siècles d'éducation française à New York* (2022).

This series of essays on the integration of indigenous languages and cultures into teaching in sub-Saharan Africa constitutes an excellent starting point for educators, researchers and policy makers reflecting on how applications and models of mother tongue and dual-language education can be applied to linguistically diverse African education contexts. *A Bilingual Revolution for Africa*, while contributing insights into multilingual education in sub-Saharan Africa, embraces the diverse and complex ways in which such an education approach actually unfolds.

The authors, often actively involved in delivering the multilingual education solutions at the core of this book, provide yet further evidence of the importance of embedding African languages in education. In particular, they underline the role multilingual education in sub-Saharan Africa can play in fostering inclusiveness in education, sustaining and/or promoting access to knowledge, and more broadly enabling greater social justice and economic growth at societal level. The rich account of the ways indigenous languages can be integrated in education systems also pointedly reveals that multilingual education approaches in Africa reflect the multilingualism in most homes. This aptly reminds us that such education approaches are best understood as attempts to bring what goes on 'outside' of classroom daily—for example, in the playground, the market, the streets, and the home—inside.

> — Clyde Ancarno, Senior Lecturer in Applied Linguistics, King's College London, UK

The evidence in favor of mother tongue-based multilingual education is not new, yet such education is the exception rather than the norm in far too many places in Africa. *A Bilingual Revolution for Africa* makes the case for education that incorporates the use of the mother tongue, but it does more than just advocate for this approach. The articles in this volume address, first of all, *why* "first language first" education is important. Some resistance to bi-/multilingual education is due to a lack of understanding of its importance and value. But the authors do not stop with why, they also address the *how*: "I'm convinced, but how do you go about it?" Some just do not think it can be done, and the *how* facet of this book gives them hope that it *can* be done.

There is attention to policy, to practice, to materials, teacher training, and deployment. There are a host of practical issues that must be dealt with. Many of the articles also address context. Not all situations are equal, and the peculiarities of each situation must be recognized, and principles gleaned that can be applied in other places. The Gambia, Côte d'Ivoire, Cameroon, Kenya, and South Africa all provide case studies that ground the theory in the reality of specific countries. Finally, I think it is important that most of the voices in this book are African. There is a tremendous amount of skill, experience, wisdom, and insight within Africa on this issue, and it is only right that Africans speak to Africans about this most important issue of how their children can best learn.

— Paul S. Frank, Senior Advisor, SIL LEAD, Dallas, TX, USA

It is ironic that bilingual education can be deemed revolutionary for Africa, where individual multilingualism is the norm. But in African schools, monolingualism has been not only usual but revered as policy, if not practice. This book shining light on exceptions to that pattern is very welcome as African educators struggle to shake off the weight of school language policy and practices rooted in colonialism and persisting stubbornly to this day. The chapters outline arguments for the new multilingualism at school that are rooted in different countries' realities; and they present profiles in practical terms—how curriculum and learning materials entail and support bilingualism, how teachers and administrators use multiple languages naturally in their work with each other and their students, how challenges can be confronted and overcome, what parents believe about mother-tongue education, and more. Readers who are well-versed in approaches to multilingual education for African students will appreciate the broad view this book provides in terms of languages and countries, as well as approaches to modifying and remedying the language policies of the past.

The authors make the point that mother-tongue-based bilingual education is not a frill. It is essential to improving education: improving systems, improving teaching and learning, improving the relevance of schools and schooling to social cohesion and national development. And it is disruptive: It is key to ending under-performing or failed praxis. This is the sense in which bilingual education in Africa is revolutionary. The revolution is justified in these chapters by references to the partiality of teaching and learning in officially monolingual classrooms where children comprehend discussions, texts, and tests only partially and teachers understand teacher guides and curricula only partially because they are not proficient in the language of school. The result is partial success where children pass on to the next grade with partial academic knowledge and skills, passively memorizing facts, but being unable to develop deep understanding. In schools that use students' own languages as they acquire others, high quality instruction can support integration of new knowledge with what learners already know. The chapters in this book—many of them written by African researchers and educators with a stake in improving education in their own countries--show what that looks like in reality.

— Carolyn Adger, Senior Fellow, Center for Applied Linguistics, Washington, DC, USA

The Bilingual Revolution Series

The Bilingual Revolution: The Future of Education is in Two Languages (2017) *by* Fabrice Jaumont (available in 11 languages)

Salsa Dancing in Gym Shoes (2019) by Tammy Oberg de la Garza and Alyson Leah Lavigne (available in 2 languages)

The Gift of Languages: Paradigm Shift in U.S. Foreign Language Education (2019) by Kathleen Stein-Smith and Fabrice Jaumont (available in 3 languages)

Two Centuries of French Education in New York: The Role of Schools in Cultural Diplomacy (2020) by Jane Flatau Ross (available in 2 languages)

Navigating Dual Immersion: A Teacher's Companion for the School Year and Beyond (2022) by Valerie Sun

Bilingual Children: Families, Education, and Development (2022) by Ellen Bialystok (available in 3 languages)

Conversations on Bilingualism (2022) by Fabrice Jaumont (available in 3 languages)

A Bilingual Revolution for Africa (2023), co-edited by Ayé Clarise Hager M'Boua and Fabrice Jaumont (available in 2 languages.

Multilingual Learning for the Arabic-speaking World (2024), co-edited by Carine Allaf, Fabrice Jaumont, and Selma Talha Jebril.

Guiding Teachers into Bilingual Education (2024) edited by Valérie Fialais and Reseda Streb

Acknowledgment

The editors extend their gratitude to all those who have supported and contributed to this book project, as well as to advocates of multilingualism and bilingual education in Africa and beyond. This project has been a truly rewarding experience, bringing together a diverse range of voices and perspectives through engaging conversations with the chapter authors.

The editors express their appreciation to Yao Ydo, Director of UNESCO's International Bureau of Education, for writing the Foreword, showing keen interest and encouragement, and to the IBE's team for their efforts in promoting multilingualism and bilingual learning worldwide. Particular thanks go Zahra Kamil Ali, Permanent Representative of the International Organization of La Francophonie for the Americas, Québec; Maya Angela Smith, Associate Professor, University of Washington, Seattle, WA; Carolyn Adger, Senior Fellow, Center for Applied Linguistics, Washington, DC; Paul S. Frank, Senior Advisor, SIL LEAD, Inc. Dallas, TX; Clyde Ancarno, Senior Lecturer in Applied Linguistics, King's College London, United Kingdom; Jane Ross, Vice-President, Center for the Advancement of Languages, Education, and Communities, New York; and Teboho Moja, Professor, New York University, United States of America and University of the Western Cape, South Africa for providing advanced praises.

The editors extend their heartfelt thanks to the chapter authors for sharing their personal stories, perspectives, and experiences: Agnès Ndiaye Tounkara, Ama E. Flora M'Baye, Pascaline A. Kouamé, Mbacké Diagne, Djeneba D. Bagayoko, Carole Fleuret, Julia Ndibnu-Messina Ethe, Michelle L. Solorio, Brenda Wawire, Maria J. Aaron, Daniel N. Obah, Pierre de Galbert, Cornelius Wambi Gulere, Feziwe Shoba, Koliswa Moropa, Tony V. Muzau, Félicien M. Maisha, Thomas Bearth, Goh Soupou, Lika Sopouh Legrand, Fan Monsia Diomandé, Siaba Sidibé, A.Tokpa Gouesse, Ari Sherris and Joy K. Peyton, Venance Tokpa, Djibrila Tetereou.

The editors also extend their thanks to The Center for the Advancement of Languages, Education, and Communities, as well as its board of directors, advisory council, and global supporters for their belief in the value of multilingualism, cross-cultural understanding, and linguistic empowerment. Special thanks to Caitlin Leib and Megan Evans for their assistance in revising and preparing the manuscript.

—Ayé Clarisse Hager M'Boua and Fabrice Jaumont

Preface

Yao YDO

Director of International Bureau of Education,

UNESCO, Geneva

If you don't understand, how can you learn?

Currently, out of seven thousand one hundred languages, nearly three thousand are in danger of extinction and only through education can they be saved. Moreover, 40% of the global population does not have access to education in a language they understand, exhibiting a precarious situation for global education. In Africa's context, eight out of ten children begin school in a language other than the one they speak at home between the ages of 0 and 6 years old. Indigenous people and speakers of minority group languages have been the most impacted by these education inequalities, which have been exacerbated by school closures during the Covid-19 pandemic. Ayé Clarisse Hager-M'Boua and Fabrice Jaumont's *A Bilingual Revolution for Africa* perfectly links the challenges of deep colonial legacies to the complex questions facing Africa's linguistic education system today.

The September 2022 United Nations Transforming Education Summit provided an opportunity to elevate education to the top of the global political agenda and sow the seeds of educational transformation in a rapidly changing world. The Summit determined that delivering on the Transformation of Education requires the promotion of traditional local cultures and endogenous knowledge and the decolonization of education. The decolonization of education involves diagnosing current curricula to reveal biases and limitations caused by colonial legacies, as well as creating an understanding of how they have shaped educational policies. Using mother-tongues as a medium of instruction and developing the linguistic capacities of education systems throughout Africa are how these key initiatives can be delivered. Indeed, language in education has the power to achieve and realize Africa's collective future potential while protecting each community's intricacies, individuality, and identity.

Multilingual education that incorporates the use of the mother tongue is key at all levels of holistic educational development. Indeed, it allows youth to fulfill their potential by providing more opportunities to access an education. In the classroom, it fuses understanding and culture by attributing value to varying linguistic identities and creating an environment where students can foster deeper relationships both to the academic content and their comrades. Using and recognizing African mother tongues in academic institutions transcends the confines of school, instills learners with pride and confidence, and empowers them to thrive in all aspects of life. For every child, the mother tongue is the foundation of their knowledge, the connection to their historical culture, and must become an integral part of their future.

Based on this premise, *A Bilingual Revolution for Africa* seeks to promote a multilinguistic education system to invigorate socioeconomic development while upholding and preserving individual cultures and traditions. As adeptly expressed by Djeneba Deby Bagayoko, languages encapsulate "people's thoughts, philosophy, view and understanding of the world." Preventing their path to extinction is the key to safeguarding patriotic values and the sense of belonging in African communities. Moreover, incorporating mother-tongue use and resources into educational systems and the wider society presents new opportunities for job creation investment in human capital and other fruitful activities that can be derived from the mother-tongue, such as alphabetizing languages and creating textbooks.

From these foundations, the education system can be revolutionized to empower students in their academic development by firmly rooting both mother-tongue and national languages in the curriculum and educational processes. The ideas subsequently outlined by the authors reflect a bilingual educational approach that will allow students to truly understand and access the content and cultural know-how they are taught while developing their capacities in a national language. This would simultaneously bolster the holistic development of future generations and, because of increasingly fluid communication, consolidate bridges across the African region.

The educational reforms under way in various African countries must prioritize the transformation of curricula to train competent Africans endowed with universal values who are rooted within and proud of their culture. Through several pilot projects, UNESCO has been working, for several decades, to promote multilingual education and the use of national languages in the first years of learning. These projects have shown that when a child starts school in the language he speaks with his mother, he attains more throughout the rest of his academic career, including mastery of other languages such as French and English. Not only does the inclusion of the mother tongue in early childhood education have positive psycho-pedagogical, emotional, and cognitive impacts, it provides an unrivaled channel through which local cultures and values transpire within schools.

However, there is no denying that challenges to this vision of transforming educational systems throughout Africa lie ahead. The first hurdle includes dispelling current false perceptions regarding the paradigm of bilingual and mother tongue education. Significant research leading to the production of invaluable publications like *A Bilingual Revolution for Africa* must continually challenge misconceptions and doubts about the infallible rewards of providing bilingual education. Pedagogical methods and learning resources must also be adapted to deliver this goal. The evolving attitudes toward bilingual education can then act as a vector for building peace in the minds of men and women.

I would like to thank and congratulate all the authors and contributors involved in the making of *A Bilingual Revolution for Africa*. This work sets the current multilingual scene excellently in the African context while tackling difficult and complex questions about the nature and necessity of a bilingual approach to education.

In addition, by studying many countries, the authors provide incredibly detailed insight into the linguistic approaches and needs of a variety of states while astutely linking them back to the wider African community. This work provides a vital contribution to the cause of multilingual education and its goal of empowering future generations.

Introduction

Ayé Clarisse HAGER-M'BOUA and Fabrice JAUMONT

Language is a powerful tool that shapes our identity, connects us to our culture, and allows us to understand and appreciate the diversity of human cultures. In Africa, there are over 2,000 different languages spoken, making it the most linguistically diverse continent on the planet. This creates a unique and complex environment for education, particularly for children who are in the early stages of language acquisition. The native or first language of a child plays a critical role in their cognitive development and perception of the world around them. It is through language that children learn to communicate, understand their environment, and make sense of their experiences. Children who have access to their native language during the early stages of language acquisition tend to develop stronger cognitive abilities, which can benefit their academic performance and overall well-being.

However, despite the clear benefits of multilingualism and the importance of native language in child development, many education systems in Africa continue to prioritize colonial languages such as English, French, and Portuguese over indigenous languages. This results in a lack of educational resources and opportunities for children who speak their native language, which can lead to educational inequality and a disconnection from their cultural identity.

In response to this, there is a growing need for multilingual education programs that value and support students' linguistic and cultural backgrounds. These programs prioritize the use of the child's native language as a means of instruction and aim to promote multilingualism as a valuable asset. They also recognize the importance of preserving indigenous languages and cultures, and work to ensure that these languages are not lost due to the dominance of colonial languages.

Overall, the need for multilingual education programs in Africa is stronger than ever. By prioritizing the use of the child's native language and promoting multilingualism, these programs can support the cognitive development and academic success of children, as well as the preservation of linguistic and cultural diversity.

How can we re-evaluate and re-conceptualize the way we approach and think about multilingualism in education? What can we learn from Africa's linguistic situation and apply to other multilingual regions? How can we create more inclusive and empowering educational environments that promote multilingualism as a valuable asset rather than a hindrance? These questions will be explored in this book.

The authors, including educators, researchers, and field workers, provide diverse perspectives on bilingualism and education in Africa. They discuss local applications of various models of bilingual education and strategies for promoting and expanding these programs in different countries and sectors. The importance of African languages in the quest for linguistic integration and sustainable development throughout the continent is emphasized. The authors argue for the development of African languages and their use as scholarly languages to enhance overall development. The mission of promoting bilingualism, intercultural understanding, and the empowerment of multilingual families and linguistic communities through education, knowledge, and defense is crucial for the development of African languages and their integration into society.

This comprehensive work, comprising of 17 essays organized into four distinct categories - bi/multilingual programs, cultural diversity, reduction of inequalities, and the expansion of access to quality education - presents a positive and constructive vision for the future while addressing and dispelling the myths and preconceptions surrounding bi/multilingualism and education in Africa. The text specifically focuses on the ignorance and obstacles that have hindered the development of bilingual learning as a strategy for inclusivity, equity, and quality, as well as an effective means to achieve economic objectives such as capacity building and economic growth, and to develop the linguistic skills of children from diverse linguistic communities in Africa's multilingual environment.

Regarding bi/multilingual programs, the text delves into the advantages of Dual-Language Learning, through several different contributions. Drawing on the results of research work conducted on multilingualism, it highlights that dual-language immersion programs facilitate biliteracy - the ability to speak, listen, read, and write with ease (skills) in two languages, by taking advantage of the propensity for young children to acquire a language. This emphasizes the importance of bilingual education in fostering multilingualism in children, providing them with a competitive edge in today's globalized world.

In her essay, Agnès Ndiaye Tounkara, the coordinator of the French Heritage Language Program (FHLP), addresses the importance of linguistic heritage and proper practices for its acquisition and preservation. The mission of the FHLP is to assist francophone students living in the United States in integrating into American society by valuing their French language heritage. This mission is echoed in the work of Clarisse Hager-M'Boua, Flora M'Baye, and Pascaline Kouamé, who discuss the use of the mother tongue and French as languages of instruction in public primary schools in rural areas of Côte d'Ivoire to improve the quality of education for young Africans. Mbacké Diagne also stresses the importance of the use of first languages in sub-Saharan Africa in his essay "A bilingual revolution in sub-Saharan Africa: Particularities, scope, and limits."

Djeneba Bagayoko, in her essay "Mother, teach me: On the importance and possibility of decolonial multilingual education through African mother tongues," emphasizes the role of the mother in ensuring the proper acquisition of a child's first language. This sentiment is echoed by the celebrated intellectual Gloria Anzaldúa, who states that "I am my language. If I cannot be proud of my language, I will not be proud of myself."

Carole Fleuret and Julia Ndibnu-Messina, in their essay "The place of heritage languages in the Cameroonian and Ontario school systems: the current state and prospective view," examine the challenges faced by students in Francophone schools in the province of Ontario in Canada with the arrival of Francophone immigrants, particularly those from sub-Saharan Africa. Michelle Solorio, in her case study "Our languages in school, that's like a bar of African gold: Parents' and teachers' visions for multilingual education in Côte d'Ivoire," explores the ideas of parents to roll out learning models of existing local languages and to construct an education system in which the use of a language in the classroom corresponds with its use in students' communities.

Brenda Wawire, through her work "Translanguaging in indigenous Kenyan languages: Including all learners, not silencing them," promotes and raises awareness of the importance of pedagogical practices of translanguaging that encourage the use of the indigenous languages of Kenya among readers and educational stakeholders for equity, inclusion, and better quality of education. Similarly, Marianna Aaron, in her work "Improving the quality of education in Africa using African languages for teaching," argues that the generalized use of English as a medium of instruction in the anglophones countries of Africa has led to a lack of quality education and that the use of African languages for teaching can improve the quality of education in Africa.

In his essay, Felicien Maisha addresses the question of why a mix or translanguaging of languages is allowed in schools. In his work, entitled "The need for bilingual education for the promotion of regional integration of the communities of the East of the Democratic Republic of Congo," Maisha argues that allowing a mix of languages in schools serves as a tool to promote linguistic cooperation among populations within the DRC, as well as with neighboring countries in Eastern Africa. This, in turn, ensures that bilingual students will have more employment opportunities and greater cultural and linguistic fulfillment.

Bearth and his collaborators also place an importance on "linguistic insecurity." They highlight the need for mother tongue literacy in early childhood, as demonstrated by Ari Sherris and Joy Peyton in a national project on the Gambia, as well as in a separate project on Ghana.

Furthermore, Venance Tokpa, through his essay "The challenges and relevance of tone didactics," addresses the concern for the transmission of tones to students in PEI schools in Côte d'Ivoire. He provides useful elements that can help to facilitate and improve the quality of teaching and learning of national languages in PEI public elementary schools.

Djibrila Tetereou, using the example of "Fulfulde-French bilingual education: advantages and solutions to the difficulties encountered," argues that dual-language education, i.e., a teaching program that utilizes both the mother tongue and a second or foreign language (such as English or French), is the only effective means of achieving inclusivity, equity, and quality education in Africa. His objective is to "show the advantages of Fulfulde-French bilingual education for pastoral populations that have been marginalized by the formal education system in Togo due to their mobility with cattle herds."

Overall, these authors and researchers highlight the importance of valuing and preserving linguistic heritage in education and the role of first languages in improving the quality of education for young Africans. They also address the challenges faced by students in multilingual and multicultural educational contexts and the importance of inclusive and equitable pedagogical practices. In general, they agree that promoting bilingual education and mother tongue literacy can have numerous benefits for both individuals and communities.

I - LANGUAGE AND CULTURAL IDENTITY

1. Creating space for students' linguistic and cultural heritage in the French classroom: the example of the FHLP in the United States.

Agnès NDIAYE TOUNKARA
FACE Foundation

Every year, hundreds of students recently immigrated from Africa or Haiti enter our French Heritage program classrooms in New York with mixed feelings: they are happy to be at school, relieved to find friends who speak their languages, full of anticipation and curiosity, but also fear. These students are only 15 to 18 years old, freshly arrived from Senegal, the Ivory Coast, or Guinea, in pursuit of the American dream and discovering an educational system radically different from their own, in a language they barely know how to speak. They speak Wolof, Bambara, or Susu and French, a language they often encountered for the first time in school despite dreaming, imagining, and thinking in their mother tongues. Those are also the languages they speak at home here in the United States with their parents or the family members who host them.

Nowhere, or very rarely in their future plans, does French appear. On the contrary, it is often seen as an obstacle in their path towards integration in a country where English seems like the only way to achieve their dreams and where their multilingualism is often presented as a deficiency, an impediment to their academic success. Moreover, the students don't speak the standard French, the Parisian French, with the 'right' accent; they frequently make errors in grammar and syntax, and, up until now, the teaching of the language has often focused on these shortcomings.

The mission of the French Heritage Language Program is: "to make French an asset that can help francophone students integrate into American society." This is an ambitious goal, in this context, one might say. However, the 'heritage approach' is particularly suited to the needs of these students and explains why this program has sustained the test of time and reached thousands of students in the past 17 years.

Indeed, our work is not only focused on teaching French; it is first and foremost about the reappropriation of the language by the students by adapting the content of our language classes to the realities of our students and allowing their national languages in the classroom, alongside French. It is also about deconstructing the linguistic insecurity acquired through years of traditional education in which the objective was the acquisition of a 'correct French.' And finally, it is truly an American, pragmatic approach embodied in our mission: to make French an academic and professional asset.

French becomes a part of the students' identity in our classrooms, the anchor that ties them to their cultures, the common thread between them and their francophone peers and, more widely, with the francophone world in its entirety, and a bridge leading them to integration into a society that is radically different from the one they come from.

Our hope is that our program serves as a model, generates reflections, and illustrates that it is possible to teach French without excluding the languages of the students. This is one of many paths towards a true form of bilingualism, in which French would no longer be considered only as an imposed, colonial language but also as a desired language that coexists with others.

The French Heritage Language Program (FHLP), despite its name in English, is a program of the French Embassy, hosted by the FACE Foundation (French American Cultural Exchange), a French American organization whose mission is to promote exchanges in the arts, education and culture between France and the United States. Its mission is francophone at its core, perfectly aligned with the cultural services of the French Embassy: to promote the French language around the world and grow the community of francophones and Francophiles in the United States. It also embodies a new reality that has been reaffirmed by President Macron and confirmed in the last report of the Francophone Observatory: The French language does not belong to France alone and the future of French will play out outside of France.

The program is also very American, a perfect example of philanthropy practiced in the United States: it was born as the initiative of a private, American philanthropist and former French professor, Jane Ross, who, after having identified a need for French courses in the International Network for Public Schools (INPS), collaborated with the cultural services at the French Embassy in the United States in order to create a program for newly immigrated students in the United States who receive their education in underfunded American schools where French is not offered. Today, the FHLP is funded by both the French government and private donations in the United States.

This unique, institutional model brings together private stakeholders, institutions, and public members, and allows them to establish partnerships with public and private bilingual schools and nonprofit organizations and to serve communities who are out of reach financially or geographically.

Since its establishment in 2005, this program has helped more than 5,000 young girls and boys in New York City, as well as those in Miami, Boston, and a few cities of Maine. In New York, the students meet after school to maintain and improve their skills in the language under the direction of a teacher, working in French on projects connected to their own cultural heritage and their realities as new immigrants to the United States. These students, too often faced with systemic challenges in their schools as African students, could reinforce their linguistic skills in French in a way that can, in return, help them to learn English. Multiple studies conducted in the United States have shown that students who learn to read in a second language can transfer their skills and overall comprehension from their mother tongue, facilitating their acquisition of other language skills in a second language. They also have a unique opportunity to capitalize on their skills in French at an advanced level (Advanced Placement French), potentially providing them with credits at universities. The program does not only help these young, francophone immigrants in preserving their French skills; it also facilitates their academic adaptation and their ability to make French an asset in their studies and their future professional life.

The FHLP also celebrates the diversity of the French speaking world and allows students to see themselves in the pedagogical resources which largely tap into their cultural heritage through literature, media, cinema, and theatre from their countries of origin. Finally, because the students are each at different levels of French, they tend to resort to the use of their mother tongues if they, for example, work in a group to understand a new concept.

French, initially seen only as an imposed language of colonizers, has become, for those students in the United States, a minority language, a heritage language. It is a language that allows these young francophones to maintain connections with their culture and their country of origin, to build bridges between them and the other francophones in school as well as the rest of the world, and their future professional life in a more and more globalized world.

In the United States, the term 'heritage language' is considered more inclusive and is favored over the term 'minority language' which tends to be the standard in Europe and often holds a certain stigma attached to "minority groups, immigrants, and indigenous peoples". This expression refers to a language spoken in the home in a context where another, majority language is spoken outside of the home. It encapsulates languages other than English, languages of immigrants, of refugees, and of native peoples. The speakers of heritage languages in the United States are individuals who are bilingual, at minimum, but often multilingual. They practice both the dominant language of the country where they live and their mother tongue(s), and their heritage language(s).

Joshua Fishman identified three types of heritage languages: indigenous heritage languages, migration heritage languages, and colonial heritage languages.

In the context of America, French is both a colonial heritage language and a migration heritage language, spoken by the children of immigrants from francophone countries who speak other languages at home. With education in English at all times, these children often speak a majority language more fluently than their heritage language(s).

The definitions of the term 'heritage language' vary as well: they range from extremely narrow definitions requiring a certain level of the language to more flexible definitions that only presuppose a connection, whatever this may be, between the speaker and the language. One of most frequently cited definitions of this concept comes from Guadalupe Valdes in an article published in 2001: she considers a 'heritage learner' to be "an individual who was raised in a family where a language other than English was spoken." In general, the speaker of a heritage language speaks this language but there are certainly cases where they do not. From time to time, these speakers are bilingual in the language their family speaks and English, but with different degrees of fluency. This definition stems from a view of bilingualism seen as a continuum along which the respective importance of an individual's two spoken languages varies following a certain number of factors, including time.

This perspective on bilingual competence as a linguistic repertoire of all spoken languages by an individual rather than the sum of two monolingual understandings has also been explored in Europe. Numerous works, less known because they had been written in French, attack the myth of the bilingual who masters a second language and is able to speak as if it is their native language. As early as 1997, multilingual proficiency and multiculturalism were being discussed by the European Council. However, it was in the United States where the research field around heritage languages was developing, starting with the principle that students who speak a heritage language not only have specific linguistic needs, but also psychological and emotional needs.

First and foremost, the 'heritage' approach is a critical outlook that supposes teachers are conscious of a fictious hierarchy existing between languages, created by relations of power and domination between different countries. It also supposes these teachers question the role of these power relations evidently present in the classroom. In heritage language classes, students and teachers are co-bearers of knowledge; the student is an expert of their maternal language and use it as a tool to acquire other skills.

The heritage approach is also a multicultural approach built on the premises that the cultural and linguistic capital of students are essential resources in the classroom, insuring the engagement of students in their process of learning. When the teacher adopts a co-learner position rather than an expert position, it encourages students to be comfortable with their identities, sending a strong message to the students that their cultural identities are valued and welcomed in classrooms, and showing they have something to bring to the learning environment.

We know that bilingual students are not the sum of two monolingual individuals who live side by side. That's why the heritage approach is also multilingual. It is therefore vital that the teacher creates, in class, an environment that encourages student's language practices and gives them authentic opportunities to use what they have in their repertoire. This also implies less airtight borders between languages and the use of metalinguistic practices like "code switching" (alternating between two languages in the same exchange) or "translanguaging" that relies on the idea that an individual who speaks multiple languages, in all situations where they can express themselves, doesn't choose one language or another but instead utilizes a complex language system, composed of all their language resources.

By bringing national languages into the classroom, students are sent a strong message that their cultural identities, carried by their national languages, are valued, which guarantees or encourages their active engagement in their learning. Some authors go further with this idea: when heritage language speakers don't see their identity reflected in classrooms, their learning suffers. In these situations, they aren't capable of connecting with the content presented in their lessons, causing them to become discouraged and lose their motivation to learn.

The 'heritage' approach is also socio-affective and considers the emotional and psychological needs of students. The modern hierarchy created between the different variations of languages and accents establishes linguistic insecurity among speakers that, from time to time, causes resistance to the use of a heritage language. Above all, they are criticized for their accent or for variations of the language they use, which are considered as incorrect.

This critical approach, this particular pedagogical practice, this multilingual environment where students and teachers learn together, are the ingredients guaranteeing the students' engagement in their learning. Not only does it allow the integration of the cultural dimensions of language, but it also acknowledges the sociolinguistic and identity dimensions involved.

This approach is particularly relevant in Africa where most students are multilingual and where the educational systems, inherited from colonial powers, were implemented without taking cultural and linguistic realities of the countries into consideration. Students come to schools where the language of education is completely unknown to them, armed with knowledge derived from their heritage language as well as resources that are often ignored. While they can speak French, they are frequently corrected on their accents or any variations of the language they may use. Our African-Francophone students practically all have the memory of a collar or other object they were forced to wear should they dare to speak their mother tongues in school. Senghor, in the 1960s, spoke of a "suffering felt by a child confronted with a foreign language when they arrive at school that destroys all their chances of succeeding."

Students come to the classroom with a linguistic and cultural identity; if they are able to see it in the curriculum and celebrated in class, they can adapt and participate in their own learning. This adaptation is, from my perspective, fundamental to the success of French teaching programs. This is true for our students in New York, but it is also true for African students who learn in French.

The other determining factor, largely influenced by the way in which learning is conducted, is the capacity of programs to maintain a desire for French. Indeed, for our students, the practice of French results in a permanent negotiation between learning English and maintaining other languages they speak in their homes. This determines that the desire to learn French must be proportional with a desire to maintain a connection with their original country, a desire to be a part of a francophone community but also a desire to have access to more academic and professional opportunities with the sentiment that their use of the language can award them tangible benefits.

In the United States, the desire to learn French is already present, both as a reflex of speakers to preserve their own culture in the face of another that can wipe out everything in its path and as a trait of union, a buoy of linguistic rescue, but also, from a more pragmatic point of view, like a strategy or an investment, a bet on bilingualism as an asset and on its ability to give its speakers an edge on the job market.

This is what I hear directly from students who often find themselves amongst francophones in their schools, who all have an anecdote about the friend they met on the first day of school who helped them to navigate their first few months in the United States; we also see it in our students' surveys highlighting the community our program has created for them, but also as an opportunity to differentiate between an academic or professional framework. With their parents, who don't want their children to lose their French, they see it as a link between their roots. I often hear the same from the representatives of francophone communities who contact us from Maine, Wisconsin, Michigan, or Georgia, wanting programs for their children born in the United States that don't speak French or for their francophone children who recently arrived and are beginning to lose their language skills.

In an African context, the desire to speak French has to be built up and directly linked to individual learning experiences, allowing the learners to create an image of the perfect speaker and establish a desire to belong to a francophone community. I borrow this notion of 'desire' from Francois Grin, who, in his COD (Capacity Opportunity Desire) model, defined it as one of the main ingredients of successful revitalization politics of minority languages. It is interesting, within an African context, to explore and reflect upon the conditions in which French can cohabitate with other national languages. It refers to, according to the author, the "subjective tendency of learners towards a motivation and particular behaviors as an investment of time, energy, or resources in order to learn a language because the mastery of it can establish concrete benefits, or, because there is, on the part of the learner, a subjective desire to be associated and take part in a community of speakers of the language in question."

In francophone Africa, the opportunities to use French and the benefits of its use can be abundant: according to research published in the latest report of the OIF, French is considered to be both important and indispensable, as a vehicle of knowledge, as a language of school and as a language of the elite. However, after conducting a survey for this report, it was found that 57% of individuals survey considered French as a language imposed upon them and, despite measures in place, 50% of learners in primary school in francophone Africa do not possess a sufficient level of competence in the language.

From my perspective, the capacity of the education systems to create the desire for this language will be the determining factor. We can't change the history of the establishment of the French language on the African continent, and, without a doubt, its influence has created complex perceptions and relationships we have with the language. On the other hand, we can change the way we teach it today and adopt a critical, multilingual, and multicultural approach where student's cultural and linguistic heritage has a space in the classroom. We can adapt the contents so it includes the local cultures and make a larger space for the inclusion of national languages. Only speakers can claim ownership of a language, recognize it, and have the desire to speak it.

What I am trying to do with this chapter is express my hope and to inspire reflections based on the experiences of the French Heritage Language Program. I am aware of the multiple obstacles we may face: the number of national languages, the daunting tasks to alphabetize in these languages, the needs of different formations of students – I could go on. I also see some models and glimmers of hope: the ELAN programs, for example, aims to improve the quality of primary school instruction in African countries since 2012. A francophone initiative promoting bilingual education, in particular in sub-Saharan African countries, ELAN programs promote the teaching of both the African languages and the French language. In France, there has been a greater emphasis on multilingualism in the field of education (a movement slightly forced by the presence of more and more multilingual, immigrant students in classrooms in France).

The OIF (Organisation Internationale de la Francophonie) has been promoting multilingualism and campaigning for the development of national languages since 1975. In its 2018 report, the OIF identified "the harmonious articulation between French and national languages" as being at the heart of the future of francophone Africa. The authors even go further and add that it is not about only a cultural reality, but a necessary condition in order to succeed in educational processes. The last report of 2022, after having shown that "the majority of French speakers and those who acquire their first understandings of the world in French live on the African continent," requiring us to recall "that it is necessary for students to recognize themselves in academic content, even if they have been operating in French." On the back of this report, we can read that history lessons should start by "our Malinke, Peul, and Kongo ancestors..." and I add that they should be taught in French, but also in Wolof, Fulani or Ewe.

2. Assets and Advantages of Bilingualism: The Acquisition of French as a Foreign Language

Clarisse HAGER-M'BOUA, Flora M'BAYE,
Pascaline KOUAME
Alassane Ouattara University

To face the challenges of the globalized world, Côte d'Ivoire attempts to achieve Sustainable Development Goal (SDG) 4 as follows: "Ensure inclusive and equitable quality education and promote lifelong learning opportunities for all". Indeed, national education is the pillar to reach the targets of each of the 17 sustainable development goals as we noticed through the 2030 Agenda. And so, the purpose of the Programme d'École Intégrée (PEI), a program for basic education from the MENA (Ministère de l'Éducation Nationale et de l'Alphabétisation) Côte d'Ivoire, is to use the mother tongue alongside French as the language of instruction. Therefore, there is a need to develop the selected languages (10 Ivorian languages), and to be codified for the PEI program, which would result in an "inclusive and equitable quality education" in Côte d'Ivoire by incorporating those 10 languages in addition to French, the official language of the country, in the educational system. The use of both mother tongue (L1) and French (L2), a simultaneous approach (unlike a sequential approach: L1, and later L2) in PEI schools is, in fact, an asset for harmonious literacy and numeracy development among public primary school students, mainly those living in rural Côte d'Ivoire.

Language plays a major role in the implementation and success of all sustainable development programs and projects in Sub-Saharan African countries, not only in terms of communication, but also in the involvement of different communities in this African multilingual environment. That is the reason why Bearth (2013) designates language as "the 4th leaf of the clover of sustainable development".

In fact, to be able to hold up over time, the economy of each country in Sub-Saharan Africa must have a qualified workforce, which means a population with skills in not only the language of communication (English or French), but also the necessary abilities: academic knowledge and know-h required by national and multinational companies as well as by the world economy. Unfortunately, many Sub-Saharan African countries do not have the conditions needed for an inclusive and equitable quality education and for lifelong learning opportunities for all as indicated (SDG 4). Likewise, professional training for capacity building of young people in the developing countries of Sub-Saharan Africa remains a big issue, mainly because of the language barrier. The language used for training is not the spoken language of many of the young people. In this chapter, we will first discuss biculturalism, defined as an asset for the populations of Sub-Saharan Africa, particularly for those in Côte d'Ivoire. François Grosjean reveals in his article titled *Quelques réflexions sur le biculturalisme* that among the many articles in linguistics, few scientific works have addressed the question of biculturalism. Indeed, although the term biculturalism is often used in literature on bilingualism, it often has no established definition, and its insertion in library files remains uncertain. Yet, the reality is that many bilinguals are bicultural. We will analyze some theoretical reflections discussed by the author for more clarity on this subject. Next, we will examine the advantages (both cognitive and linguistic) that bilinguals possess due to the double phonological system (alphabets), lexical knowledge, reading performance and text comprehension (cf. Floccia et al. 2018; Berens et al., 2013; Serra, 2007), considering a methodology for the acquisition of French, the official language of Côte d'Ivoire, as a foreign language. Since the 2000s, the Ivorian education system has gone through a crisis: most primary school students could not read or write. To remedy this, it will be necessary to revise and restructure education at its base; that is to say, literacy and numeracy must be acquired in the first years of primary school. Finally, we will illustrate the steps towards the acquisition of French from the mother tongue within the framework of a basic education program that uses both the mother tongue (L1) and French (L2) as languages of schooling during the first four years of primary school for instruction in reading and writing in French.

1. Assets of bilingualism

1.1 Bilingualism in Côte d'Ivoire

Studies on bilingualism conducted by Grosjean (cf. Grosjean, 1993) define bilingualism as "the capacity to produce significant statements in two (or more) languages, mastery in at least one form of linguistic competence (reading, writing, speaking, or listening) in another language, alternating between the use of multiple languages." Using this definition, we can understand that, in the entire world, the phenomenon of contact between languages is one of the most pertinent factors encouraging the bilingualism of an individual or a community. In sub-Saharan Africa, many countries are faced with the situation of bilingualism. Such is the case for Côte d'Ivoire, where the French language was diversified following contact with local/Ivorian languages. Indeed, the cohabitation of French and local/Ivorian languages has favored a linguistic amalgamation over the decades. This mix of languages has given birth to multiple varieties of French, specifically: Ivorian French, popular Ivorian French, and Nouchi (a pidgin). This diversity demonstrates the lack of mastery of standard French in all its contours by the Ivorian population. It should be noted that standard French or its varieties are used by the Ivorian population depending on the level of education (secondary school, high school, or university) or the living environment (urban area or rural area) of the population. For François Grosjean, a psycholinguist, bilinguals are "people who make use of two or more languages (or dialects) in their life on a day-to-day basis."

Grosjean explains that "this includes people who have an oral competence in one language and a writing competence in another." Following the definition of a bilingual individual given by the author, we can retain two categories of bilinguals in Côte d'Ivoire. The first category concerns the population who became bilingual through colonization. In fact, these are people who were originally monolinguals or even already bilinguals (use of two local languages), but who, in order to have full access to public life, became bilinguals or multilinguals out of necessity, adding French alongside their native language/s. In this way, the different roles assigned to the

French language make it the only medium of national identity and unity, the language of social promotion, the language of education, and the official language of the country. These multiple attributes of French have boosted the existence of different types of bilinguals. There are those who use multiple local languages in addition to standard French and/or a variety of French and those who limit their usage to two local languages alongside standard French and/or one of the many varieties of French. There are also bilectal bilinguals, or those who do not use standard French, but one of its varieties. This is a marginal group of the Ivorian population who, very often, are less or not educated despite growing up in an urban environment.

In addition, we have people who, due to their social class, function, prefer to actively use French and its different varieties depending on the context. There are also exogamous spouses who, due to their linguistic heterogeneity, prefer to alternate between standard French and one of the varieties of French within their relationship. Thus, most of the population has become bilingual according to their degree of comprehension of the French language (the low level as well as the high level), making the manifestation of their biculturalism not always obvious. On this subject, Grosjean (2018) explains in these terms that "a bilingual person is not always bicultural if she/he does not participate in the life of two cultures."

Thus, the particularities that make the manifestation of proper biculturalism inexistent within the Ivorian population are related to the different ways in which this population has become bilingual.

1.2 Typology of Ivorian biculturalism

Throughout our research, we have noticed four categories of bilingualism in Côte d'Ivoire. The first category is comprised of individuals born to parents of different ethnicities: children coming from mixed marriages. This is a group of people who become bicultural based on the affiliations of their parents. Most often, in these mixed households, it is Ivorian French – one of the most spoken varieties of French – that is prioritized as a language of communication. These children generally have no idea about the cultures and languages of their parents; instead, they superficially acquire the culture conveyed by the French language. The second category is made up of monolingual children who became bicultural through their education. They have their mother tongue (L1) and learn French as a second language (L2) at school. Most students educated in Côte d'Ivoire are concerned with this category. The fact that only French is taught at school means that the children who do not have French as their mother tongue use their L1 as a crutch to help them understand what the teacher says. However, due to the non-mastered French culture, the acquisition of standard French used in school is done using many imitations of the local languages. On this subject, Grosjean (2018) evokes the impact of the principle of complementarity on the dominant language according to the idea that if a language is used in a limited number of domains or activities, the number of speakers is bound to decrease and there is a strong chance it will not be as developed as a language that is used in a wider range of contexts. This is the case for Ivorian languages. The third category is made up of children who are not only in bicultural families but also become multicultural due to school (coming into contact with French culture and language). These children, due to the bilingualism in their families, acquire French as their mother tongue. The languages of their parents, alongside their respective cultures, appear less attractive to these children. Once at school, they learn, partially via academic French, the culture of the French language. In the fourth category, there are children born to parents of different races. They are mixed-race and learn, in general, the language of communication chosen by their parents and their chosen culture as well, particularly that of their host country.

Nevertheless, it is important to note that biculturalism constitutes an advantage for the development of bilingualism in a community. The ability to appropriate different cultural codes allows for a community to develop and learn languages stemming from these cultures. For school children, the second language is well acquired at school if it is associated with the culture of this language. The implication of cultural values in education will allow students to have a richer vocabulary, an open mind to other cultures, and a view of the world that is much more diversified. We also argue that a community which evolves within a bilingual environment presents advantages on an intellectual, professional, and economic level.

2. Advantages of bilingualism

One of the results of contact between languages is the capacity for one person to speak two or more languages. Any individual who speaks more than one language is, then, considered to be bilingual. In our current society, with globalization, the number of bilinguals has grown significantly. Indeed, bilinguals appear, to be special individuals considering the importance and the advantages of bilingualism. However, before speaking of bilingualism, it is necessary for us to provide a definition of bilingualism. In fact, a multitude of definitions of bilingualism exist, but we will focus on the one proposed by Van (1972: 117-118):

> Bilingualism consists in being able to express oneself without difficulty in two languages with an identical degree of precision in each of them; it is the presence of two languages that brings about a set of linguistic, psychological, and sociological overlaps likely to cause a conflict of language and therefore of identity. It is about the alternative use of two languages that the speaking subject employs in turn for the needs of his expression.

A bilingual person is often appreciated and, at times, a subject of jealousy in his environment. In the paragraphs that follow, we attempt to present some advantages of bilingualism at school (learning of school subjects), in professional life (English as lingua franca), and at university (the use of English as medium for scientific research, results, reports).

2.1 The advantages of bilingualism at school (education system)
Various studies have shown that a child who speaks two languages learns quickly and easily (Floccia et al., 2018; Berens et al., 2013). A bilingual child entering school with this aptitude has a greater chance of succeeding in his studies than a monolingual child. In Côte d'Ivoire, mainly in the Gontougo region, most children are bilingual. This bilingualism is a product of the presence of two local languages, specifically Bron (or Abron) and Koulango. A study conducted by Seka Y.A. and Niamien C. (2016), titled *Bilinguisme et développement cognitif à l'école primaire : une étude expérimentale à partir du terrain de la*

région de Bondoukou, indicates that this region "is overflowing with a number of children whose cognitive performances appeal to the popular imagination." The objective of the study was to analyze the effects of bilingualism on the cognitive development of educated children (students) in the Bondoukou region.

After conducting different evaluations, the results reveal that bilingualism seems to have a positive effect on lexical production. According to those two researchers, bilingualism favors proficiency in the pronunciation of inverted syllables, and that multilingual children produce better school outcomes, because they possess superior cognitive abilities. In fact, bilingualism bears a positive result on the reflection of the learners, as shown in the supporting work of Colombat (2011)[1] cited by the two researchers: "...bilingual children have intellectual advantages, more mental flexibility, more creativity, more originality in their ways of thinking, and can more easily identify two or three solutions for a problem. They can more easily find many answers to a question or a problem." It is, therefore, necessary to promote bilingualism (bilingual education) in education systems.

2.2 Use of English in professional life

Bilingualism is advantageous in all domains and rewarding to everyone, especially in a professional environment. Today, in Côte d'Ivoire, being bilingual is a big advantage in the professional world. Indeed, a person looking for a job who speaks English in addition to French will find a position more easily than a person who only speaks French; this is because English is the language of the global economy. In a multinational company, for example, a bilingual employee has more opportunities, more responsibilities, and more privileges compared to a monolingual employee. The bilingual employee can easily obtain a promotion to a higher position within the company, which will likely include a more consistent salary. In a country like Canada, the importance of bilingualism in the professional world is well demonstrated. According to the former mayor of the town of

---

[1] Colombat, K. (2011). The benefits of bilingualism.

Moncton, Brian Murphy, cited by Leblanc M. (2014)[2], "bilingualism has become an integral part of the business world, which makes our town an interesting place to live. All that divides us has been put behind us, and we can now use bilingualism as an asset."

A bilingual person in his industry can be asked to supervise projects with foreign partners, or to go on business trips in several countries to represent his company. In other words, bilingualism opens the doors to the world through business trips. Thus, it is possible to discover different cultures of the world. As we discover a new culture, we allow others to learn about ours as well, which will lead to the enhancement of different cultural heritages. In short, we agree with Leblanc M. (2014) through his previously cited article that being bilingual is beneficial for an individual's professional life: *"The case studies we have presented allow us to conclude that, in regard to the aforementioned salary gaps, bilingual francophones have a clear advantage over monolingual francophones, hence their personal income is, as we have shown, noticeably inferior to that of bilingual francophones."*

2.3 English as a medium for scientific activities

Sub-Saharan African countries must promote bilingualism in all domains, but especially in the academic world, with English learning. Today, English is a necessity for students in the same way it is for professors and researchers in pursuing the goal of being more competitive in international rankings. For scientific activities within a university, speaking English alongside the official language of the country (Benin, Burkina Faso, Côte d'Ivoire, Guinea Conakry, Mali, Senegal, Togo) is very important for communication with professionals during conferences and symposiums. English has become an ideal language of exchange in the scientific field. Moreover, most books and scientific publications are published in English. A monolingual researcher (unless he/she is an anglophone) will have more difficulties conducting research because non-fluency in English constitutes a handicap for him/her. Being able to speak in English is vital for any researcher in modern times because it provides individuals with opportunities and possibilities to participate in

---

[2] Leblanc, M. (2014). The advantages and benefits of bilingualism in Moncton: Between discourse and reality. Linguistic minority and society. (4). p. 154 - 174

research activities, symposia, in-person, or online conferences with researchers from different countries.

The advantages of bilingualism are undeniable in terms of linguistic and cognitive abilities. Therefore, it would be wise for the French-speaking countries of sub-Saharan Africa, such as Côte d'Ivoire, to integrate into their education system the use of not only the mother tongues (local languages) and French, but also of English so that the students from these countries become bilingual (mother tongue and/or French and English) like those from English-speaking sub-Saharan African countries such as Ghana (English and French).

3. Acquisition of French as a Second Language

For a proper acquisition of French as a foreign language among students from French-speaking sub-Saharan African countries, it is necessary to proceed step by step according to Maria Montessori's pedagogy. Indeed, for the Italian doctor and pedagogue, "all children possess universal capacities that permit them to acquire knowledge." Among these capacities are linguistic capacities as well as cognitive capacities necessary for all kinds of school learning (from early childhood - three years old - to 18 years old) and subsequently professional and/or university training (adult of 18 years or older). The mastery of the second language (French), the official language, is crucial for the people of the francophone countries of sub-Saharan Africa in general and particularly for the people of Côte d'Ivoire because, unlike the people of European countries and the United States of America, English, Portuguese, or French, depending on the country, is considered to be the official language of the country and the language of culture (and very often the only language of instruction: the teaching language), but it is not the language spoken by most of the local population. In fact, the populations of sub-Saharan African countries are compounds of different linguistic groups/communities; and each community has its own language that, quite often, differs from that of other communities within the country. Therefore, it is the mother tongue that is used on a day-to-day basis in the multilingual African environment.

What can be done for the populations of sub-Saharan African countries to ensure that they master the official language of their country? As an answer, we suggest the acquisition of the official language, or second language, from childhood (3 - 5 years old) using both the mother tongue or first language (L1) and the second language (L2) as languages of schooling during the first four years of primary school. To reach this target, it is necessary to use a simultaneous approach (Dual-Language Learning) for a mother tongue-French program. Indeed, speaking about the didactics of a foreign language, Borel et al. 2009 have said:

More specifically, unlike working in L1 which gives students the illusion of easy and immediate understanding, and which allows approximate expression, working in L2 makes it possible to create new automatisms (…) at the level of comprehension, precision of expression and metalinguistic reflection. This is particularly the case when disciplinary concepts are introduced for the first time in the L2 without having been previously covered in L1. Several teachers interviewed show themselves to be particularly aware of the importance of the processes of deconstruction and defamiliarization linked to the use of a foreign language. (Borel et al., 2009, p. 219).

According to the authors, the teachers surveyed highlighted the investments that drove them to focus both on disciplinary content (the goal) and language (the means of communication). In addition, they found a certain number of advantages of using an L2 in the learning-teaching of an NLD (nonlinguistic discipline). This confirms our hypothesis for bilingual education: acquisition of French (L2), by using the linguistic and cognitive abilities developed in the mother tongue, will allow the students to learn better, acquire the French alphabet, sound <=> letter correspondences (fundamental to reading and writing) along with the French lexicon and reading skills (reading in French).

To achieve this, it is necessary to first develop the mother tongue (local language) by making it pass from a spoken language to a written/standard or codified language (alphabet, vocabulary or dictionary, grammar), then develop pedagogical tools for the bi-competent teachers (pedagogical documents, worksheet), textbooks for students (lesson books, exercise books), and finally to teach the written form of the mother tongue, a language which they have already mastered orally, to the students. The acquisition of the written form of the mother tongue, which has become a written/standard language, and therefore used as the language of schooling in addition to French, will allow students to better acquire French, their second language. Below, we provide the different steps in the learning process of the two languages simultaneously: first, the alphabets of L1 and L2, phonological awareness (correspondence between sounds and letters or groups of letters of the alphabet of L1 and L2), then the mental lexicon (knowledge of familiar words and their synonyms/antonyms in L1 and L2), and finally learning to read and write in L1 and L2: reading/writing letters, words, sentences, and texts with comprehension questions in the mother tongue as well as in French, being therefore bilingual.

3.1 The phoneme

Surveys carried out with mother tongue (L1) and French (L2) tests in several EPP and PEI schools in villages in southern Côte d'Ivoire, in the frame of the TRECC program[3], revealed that only 20% of CM1 students (those in the 5th year of primary school) know how to read correctly. At the time of the TRECC survey, students in Cours Préparatoire 1 (or CP1) in EPP schools had only a few months of exposure to French, the second language (L2). Those in Cours Élémentaire 1 (or CE1) had two years of exposure to French. And those in Cours Moyen 1 (or CM1) had been exposed to French for four years. Concerning the students at the PEI schools, those from CP1 had no exposure to French. As for students in CE1, they had only a few months of exposure to French. CM1 students had, in total, two years of exposure to French after four years of primary school, which explains their insufficient performance in reading compared to the performance of CM1 students in EPP schools. We conclude that these results on the level of reading performance for public primary school students in rural Côte d'Ivoire are due, in part, to the fact that these students, in particular those from the Programme d'École Intégrée

---

[3] Transforming Education in Cocoa Communities (TRECC). This is a survey of public primary schools in three villages in the Adzopé region (for the Atié language), namely: Anaguié, Bécouéfin and Moapé, and in three villages in the Sikensi region (for the Abidji language): Elibou, Gomon and Yaobou.

(PEI), are exposed to French late (for more details see Jasinska et al. 2017c). However, it is now clear that the reason this writing/reading performance is insufficient is due to the absence of phonological awareness among public primary schools' students of Côte d'Ivoire, both in EPP and PEI schools.

- Phoneme identification

This test is used to identify the sounds (phonemes) of the students' L1 (Local Language) and L2 (French), then to demonstrate the pertinence of phonological awareness as a basic method of knowledge among students. They have the task of identifying and pronouncing the first sound of a familiar word out loud. For example, the teacher asks the students: "What is the first sound of the word /tî/ 'arbre/tree' (in abidji)?" The students must provide the correct response to the teacher, specifically: the first sound of the word /tî/ 'arbre/tree' is [t]. This test, like all tests of phonological awareness, calls for the use of an individual's lexicon (their knowledge of words in the language in question); hence the importance of an established lexicon in L1/L2 (for example the lexicon Abidji/French) in learning the two languages of schooling.

- Phoneme segmentation

This test of phonological awareness allows students from EPP and PEI schools to be able to say, out loud, one by one, the different sounds (phonemes) of familiar words (example: /bá/ [in abidji] 'corde/rope' => /b/ /a/: two sounds, two phonemes). It is important to note that all phonological awareness tests, in particular this test, reliably and precisely measure students' phonological awareness. These are strong predictors, by means of both oral and written exercises, key reading and writing competencies: the "fundamentals of reading and writing."

3.2 The lexicon

The other key skill for learning how to read and write is knowledge of lexicon (vocabulary). It is important to note that the debate on the related question of writing abilities in local languages is not limited to Côte d'Ivoire. Other Sub-Saharan African countries are equally confronted with this problem: most Africans speak their mother tongue, but do not know how to write or read a text in this language. This is due to higher rates of illiteracy, but also the absence of a structured corpus (lexicon/dictionary, written texts). Therefore, the goal is elaborating the corpus, at least in terms of the lexicon for learning the written form of mother tongues, which then become codified/standard languages that can be used as languages of schooling. Indeed, scientific research conducted in Switzerland and other countries has shown that, among the factors impacting the quality of language acquisition (bilingual didactics): exposure to two languages simultaneously, on the one hand, and the age of the student at his/her first exposure to the second language, on the other hand, are co-determinants of phonological awareness, lexical knowledge (mental lexicon), and reading and writing performance among bilingual students, and in general, a deciding factor for better performance in school (cf. Floccia et *al.* 2018; Berens et *al.* 2013).

- Knowledge of synonyms of familiar words

In addition to phonological awareness tests, there have been, during the survey conducted by the TRECC program, tests of lexical knowledge (vocabulary) adapted from the USAID Early Grade Reading Assessment (EGRA) for francophone countries in Western Africa. The goal of these tests is to encourage students to reflect on the familiar words provided and generate a synonym for each, in order to evaluate the level of their lexical knowledge ("mental lexicon," as indicated by Goswami, 2015). This test reveals the understanding that students have not only of their native language (L1), but also their second language (L2), namely French. The teacher proposes a word to the students in their native or second language, then asks them to identify a word that has the same meaning in the given language (L1 or L2). Examples: in Abidji (L1) => bwɔ́ "father" = àpá "daddy"; in French (L2) => père "father" = papa "daddy."

- Knowledge of antonyms of familiar words

Like the synonym test, the instructor presents familiar words to the students and prompts them to provide a term with a contradictory definition (having previously introduced and illustrated the concept of antonyms). The students are then invited to reflect and give a word that is opposite to the one provided by the teacher in the mother tongue or in the second language. Examples: tépèpɷ "bad person" ≠ ténámɷ̀pɷ̌ "good person" in Abidji (L1). For French (L2), we have the words méchant "bad person" ≠ gentil "good person" ("méchant" being the antonym of "gentil").

3.3 The text

The tests are expanded upon the comprehension of oral texts and written texts. For students at the CP1 and CE1 levels, the test utilizes a small text (six sentences, for example), and, for students at the CM1 level, the text is a bit longer. Orally, the students are tested on their capacity to understand a text they listened to then respond to comprehension questions (five questions maximum). The text is read by the teacher (a native speaker for the tests in the mother tongue) two times back-to-back in the given language. For the written portion, the texts in the mother tongue are transcribed following the orthography of Ivorian languages (cf. ILA, 1976). The texts in L1 and L2 change depending on level of study (CP/CE/CM). The students are free to start the test in L1 or in L2. They respond to comprehension questions only in the language of the text (L1 or L2). In this way, public primary school students in Côte d'Ivoire will be perfectly bilingual: mother tongue/French, and then mother tongue and/or French/English from CM1, in the manner of students from private primary school in Côte d'Ivoire or public primary school students in Cameroon, Canada, Switzerland, Zambia, and many others.

3. Bilingual revolution in sub-Saharan Africa. Particularities, scope, limits, and perspectives.

Mbacké DIAGNE
Université Cheikh Anta Diop

To write about the necessity of multilingual education in Africa, for us, is a matter of patriotic, pan-Africanist commitment and a fight for sustainable socio-economic development for African countries in general, especially for countries south of the Sahara. This commitment is fueled by the conviction that Africa can only launch itself further in the quest towards development by resorting to its own human resources, along with their knowledge and know-how. African knowledge and abilities, especially traditional ones, can only be exchanged properly through African languages. In other words, the issue of education and training is an essential condition for the overall development of the continent and for a better future for the African people. The realization of this condition should not consist of completely replacing the typical experience of monolingual education using a foreign language that had been previously established as an official language since the beginning of independence. Instead, it should ensure the second and opening phase of global education is rooted in the culture and first language of the child (the African language). Such a system of multilingual education and training would make it possible to enhance the value of African knowledge and know-how, providing sub-Saharan countries with quality human resources. This is why the promotion of multilingual education using French and a child's mother tongue within the same classroom setting is a subject of great interest to us.

We believe that multilingual education provides a needed voice to sub-Saharan African countries such as Senegal in terms of the solutions it can provide - not only to the problems education systems face in achieving universal, sustainable, and quality education, but also to the problems of socio-economic governance that hinder the development of these African countries.

We first attempt to provide context to these situations in Africa, then identify the sociolinguistic and historical specificities in a comparative approach with other contexts (e.g., those of the Western world) before finally defining the terms of the implementation of multilingual education.

Subsequently, beginning with the experiences in Senegal, we attempt to show the extent to which multilingual education can disrupt our typical educational convictions and practices, as well as how it can help to remove many obstacles to the achievement of a quality education system. Finally, we discuss the limitations that can slow down the march towards this multilingual revolution in sub-Saharan African education systems and the solutions that can be presented within them.

The sociolinguistic context of sub-Saharan Africa: the case of Senegal

The linguistic governance of formerly colonized African countries can lead to the belief that sub-Saharan Africa is a region that refuses to speak its own languages. Post-colonial Africa has proceeded by domesticating foreign languages that occupy the public space, developing favorable material and environmental conditions to their maintenance as official languages. This type of governance, which has excluded the use of these countries' national languages within the media of education and work, is out of place because it is based on a model copied from the former colonial homeland. It only benefits an educated minority to the detriment of the majority of the African population who have been excluded from this national conversation. In Senegal, a profound gap in communication exists between the government and the population, impeding the implementation of a participatory approach to socio-economic emergence.

However, in Senegal, each of these languages has naturally taken on a role in the way of life of these populations. The officialization of the natural statuses these languages have already acquired would be a good step on a national level for the promotion of indigenous languages and the strengthening of economic emergence in Senegal. This would constitute a strong act of valorization, a powerful element of socio-political integration and an immeasurable component in the emergence of human resources using a high level of competence, capable of leading state policies towards the achievement of even better school results. Unfortunately, the reality in sub-Saharan Africa is that these policies are conducted in the foreign language of a former colonial power.

In the case of Senegal, French has remained the only official language of work and communication since independence in 1960. However, less than 20 percent of the overall population has a level of proficiency in this language that allows them to use it appropriately in their daily activities. This monolingualism excludes more than 80% of Senegalese citizens from a monolingual governance which conducts itself only in French. However, these excluded individuals speak and function daily in their mother tongue or first language. All sectors of the state suffer from this type of language planning, especially the education system. African systems of education struggle to reach performance thresholds, despite the significant financial efforts made by the Senegalese state within the framework of its Program for the Improvement of Quality, Equity, and Transparency in the Education and Training Sector (PAQET-EF).

Despite the increase in education access since the implementation of the Ten-Year Education and Training Plan (PDEF) in 2000, followed by the Education and Training Development Program in 2010, dropout and failure rates remain high. The completion rate for all combined levels of education is very weak. Offering education only in French appears to be inadequate and has not been adopted by all actors in education, especially African parents. French language schools are often rejected by part of the population who have taken the initiative to develop other educational opportunities more in line with their cultural experiences and aspirations. Evidently, the French school model is, in a way, disconnected from an African background and does not speak the same languages of the communities it attempts to educate. Language, both literally and figuratively, is the main obstacle to quality education adopted by and adapted to African populations.

Many studies, as well as several internal and external evaluations, have proven that a curriculum based in French language alone does not facilitate learning and distorts the pedagogical and didactic foundations of teaching and learning. Each of these evaluations demonstrates the low proficiency in French among the majority of learners after ten years of monolingual schooling. However, the obstacle of foreign language within an educational system that rejects the first language of the African learner was seen very early on by the Senegalese instructor. The cognitive barrier of a foreign language is established the moment the African child enters school and is forbidden to use their first language after six to seven years of environmental immersion and mastery in it.

This assessment allowed Senegal to think about the use of national languages in school alongside French very early on and, through history, has proven to become a useful tool for the education of Senegalese children. Many bilingual education programs have been implemented by the Senegalese government, attesting that, to increase the quality of the educational system, education should begin in the first language of learners. This is how an irreversible, bilingual revolution was born in Senegal. But before coming to the description of the process of this bilingual revolution, it seems necessary to discuss the contextual realities of how bilingualism is implemented in sub-Saharan Africa.

The particularities of a revolution in sub-Saharan Africa

Without going into too much detail, bilingualism, in general, can be understood as the presence of two languages in the same communicative situation where an individual can express himself correctly in either language. In the field of education, learners must be able to make their first acquisitions in and through their first language (L1) before they can invest their skills in and through a second language (L2). Bilingualism experts at the Ministry of Education in Senegal define this concept by stating that:

> Bilingual/multilingual competence occurs when a speaker is able to use two or more languages to meet communication needs in specific social contexts. At the school level, it will be

a matter of helping the child to acquire and integrate adequate resources on the two languages and cultures concerned, as well as skills in transferring from his or her first language to the second language in teaching-learning situations. (MOHEBS Teacher's Guide, 2022).

In the context of sub-Saharan Africa, this is a didactic bilingualism in a teaching-learning situation that makes use of two languages: the first language (often the mother tongue) of the learner and another language to boost the quality of education, to improve education, and to reconcile the language of schools within its environment. This is indeed a bilingual revolution, but the ins and outs of it are very particular and different to those taking place within the contexts of European and American countries.

The sub-Saharan African context is one consisting of a high level of linguistic diversity, an ecosystem comprised of thirty to over two hundred languages from one country to another. These languages have only recently been given access to the written code, resulting in extracurricular environments that lack written documentary resources and languages whose written form is not yet widespread and mastered by the majority of its speaking population. This situation results in the absence of a literate environment where learners can find the codified national languages outside of a school environment. For the most part, their parents are unable to read in their own language and are therefore incapable of helping their child learn at home.

Thus, the bilingual revolution in sub-Saharan Africa is hindered by both the abundance of languages within each country and the social status of these languages, marked by oral rather than written use. This is in contrast to forms of bilingual revolution in other contexts, such as those in Europe or the United States, where the languages present in the school environment are, for the most part, languages with a long written tradition, outside of the learning environment, in public and/or within the familial context.

The bilingual revolution in sub-Saharan Africa requires more investment in human, intellectual, and financial resources and also requires much more time to be implemented.

Senegal: a long-term experience of scholarly bilingualism

In spite of these obstacles, countries like Senegal are attempting, in a very committed way, to revolutionize their educational systems by integrating national languages as the first language of acquisition (L1) for students alongside French, the second language (L2).

Slowly but surely, Senegal has launched its own bilingual revolution, a process that has played out for half a century. This revolution began with the codification of the country's languages. The first six to be codified were tried out in both formal and informal schools repeatedly. They were implemented as indicated below (excerpted from MOHEBS Guidance Document, 2019 version):

- Televisual classes (TC) and non-televisual classes (NTC). The use of national languages in schools has been on the agenda of the Senegalese government since 1971 and was first experimented with in classrooms between 1977 and 1984. These classes relied on the support of media such as television and radio to teach national languages in elementary school. During the 1980-1981 school year, there were only about 15 classes, all in Wolof, with the exception of an experimental class in Seereer. The experiment lasted six years and ended in 1984.
- Experimentation from 2002 to 2008, or "Trial" (MAE). Beginning with the 2002/2003 school year, the nation of Senegal opened 155 IC classes every two years, bringing the total number of classes to 465, to experiment with bilingual education (LN/F) in elementary schools using six national languages (Wolof, Pulaar, Seereer, Joola, Mandinka, and Soninke). The program covered all levels of elementary school across the entire country, with 10 or 15 classes per region as needed. In the CI, L1 is used as the only medium and object of instruction. The outline for the progressive introduction of French was established as follows: The first generation of these students took the CFEE and 6th grade entrance exams in 2008 under the same conditions as students in traditional classrooms with satisfactory results.
- The School and National Languages in Africa Project (ELAN-Africa). Under the direction of the OIF, through the Institut de

la Francophonie pour l'éducation et la formation (IFEF), this initiative has had three phases since 2012. During the first phase, ELAN consisted of experimentation involving the first six codified national languages (Wolof, Pulaar, Seereer, Jola, Mandinka, Soninke) in 9 regions of the country. This experimentation involved 60 classes from CI to CE1. The didactic approach to bi/multilingualism proposed in the ELAN orientation guide, based on the CEB, emphasizes the links between French and national languages in order to better understand the transfer process. Based on the positive results of the evaluation of the experimentation of the first phase, the second phase (2017-2023) consists of supporting the Ministry of National Education in the definition and deployment of the Harmonized Bilingual Education Model (MOHEBS). The third phase will continue the implementation of MOHEBS with a focus on the assessment of student learning.

- Community Elementary Schools (CES). Created in 2002 by the "Education and Health" Foundation, these schools are found in the localities of Thiès and Kédougou. The process for introducing national languages in these schools is identical to that of the MAE. In addition, school-age students receive training in local trades such as gardening and horticulture. The objective is to make the student capable of transforming their environment and community. The new name of the Rural Elementary Community School (ECE) defines their location in rural areas. This experimentation stopped in 2012 due to lack of financial support.

- Associates in Research and Education for Development (ARED). Bilingual Education Program. The NGO ARED seeks to promote quality education in African languages for grassroots communities through training, publishing, and pedagogical innovations and action research. Since 2009, in partnership with the Ministry of National Education (MEN), a bilingual Pulaar/French and Wolof/French program has been running in formal elementary schools. This experimentation is based on three domains (Language and communication, mathematics, and ESVS) of the Basic Education Curriculum (BEC), covered in 2014-2015, 208 classes – 14 including 8 classes of CE2, 99 classes of CE1 and 101 classes of IC distributed in 4 Academic Inspections of the country (Dakar, Rufisque, Kaolack and Saint-Louis) and concerned the first two stages of elementary school (CI-CP and CE1-CE2). The experimentation also concerned the third stage (CM1-CM2) and reached a total of 10,500 students. ARED's approach to bilingual education, which is community-based, is part of the CEB framework and is characterized by the simultaneous introduction, alongside Wolof and Pulaar, of reading in French (L2) starting in first grade. This gives it the name of 'real-time bilingualism.' In its implementation strategy, the NGO ARED's bilingual education model emphasizes teacher training, production of teaching materials, community involvement and monitoring and evaluation.

- The Program of the Association for the Development of the Saafi Language (ADLAS). In 2008, ADLAS started to run a mother tongue-based preschool program. The targets are 3-, 4- and 5-year-olds. ADLAS has built and equipped 15 schools for 30 classes, including 15 large sections and 15 medium sections with funding from the Norwegian government. Since the beginning of the school year in October 2011/2012, in partnership with the Government of Senegal under the funding of Hewlett, ADLAS introduced Saafi/French bilingualism with the opening of ten test classes including 3 CP classes and 7 CI classes.

- The Multilingual Education Project (EMiLe). In partnership with World Vision Senegal, ONECS, SIL, and with the support of the IEF of Fatick, EMiLe has developed a bilingual Seereer-French program. EMiLe first moved from a preparatory phase in 2009 to 2013 to an introductory phase in September 2013, with the launch of 12 pilot classes. Since the implementation of the experiment in the CI class, the L1 medium occupied 90% of the teaching time compared to 10% of the time for L2. This schedule format is gradually rebalanced to give a slight advantage to French at the end of the primary cycle. It takes place as follows: in CI, L1 occupies 90% of time, L2 10%; in CP,

L1 70%, L2 30%; in CE1 and CE2, 50% L1, 50% L2; in CM1 and CM2, L2 dominates with 60% against 40% for L1.
- The Reading For All Program. This is an initial reading program in Wolof, Pulaar and Seereer conducted throughout the first three years of schooling across six regions (Kaolack, Fatick, Kaffrine, Diourbel, Louga and Matam), the MEN, developing its experimentation in the Academy of Saint-Louis within the framework of a direct agreement between governments (G2G). This experimentation, planned for a period of five (5) years (2016-2021), concerns the CI, CP, CE1 classes of 3,890 schools and 100 Daara.

Scope, limits, and perspectives of bilingual teaching and learning in Senegal

Scope, limits

Today, Senegal has accumulated these experiments, generating a multitude of positive results, especially those at the level of reading and writing mastery, improving skills in mathematics and science, and the opening of schools to the environment of national languages.

Nevertheless, difficulties were noted by experts and must be addressed:

- Lack of a proper command of reading and grammar skills of the national language by some teachers;
- The uncontrolled mobility of teachers already trained in bilingual education;
- Low parental involvement;
- The almost non-existent funding by the state, leading to the delay, or even absence, of textbooks and various other teaching aids.

Having drawn upon many lessons after half a century of experimentation, the country of Senegal has decided to resolutely commit itself to the increase of first-language use among pupils in formal school through a program that will be implemented based on a Harmonized Model of Bilingual Education in Senegal (MOHEBS). As of October 2022, this model will govern all interventions in the field of bilingual education, regardless of who initiates them.

In the future, Senegal will extend MOHEBS bilingual education to all CI classes throughout nine regions of the country.

The MOHEBS

Here is what the MOHEBS states verbatim:

> The type of bilingualism proposed in the current model is based on the principle of national language(s) and French use as a medium and object of learning throughout the elementary cycle. In the CI, the national language (L1) is the main medium of teaching/learning. French (L2) is taught orally from February onwards. In the CP, reading and writing in French begin at the start of the school year. Learning mathematics in French begins in the second trimester. In the second stage (CE1 and CE2), the national language and French are used as a medium in a functional balance. In the third stage (CM1 and CM2), L1 is maintained while French is the main medium of instruction.
>
> [In] Language and Communication, language is taught using the national language at the beginning of IC: French is introduced from February; reading and writing in French begins at the beginning of CP.
>
> [In] Mathematics, from the CP's second trimester, French becomes, alongside the national language, a medium for mathematics.
>
> [In] ESVS and EPSA, during the first two years (CI/CP), ESVS and EPSA are conducted exclusively in L1 and for the last four years in the national language and French.

Through MOHEBS, Senegal has brought about a technical solution to the operationalization and implementation of its bilingual revolution. I hope that Senegal's example will be followed by all French-speaking African countries that have yet to take this step.

Conclusion

In essence, we have shown here that it is necessary for sub-Saharan Africa to carry out a revolution of national education systems by introducing the mother tongue or primary language of African children, thereby boosting the quality of education and training of

African youth and, finally, allowing for adequate human resources for the continent's sustainable development. However, this bi/multilingual revolution will unfold within a sociolinguistic context that is very different and more complex than those of the bilingual revolution in the West or elsewhere outside of Africa.

Despite the complexity of the sub-Saharan linguistic ecosystem, countries such as Senegal have resolutely embarked on their bilingual revolution, using African languages as mediums and objects of instruction prior to and alongside the language of the former colonizing country. Senegal already possesses its own tool and program document, the MOHEBS, enabling the country to engage in an increase in the scale of national language-French bilingualism.

4. Mother, teach me: On the importance and possibility of decolonial multilingual education through African mother tongues

Djeneba Deby BAGAYOKO
University of Paris Diderot

One thing that I became aware of in my traveling recently through Africa and the Middle East, in every country that you go to, usually the degree of progress can never be separated from the woman. If you're in a country that's progressive, the woman is progressive. If you're in a country that reflects the consciousness toward the importance of education, it's because the woman is aware of the importance of education [...] So one of the things I became thoroughly convinced of in my recent travels is the importance of giving freedom to the woman, giving her education, and giving her the incentive to get out there and put that same spirit and understanding in the children (X, 1964).

These are the words as uttered by Malcolm X in 1964. He understood the importance of intellectual emancipation not only for men, but also for women and especially mothers who are tasked with passing down information, wisdom, and knowledge to future generations.

It is often said that a mother is a child's first teacher, so why are her words, her tongue, African mother tongues neglected and relegated to a secondary place, in the shadows, away from the spotlight of education, officialdom and formality? Just as a mother's breastmilk fortifies an infant's body, bones, immune system, so does a mother's tongue strengthen the baby's brain providing it with the tools to give voice to their thoughts, express their emotions, connect with those who share the same or similar cultures and the ability to fully express their potential. A mother's tongue is the most powerful and comfortable weapon one can yield. There is no fear of making mistakes or expressing themselves incorrectly for we are born with it. She is our life companion.

In many countries across the world mother tongue is synonymous with official tongue. The idiom spoken at home is the same one we hear on TV and use in school. Africa, on the other hand, separates those spaces by relegating a mother's tongue to the house, family, market and the official language (usually inherited from colonialism) to more sophisticated areas or places that are deemed intellectually superior for example schools, courtrooms, or hospitals. When education starts the African child is cut from their home twice: there is a physical distance with the parents and a cultural and intellectual separation exemplified by the imposition of a foreign European language.

Languages are not just the collection of sounds and words. They include a people's thought, philosophy, view and understanding of the world. Without those pillars, or by forcing those belonging to a strange and far people, how can a child effectively and efficiently build their intellectual and cultural humanity? And by expanding on this question how can a nation grow and develop if they refer to standards, rules, and structures they haven't come up with?

The only way, from an educational standpoint, to have strong and smart people and citizens is by putting in place measures that will help them fulfil and amplify who they already are. It is easier to follow and add onto the work that has been done at home thanks to the mother tongue than to undo six or seven years of life lessons and start from scratch with alien concepts. In order to contribute to the growth of Africa we need to put mother back at the forefront and let her teach.

When your mother's tongue is confined to the home and space is not made for her in schools, universities, embassies, and someone who dares speak it in those institutions is punished or mocked the underlying message that is being conveyed to the speaker is that their primary language is not worthy of those places. It creates the idea that that idiom is not refined, that it is wrong and that it doesn't have the range to occupy formal settings. However, when you think that Cheikh Anta Diop translated part of Albert Einstein's theory of relativity into Wolof you understand that African languages do have the range and flexibility to be used everywhere.

The Comb, a BBC podcast, dedicated one episode to African languages titled *Losing my language*. The interviewees who hailed from South Africa, Nigeria and Ghana recounted their experience. One person's story, Khahliso Amahle Myataza, struck me the most. She has a beautifully rich Sotho name meaning « the act of bringing happiness to someone's life, being the positive aura » (Myataza, 2021). Before starting primary school, she spoke three South African languages fluently but when she began her education, it required her to only speak a language she wasn't familiar with: English. Because she didn't yet master it, her schoolmates made fun of her and even reported her to the head of the school when she spoke in Sotho. Now at seventeen she may have gained an international language but lost Sesotho, Zulu and Xhosa. And with it she lost stories, wisdom, proverbs, and sayings. The participant from Ghana, a teacher who wanted to be kept anonymous, shared how education in a foreign language limits students who may understand and know the answer to questions but can't articulate them in English. The punishment inflicted on the school body and students has a detrimental effect as everyone polices each other. Dropout rates are high, students experience bullying from those who master European languages and in their quest for integration at school they lose their community and become unable to relate to their families (Myataza, 2021).

If a mother tongue is deemed inferior subsequently mother herself is inferior. When you attack the status of a language, you're attacking all its speakers, teachers and their intellect. Lisa Delpit, together with Theresa Perry, edited a book about the possibility of using Ebonics[4] in schools titled *The Real Ebonics Debate: Power, Language and the Education of African-American Children* and wrote:

> I can neither be for Ebonics or against Ebonics any more than I can be for or against air. It exists. It is the language spoken by many of our African-American children. It is the language they heard as their mothers nursed them and changed their diapers and played peek-a-boo with them. It is the language through

---

[4] A diasporan African language spoken by African-Americans.

which they first encountered love, nurturance, and joy (Delpit, 1998).

Replace Ebonics and African-Americans with any other diasporan or continental African idiom and nation and the sentiment still stands. We can't be for or against African languages. They exist. So let us let them be.

Most nations in the world have a schooling system where the official language of the country is used to teach. If you are in Italy it is Italian, if you live in France you will study in French and if you live in Japan, it will be Japanese. The difference between those countries and states like Mali, Senegal, or Kenya is that we have multiple languages coexisting and a colonial linguistic heritage. African nations have had colonial European languages imposed onto them and this relic is still very present today. What we want to achieve is not the mere replacement of a colonial language by an African one while overshadowing other national African languages. We need to find ways where everybody's mother tongue has its rightful place on the stage and under the spotlight.

One continent, fifty-four countries, more than two thousand languages. There is immense richness on the African continent, from its natural resources to its cultures, histories, and tongues. How do we value all of them? Let's reimagine the education system and how classes are organized. They are generally separated by age with children of all creeds and ethnicities finding themselves together for several years. What if we additionally divided them by mother tongue? One school with different classes that will best suit each student's needs. Now, there will be legitimate fear that such division will deepen tribalism and foster segregation, but there is no such risk because the benefits outweigh this concern. For starters, ethnic and cultural differences already exist so why not use something we have and turn it into a positive? Differences are not the problem, weaponizing them to carry out destructive agendas in the quest for power or wealth is the issue. Artists who capture the soul of a country and are most sensitive to humanity often use their craft to praise the diversity of African nations and their multilingualism. This is the case for Malian musical artists and singers. In *Takamba* by Habib Koité he sings in Bamanankan[5] and Koroboro[6] and he cites these Malian cities: Gao, Tumutu[7], Kidal, Bamako. In *M'bemba* by Salif Keita the singer praises Guinean and Malian jeli, and Senegalese gawlo. What are mistakenly referred to as griots[8] are called jeli in Maninka and Bamanankan, gawlo in Pulaar and gewël in Wolof. Keita mentions them according to the country's tongue paying them respect in their names. Another example is that of Oumou Sangaré in *Wayeina*. The Diva of the Wassolon sings in Koroboro and refers to Tomutu, Sikasso, Kayes, Bamako, Segou and Gao. Besides many Sahelian nations like Mali, Niger and Guinea are known for their joking relationships[9]. These are usually expressed as a game where specific ethnicities or families pick up on each other. These games are never meant to hurt or offend the other party. On the contrary, they are meant to cement and continue ancestral relationships. Africans know each other and of each other. It is just a question of formalizing and institutionalizing this knowledge.

Placing students in an environment where they can learn in the same language they use in their household will show them how much their nation and government care for them and instill a stronger sense of pride and trust in institutions consequently making them prouder and more loyal citizens. Furthermore, other African and European languages will be implemented into their educational path as years go by allowing students to mix, interact and effectively communicate with other people both within and outside the school.

I was born and educated in Italy so naturally the first language of my studies was Italian. At age eight when I was in my third year of elementary school I was introduced to a new language: English. At age eleven, when I started secondary school, French was added to the curriculum. By the time I started high school I was familiar with

---

[5] Bamanankan is the correct name for the language of the Bamana people. Westerners incorrectly spell it and pronounce it as Bambara.
[6] Songhai is the name of a people, a set of languages and the ancient Songhai Empire whose capital was Gao in modern-day Mali. Koyraboro Senni or Koroboro is how Malians refer to the Songhai language spoken in Mali. Other Songhai languages include Zarma, Koyra Chiini, and Dendi.
[7] Tumutu or Tomutu are the proper pronunciations for Timbuktu.
[8] Griot comes from the Portuguese word « criado » meaning servant.
[9] In Bamanankan joking relationships are called sinankunya and in Wolof they are known as kal.

three European languages. This successive addition of idioms into the curriculum is feasible in Africa too. If we were to take Mali as a case study, we could imagine the following: in its capital city Bamako, and more precisely in the neighborhood of Lafiabougou we have our first and new multilingual school called Thomas Sankara Elementary School. 50% of enrolled students have Bamanankan as their mother tongue, 30% Pulaar and another 20% Soninke. The school will have three classes for the Bamana-speaking students, two classes for the Pulaar speakers and one class for those who speak Soninke. In their first year of school, they all learn their native tongue (alphabet, grammar, syntax) and other subjects like math and history in their primary idiom. A full year of studies in their mother tongues strengthened by six or seven previous years of learning and speaking it with family and friends will provide students with a firm foundation with which they will be able to build their linguistic and intellectual skills. In the second year they can all be introduced to another national African language. Let's suppose that Sankara School decides that Bamana students learn Pulaar (the second-most spoken language in the school), while the Fulɓe[10] and Soninke students learn Bamanankan which is the most spoken language in the institution and Mali lingua franca. And they will learn it using their tongues as support language. Depending on the school and regional ethnic make-up each establishment, together with the participation of the local community, can decide on which national African language to introduce first. Not only will students be introduced to their schoolmates' and neighbors' cultures, this type of multilingual education also opens up different avenues to job creation. First of all, native speaking teachers will be required in schools to deepen the linguistic knowledge of native speaking students. Since most people that speak a tongue tend to live in the same area, teachers may be asked to relocate to different parts of the country. This will enrich them culturally and experience wise as they will be moving and discovering new sides of their nation. Among the teacher population, a feeling of integration, unification, solidarity, appreciation and

---

[10] Fulɓe is the name of the ethnicity while Pulaar is the name of the language. In the West, terms like Peul (from the Wolof Pël) and Fulani (from the Hausa idiom) are used to denote both.

respect for other realities will grow. Such sentiments can be passed down to their students making them conscious citizens. An additional point is the need for a standardized alphabet, writing system, textbooks and children's books. There are many scholars, writers and researchers who have come up with them: Guinean writer Solomana Kante invented the N'ko[11] alphabet used to transcribe the Malinké language of Guinea Conakry. Since Malinké is interchangeable with Bamanankan, Maninka, and Jula[12] students across Mali, parts of Senegal, Burkina Faso and Côte d'Ivoire can be taught to read and write in N'ko. The Académie des Sciences N'ko in Bamako teaches the alphabet, and it could form future teachers in its use. People like Mody Bathily and Ousmane Moussa Diagana wrote Soninke dictionaries. And Emily Joof, education advisor, postgraduate researcher, author, and founder of her independent publishing house Mbife Books, has written children's books which have been translated and are available in different languages such as Wolof, English, French and Swedish. Her first book *Mangoes & Monkeybread: Fruity Fun with Ella and Louis* is one such example. Joof's latest work is a tri-lingual children's book to teach numbers in Wolof using English, French or Swedish as support languages. Books for children are a great avenue for job creation too as they involve different actors: pedagogists, teachers, parents, cartoonists, voice over actors should they be turned into televised cartoons, artists, toymakers for educational toys. New intra-African translator positions can thus be easily created. Writers and translators will be able to work together to produce new literature from children's books to novels and non-fiction work. A similar feat is done by Mother Tongue Editions which publishes mono and bilingual books in many different African languages like Moore, Hausa and Kanuri. The resources and know-how are already present, they just need to have set guidelines for them to be as effective as possible. Another promoter for the use of African languages in education is Aziz

---

[11] N'ko means « I say » in Malinké and the alphabet was created in 1949.
[12] Jula is also written as Djoula and was used by merchants and traders as lingua franca in many West African countries.

Tarawele[13]. Tarawele is a young Malian of the Senoufo nation who is pushing for the use of Bamanankan in schools. In different videos available on YouTube, he breaks down seemingly modern and difficult subjects like chemistry and physics in Bamanankan. He reiterates that the French language stunts Africans' development and that whatever foreign concept exists, it can be localized and made to suit local realities.

Literacy, however, cannot and should not be limited to schools. A great example of how it was spread country-wide comes from Italy. Between 1960 and 1968 the Italian public broadcaster RAI produced a show titled *Non è mai troppo tardi. Corso di istruzione popolare per il recupero dell'adulto analfabeta* (It is never too late. Popular education course for the rehabilitation of the illiterate adult). Hosted by Alberto Manzi, the show had almost five hundred episodes to counter and reverse the high illiteracy rate among the Italian adult population (Farné, 2003). After reunification a century prior and after the end of the Second World War, Italy needed to cement national unity. The tool that they chose was language. Prior to 1860 what we now call Italy was a puzzle composed by different reigns, principalities and states all using different idioms. When the country unified it was imperative to find a common cultural and political basis for the survival of said unity. Many of the great minds that shaped Italian and European cultures, like Dante Alighieri, Galileo Galilei, and Michelangelo Buonarroti, came from the region of Tuscany. It thus made sense for the early politicians of the Reign of Italy to use the great literature produced by Florence, take the Tuscan tongue and turn it into the Italian language. Spreading the language reached its apex in the 1960s when a powerful tool, the television, was used to homogenize the idiom and teach adults how to read and write it.

In many, if not all, African states the internet has prohibitive costs and connection may not be optimal, especially in small towns and villages. Television and radio, however, are still relatively accessible and present in most households. These media can become extremely

---

[13] The name Tarawele is often spelled as Traoré. This spelling mimics French mispronunciation. It is important to revise spelling when we become literate in African languages so that words are written and pronounced correctly.

helpful and powerful instruments for the spread of multilingualism, literacy, national pride and unity. And it can start in a very simple way: a light, a camera, a host/teacher. Even in a simplistic setting, this type of production would still need a crew and a staff for its realization. This includes a cameraperson, someone responsible for lighting, a make-up artist, people who look after the host's wardrobe, designers, marketing and advertisement teams, the people behind the camera coming up with the theme and topic for each episode, musicians for the theme song and so on. One television show can create many jobs. Unemployment rates amongst the African youth are high and television could absorb some of it and give Africans an avenue to express their talent, innovative ideas, enthusiasm, and passion. To make this project democratic and fair and not to neglect any language, all national idioms should have a show dedicated to them. Let's take Senegal, a West African country whose lingua franca is Wolof. All Senegalese understand it so making them literate in this tongue is relatively easy. Now, Wolof isn't the only language spoken there. Serer, Jola[14], Pulaar are just a couple more ways people communicate in the country. On a pre-defined rota, the new Senegalese educational channel will play its show to teach people how to understand, read and write other Senegalese tongues. People whose mother tongue isn't the lingua franca will feel included, appreciated and will know that their cultures and languages are an integral part of the nation. Citizens whose first idiom is the most used will get a chance to learn another one and get closer to their neighbors. As for radios, a host can read books or simply have broadcasts completely in national languages which have happened for years. Audiobooks are also a powerful and helpful tool. In the process of becoming literate, a hearing support can help teach people to read their tongues more easily and quickly. Even if the Internet is costly, Africans can still use it to create channels and shows for the purpose of spreading African mother tongues. The use of television and radio doesn't exclude any other possibility.

Now the main question would be where do we find the money to invest and finance this work? We can rely on the people. As Africans, we live in communities where we combine our expertise and know-

---

[14] Jola or Diola.

how to solve our everyday issues. Africans are resourceful, talented, ingenious, and creative. Before continuing and expanding the work that has already been done in countries like Somalia, Ethiopia, Burkina Faso, Senegal, and Mali (Ouane et al., 2010), we need an awareness campaign geared towards parents, chiefs and communities. Many of them would rather their children be educated in European languages because it will afford them better chances at getting a job and more possibilities in a globalized economy. These concerns are very valid since every parent wants to see their child succeed and be economically independent. When, however, the benefits and richness of mother tongues are presented with evidence and examples, they will in all likelihood see the value in the tongue of their ancestors and become involved in their children's education in an active way. The parents will become teachers and also students as they will contribute to the scholarship of their progeny and learn school subjects with them as they do homework or draw the curriculum. Much of education falls into the realm of informality. The house is the first school and parents, relatives, and neighbors the first teachers. Mother, fathers, aunties and uncles may impart teachings by telling stories, sharing anecdotes, and by showing practical life examples (Walther, 2007). The synergy of the family and the school will create a fertile environment for intellectual growth. Nothing empowers a person more than knowledge, mental liberation and intellectual emancipation. The more the people is involved, the more they will feel useful and a core part of the revolutionary change in their town, nation and continent. Collaborating with neighboring countries that share the same or intelligible languages will also foster unity, kinship and solidarity across and despite colonial borders. Once trust is set and results yield, people, organizations and governments will become more interested in developing systems to expand multilingualism and they will provide funds for it (Ouane et al., 2010).

Earlier I mentioned how institutionalizing African idioms will instill pride in citizens since governments will proactively work to include everyone into education. Democracy is indeed another positive by-product of bi and multilingualism. Fary Ndao wrote an article for the French newspaper Le Monde titled *Au nom du savoir et de la démocratie, enseignons dans les langues africaines !* (For the sake of knowledge and democracy, let's teach in African languages!). In the paper he shares a UNESCO study that shows the following: out of twenty countries that have produced most academic literature and papers in the world, twelve have national languages that are only spoken within their borders. Some of the countries mentioned include Japan, Italy, the Netherlands, and Turkey. Although Dutch-based Creoles exist in Curaçao, Aruba, and Suriname, and Italian is spoken in parts of Switzerland, San Marino and the Vatican City State[15], these idioms are not spoken to a great degree in different countries or continents. Yet that doesn't prevent or stop their citizens from contributing to world academia, science, research and knowledge (Ndao, 2016). Not having a global status shouldn't discourage speakers of African languages from creating by using them. Another prominent figure that has long worked for the dissemination and promotion of African languages is Professor Kwesi Kwaa Prah. Professor Prah founded and is the director of the Centre for Advanced Studies of African Society (CASAS), a Pan-African organization that focuses on cultural, historical, economic, social and political research as tools for the development in Africa. He advocates for the use and homogenization of African idioms as means for development, economic growth and democracy. Professor Kwesi Prah stated that "No country can make progress on the basis of a borrowed language, understood only by a minority" (Prah, 2013). A minority indeed when we think that more than 70% of Africans don't fluently speak French, English or Portuguese while 50 million people speak idioms like Èdè Yorùbá and, if we combine native speakers and those who speak it as a second language, 57 million speak Amharic (Eberhard et al., 2021). Former colonies like Vietnam ditched the colonizer's tongue, in this case French, and have seen tremendous economic growth and progress. While language isn't its sole responsible being in tune with one's culture and history and using one's mother tongue at all levels play a huge part in a country's development (Prah, 2013). On the continent education is a privilege of the few. These few are already indoctrinated by a

---

[15] San Marino and the Vatican City State are both located within the confines of Italy.

westernized schooling and when they become part of the elite, their use and adherence to western languages and cultures separate them from local people and local realities. The ruling class runs the nation in ways that are too detached from the people and communicates with them in a language foreign to most of them. There can be no collaboration or understanding between those who rule and those who are ruled in this way. Democracy is at risk when presidents and politicians feel closer to and perpetuate western models of life and refuse to communicate efficiently and effectively with the masses. The chasm thus created will move the people further and further away from the country's representatives and the children of the nation will not see themselves, nor their interests, reflected or represented by the elite and ruling class. When a population's voice goes unheard, and the ruling class fails to communicate effectively, democracy falters. On the other hand, when language is easily understood by everyone, the destiny of the nation is entrusted to capable, proud, accountable, and aware citizens.

Taking a bi- and multilingual approach in education has the potential for unity, development and growth in Africa. The first polyglot environment I and many continental and diasporan African children encounter is the family. Multilingual schools would be a natural progression and extension of the home especially on a continent where often two African idioms and one European language are necessary to function in society. Let me give you an example of how multilingualism is weaved into a continental African's brain. While I was preparing my essay proposal for this book, I asked an acquaintance to provide me with some feedback so I could increase my chances of being selected to write a chapter for *A Bilingual Revolution for Africa*. When sending me voice notes on WhatsApp she would effortlessly switch between English (our only common language), Kiswahili and Gĩkũyũ[16] which are spoken in Kenya. Well-off families promote multilingualism for their children because they understand its value: ability to travel and study abroad, career progression, easy adaptation in different countries. Adaptation leads to integration and unity which are goals we have been striving

---

[16] Also spelled as Kikuyu or Gikuyu.

for on the continent since independence. Multilingualism may be taken for granted because it is so natural and ingrained in Africans' minds. It may also not be appreciated because African languages don't enjoy a global status. Whatever the reason may be, if we want to keep our idioms, philosophies and cultures alive we need to strive to fulfil their fullest potential. African mother tongues gift us with immense and endless possibilities: comfort, ease, empowerment, pride, jobs, unity, freedom, intellectual emancipation. Let mother teach.

II - BI-CULTURALISM: AFRICAN CULTURE AND EUROPEAN CULTURE

5. The place of heritage languages in the Cameroonian and Ontario school systems: the current state and a prospective view

Carole FLEURET
University of Ottawa

Julia NDIBNU-MESSINA ETHE
University of Yaoundé

Cameroon, a multilingual country, has 238 national languages (Bitjaa, 2004, Ndongo Semengue, 2012). The official languages, French and English, inherited from the British and French mandates of the colonial period, have divided its educational system into two coexisting subsystems. They symbolize the former federated states: French-speaking East Cameroon and English-speaking West Cameroon. The evolution of the state of politics in Cameroon has greatly influenced educational policies. These policies now center around the implementation of institutional bilingualism at all levels of education. The introduction of African languages into the education system seems to originate from pan-African struggles. In fact, a number of organizations, such as the National Association of Cameroonian Language Committees (ANACLAC) through the Operational Programme for Language Teaching in Cameroon, the Cameroon Association for Bible Translation (CABTAL) and the International Society of Linguistics (SIL), have piloted successful experiments in the teaching and use of African languages in primary education. The success of these studies has provided arguments for educational developers to be able to advocate for the integration of Cameroonian languages into the educational system. As a result, Cameroonian languages and cultures have been taught since 2008.

For its part, Canada is a bilingual country with English and French as official languages. However, depending on the province, the latter becomes a minority, as is the case in Ontario, which has about 5% of French speakers (Statistics Canada, 2016). Province-wide, the proportion of exogamous families is 69% (Statistics Canada, 2016). The portrait of the student population in

Francophone schools has therefore been transformed by, among other things, the arrival of Francophone immigrants from sub-Saharan Africa. These students represent a minority of the minority (Lajoie-Jacquet, 2007; Fleuret, 2021), which makes the relationships between the different populations involved (i.e., ethnic minorities, Francophones, and Anglophones) even more complex. The study conducted by Jacquet, Moore, Sabatier, and Masinda (2011) in British Columbia documented the challenges of African students regarding their inclusion in the school context. To fully understand the current school context, we need to briefly review the education systems in both countries.

1. Interculturality and the evolution of the education system in Cameroon

Cameroon is governed by the Education Orientation Law No. 98/004 from April 14, 1998, in its article 17. The education system is subdivided into three types of education: basic, secondary, and higher education, both public and private. These educational cycles are federated by the presence of many cultures and languages in classrooms. These have influenced pedagogical movements for centuries.

1.1 The missionary era: uses of Cameroonian languages and cultures

If Métangmo-Tatou (2019:175) seems to certify that the teaching of Cameroonian languages started in 1967 at the Libermann College in Douala, the Basel missionaries were the first to teach using Cameroonian languages (Njiale, 2009:2). Their official aim was to evangelize using the most familiar language to the target populations.

According to Njiale (2009, p.2), the first school

> ...opened its doors in 1844 in Bimbia, at the request of Joseph Merrick. Later on, other congregations were established, notably the Basel missionaries of the Protestant faith, the Pallottine Fathers of the Appotolus Catholici Society (1890) and the American Presbyterians.

All these congregations targeted a different culture for which language was, at the time, the primary vehicle of communication. Chumbow (1980, p.10) states that:

...the missionaries learn Duala and Bulu in order to evangelize the people using their own mother tongues. They translate the Bible into these languages and simultaneously provide a written alphabet that is used for writing in other forms of communication.

Alfred Saker and Joseph Merrick equipped Cameroonian languages with a culture of writing. These languages were taught with respect for the traditions of the people while conveying Bible verses. If certain biblical and preached content demystified traditional practices perceived to be negative, such as herbal medicine, the protection of the people and particularly warriors by using rites to summon the ancestors, other traditional practices coexisted without conflict. Sermons admonished many of these cultural practices, and certain elements of Cameroonian culture were eliminated from daily life in favor of prayer.

The translation of the Bible into Duala by Alfred Saker considers certain elements of Sawa culture, even if the writing is modeled on English script. African linguistic particularities are left out in favor of a stress that distorts Duala words. However, the cultural essence of Duala is preserved in the phrasing. Phrases such as "Give us this day our daily bread" are equivalent to "Bola biso da wenge kana miña mese" in Duala, which literally translates to "Give us food as days." Beyond the morphosyntax of sentences in Duala, which is different from that in French, the lexical unit "da" corresponds to "daily bread." This can be justified if it is recognized that Cameroonians do not have the same bread culture and are unable to directly translate this expression in French and English into the Duala language. They eat local food without the appetizers, main courses and desserts that characterize the Western meal. Only the main course is important. This translation is identical in Bantu languages that have been used for Bible translations.

It is quite clear that the bicultural system was set into motion as soon as schooling with evangelization was introduced. The Bible, translated into the Duala language, conformed to endogenous values so that the learners and the faithful would claim to be a part of the two cultural systems. The learners began their schooling in their first language while maintaining a connection with their culture, family and environment, evolving towards the final language of evangelization: English and/or French.

1.2 The German protectorate: 1884-1916

The Portuguese, based on the discovery of an abundance of shrimp on the Sawa coast, named the Cameroonian territory "rio dos camaroes." The Germans retained only "Kamerun." In the same vein, for nearly 40 years, local cultures continued to be promoted within the schools inherited from the Baptists. At first, in 1886, they allowed the Baselites to take over instruction in Duala, Bulu and some other national languages. The Basel mission asserted that "reading the Bible could only be learned in school, and the training of native catechists required learning to write and read" (Stumpf 1979, p.32). Two more schools were successfully opened by the Basel mission in Edea and Bali despite Von Zimmerer's intention to introduce German as the language of instruction in 1891 (Stumpf, 1979). Leconte (2015, p.7) gauges the biculturalism/bilingualism introduced by Germany in a rather depreciatory light, because for him, it is not about valuing Cameroonians or their cultures, but rather about reinforcing German hegemony:

> The linguistic policy practiced by the "Germanics" consisted of combining African languages with European languages at the basic levels of education. It was in no way a question of "valorizing" African languages, but of preventing the colonized from learning the language of the colonizer: it was feared that they would lose prestige. Moreover, the aim in the early stages of schooling was to train a workforce of colonial auxiliaries, capable interpreters, among other things, to keep the ledger books for goods exported to the homeland. (Leconte, 2015, p.7).

German and Cameroonian cultures seemed to live together harmoniously until the decree of Governor Von Put Kamer in 1895, which required the Basel people to be taught only in German. Despite the surrounding environment's multiculturalism, German became the only culture and language of education for the endogenous population. The Basel missionaries and the German government were at a standoff, as some defended an intercultural education integrating English, German and Cameroonian languages and others supported a monocultural education in German.

On April 25, 1910, Governor Theodore Seitz regulated language use: public schools used German, and Protestants opted for German-national language bilingualism, while Catholics retained German. Bicultural classroom practices were carried out through translations and, above all, through the involvement of natives who were competent in both languages and cultures. Debates on linguistic and cultural policies implemented by the Germans contributed to the destabilization of Cameroonian languages and cultures in the education system, as well as the vehicularization of a national language, notably Duala (Tabi-Manga, 2000) or Mungaka. However, to the credit of German governance, the proposal of a lingua franca (an 'Einheitsprache') would have been useful for social cohesion. Other Cameroonian cultures would have recognized themselves in it, and the debate on industrialization based on Cameroonian languages and cultures would have been partially founded in the 21st century. The development of a country in a foreign language and culture seems impossible, and only interculturality through bi/multiculturalism in schools can bring about this development. At the time of the official re-integration of languages and cultures in schools, the pedagogical methods seem to conform to those of that era, yet the French and English mandates are marked by a progressive exclusion of the latter.

1.3 The Franco-British mandates: 1919-1959

The First World War resulted in the departure of the Germans and the division of Cameroon into two parts. Njiale (2009, p.5) states that:

> France inherited 80% of German Kamerun, and England the other 20%. The Treaty of Versailles of June 29th, 1919, gave France and England the role of managing the two territories respectively. The Mandate Act signed in 1922 under the supervision of the League of Nations included the obligation for the Mandatory Powers to "increase the material and moral well-being of the populations by all means necessary...". It also recommends that they "give all

missionaries the right to enter the territories, to erect buildings there for religious purposes and to open schools..." The school becomes the first ideological instrument of the 'colonial project.' French-speaking Cameroon was subjected to an assimilationist policy while English-speaking Cameroon was subjected to 'indirect rule'.

1.3.1 The French mandate

The French assigned French missionaries to the schools abandoned by the Baselites. The number of schools increased exponentially from 22 to 150 (Ndibnu-Messina, 2010). Starting in 1920, decrees in favor of the sole use of French were widespread. Leconte (2015, p.7) specifies that it is a question of "not only colonizing and exploiting, but also 'civilizing', educating Africans in the 'good values' of Western civilization." Africans, viewed as lacking in civilization, had to be educated in the image of the agents of civilization. The Carde Law of 1921 stipulated that any offender who used his mother tongue in school or within the administration would be punished with 100 lashes, condemned to walk around all day with a debasing sign or would not be eligible for a scholarship.

The decision to exclude African languages from the educational and administrative system led Presbyterian missionaries to appeal to the League of Nations. The latter passed a three-year moratorium to conform to the cultural and linguistic monolithism advocated by France. In 1921, Aymerich signed a decree reorganizing the teaching and use of languages: "[...] No school can function if teaching is not done in French. This provision needs no justification. Between the indigenous peoples and us, a solid link will only be established through the introduction of the natives to our language. (Ndibnu-Messina, 2010, p. 65).

Two types of schools emerge from this:

- the village school where French is taught with an emphasis on hygiene and agriculture lessons.
- the regional school, where French is taught methodically and precisely.
- adult classes, where literacy is taught in French (Ndibnu-Messina, 2010)

Following the moratorium, local languages were used only for celebration of religious ceremonies. The educational institutions of the evangelists were not provided with any didactic material so as to make them aware of their offense: the use of the languages and cultures of a territory devoid of civilization. To this day, the signs of cultural rejection by Cameroonians are remarkable and seem to be reinforced. The rupture carried out at the time of French administration has generated an identity decline. Some individuals recognize themselves as Francophones and not Basa, Beti, Duala and other Cameroonian ethnic groups, fighting not for bi/multiculturalism but rather for recognition as Francophones. Pie Claude Ngumu (1985, p.20) acknowledges that:

> There was indeed a tragic moment of rupture with our natural cultural foundation, a rupture that, coupled with the imposition by the outside of cultural practices and civilizational patterns in our societies. We have internalized these models because they were taught to us in school, and we continue to teach them to our children today.

Biculturalism has become a way out of this crisis, and Cameroon, rich in its cultural diversity, symbolizes the successful cohabitation of several cultures and languages, both at school and on the street.

1.3.2 The English mandate

The English were slow to make their presence felt in Southern Cameroon, a region which was still attached to the central administration of Nigeria. It was in 1925 that the Nigerian Educational Board decided to introduce national languages in schools (Stumpf, 1979). The linguistic cohabitation between English and the national languages went smoothly. The number of English-only schools multiplied, and the number of scholarships offered to students enrolled in them increased. The Basel missionaries, despite their enthusiasm for teaching in the local languages, declared schools to be English-speaking in order to benefit from the bonuses offered by the English administration. However, as independence approached in 1958, "the autonomous government of Dr. E.M.C. Endeley decided to prohibit the teaching of Cameroonian languages in this part of the country" (Ndibnu-Messina, 2010). Africans themselves campaigned for cultural and linguistic monolithism, relegating African languages and cultures to the tribal level. This does not impede on the strong ethnic roots of these populations already accustomed to a bicultural education.

The cultural stigma attached to the school by both the agent of this prohibition and Cameroonians has contributed to the latter's lack of connection to local cultures. However, even if Cameroonian languages are not used or taught in school, pupils come from different ethnicities and cultures, and teachers must recognize this. This recognition is illustrated by the behavior of the latter and by the evolving pedagogical models that provide for a feeling of pride in cultural anchoring.

1.4 Independence: from 1960

The independence of Cameroon in 1960 founded first the federal Cameroon and, in 1972, the united Cameroon. Despite Cameroon being united, the school systems coexisted and were not standardized. Each sub-system retained its particularities. Institutional bilingualism became the prerogative of unification, which did not fail to generate controversy.

Njiale (2009, p.7), while commending the quality and quantity of schools and schooling up to the 1980s, notes the subsequent characteristics:

> The school participates in the construction of the nation-state and the single party; English and French are adopted as official languages and of equal value in the field of education; this choice, which reaffirms the national option of biculturalism, is based on local and republican values; the educational ideal includes: the promotion of bilingualism; the guarantee of equal access to education for all; the preservation and reinforcement of national unity and contribution to economic and social development; as an achievement of the colonial era, the principles of secularism, free choice of schooling for parents and freedom of education for missionaries are recognized; the educational effort of the missionaries supported by subsidies; in terms of its purposes, the school is part of a universal, utilitarian and productive ambition; it integrated the notions of instruction, knowledge,

know-how and being; on the whole, the schooling movement was largely transformed, sometimes adapting to local realities.

All these characteristics did not counteract the effects of the Carde law of 1921 nor that of EMC Endeley. The pan-African struggle became that of linguistics, wanting to promote the effective integration of Cameroonians and interculturality within teaching. However, the speeches made by Presidents Ahidjo and Biya emphasized the need to cohabitate and promote the cultures and languages of the land, because these are the future of Cameroon.

This momentum has been displayed through experiments in language teaching programs such as the Operational Program for Language Teaching in Cameroon (PROPELCA). PROPELCA, in its strategy of integration of Cameroonian languages and cultures into the Cameroonian educational system, has offered an opportunity to train young people in an intercultural perspective. The trilingualism of Tadadjeu (1982) operationalized all experiments in teaching Cameroonian languages in the field. Subsequently, in the 2000s, other programs reinforced the results of PROPELCA. School and Languages in Africa (ELAN-Africa), piloted by IFEF since 2012, has contributed to the expansion of bi/multilingual and bi/multicultural education in Africa, and particularly in Cameroon, where ELAN is implemented by the Ministry of Basic Education, with 43 experimental schools to date using 5 national languages (Ewondo, Basa, Ghomala, Fufdulde, and Duala).

The metamorphoses of education systems symbolize the dynamics of cultural cohabitation between peoples. The contexts of "language wars" or culture wars between exogenous and endogenous languages spare no territory. While certain laws on bilingualism and biculturalism are applied early on in countries, such as Canada, for example, Cameroon has taken unique steps to reduce the speed of official multicultural integration within educative policies. The following paragraphs highlight the particularities of Ontario which, in some respects, are like the Cameroonian education system.

1.5. The Ontario School System

Canada is made up of ten provinces and three territories. It is important to note this because each province has its own policies, and education is no exception. Ontario is the most populous province in Canada, and it is also where we find the largest number of Francophones outside of Quebec (about 5%) (Statistics Canada, 2016). However, French remains a minority language, which makes Ontario's sociolinguistic context complex due to the durability of the French fact and the inclusive education advocated in school policies.

The Canadian Charter of Rights and Freedoms (section 23), approved by the federal government in 1982, guarantees every parent, residing outside Quebec, the right to have his or her child educated in a French school system. In other words, the section clearly states that:

> Citizens of Canada (a) whose first language learned and still understood is that of the English or French linguistic minority population of the province in which they reside, and (b) who have received their primary school instruction in Canada in English or French and reside in a province where the language in which they received that instruction is the language of the English or French linguistic minority population of the province, have the right to have their children receive primary and secondary school instruction in that language. [Further], any Canadian citizen whose child has received or is receiving primary or secondary school instruction in English or French in Canada has the right to have all their children receive primary and secondary school instruction in that language. (Canadian Charter of Rights and Freedoms, 1982).

The enactment of article 23 thus entitles parents and their children to an opportunity to be educated and live in French. In turn, this also signifies linguistic, cultural, and political rights that the school and individuals will pass on, thus ensuring the group's social capital and ethnolinguistic vitality (Landry, Allard and Deveau, 2010; Magnan and Pilote, 2007).

However, in Ontario in particular, it was not easy to establish a French-language education system. In fact, recognition of this right to education was only achieved after a bitter struggle, as the government at the time passed Regulation 17 in 1912, prohibiting the teaching of French in all schools in the province (French Language Education in Ontario, n.d.). As soon as the law was enacted, francophones organized to demand their rights. This regulation was not abolished until 1944, but it was not until 1994 that francophones obtained full control of their school system (ibid.). This stubbornness has paid off, since there are now 12 French-language school boards in Ontario and 471 public or Catholic schools.

Although there is an ideological distinction between secular and denominational schools, they share a common mission: that of a French-language educational system:

> French-language education has a very important social authority, stemming from the Canadian Charter of Rights and Freedoms. In addition to ensuring the success and well-being of children and students, French-language schools have a responsibility to transmit the French language and francophone culture. French-language education is a continuum of learning from early childhood to postsecondary education, including training for employment. (French-Language Education in Ontario, 2017).

In order to ensure the sustainability of the French fact, Ontario's French-language schools have adopted the linguistic organization policy, which was developed in 2004. This policy:

> ...was expanded with the intention of better responding, in a minority context, to the specific needs of French language communities in Ontario and their educational institutions. This policy enables educational institutions to increase their capacity to create teaching and learning conditions that promote the transmission of the French language and culture to ensure the academic success of all students. (p.1)

In summary, it is clear the policies in place are aimed at strengthening and preserving Francophone unity both linguistically and culturally. However, as we have mentioned, the school population has become much more diverse in recent decades, and the very concept of a francophone needs to be redefined.

1.6. Francophone status in Ontario

Considering what we have presented, we can understand the fear experienced by Franco-Ontarians of being assimilated into Anglophones. This stance, which is both legitimate and defensive, poses several problems, which illustrates its complexity. First of all, the term "native-born Franco-Ontarians" implies that there are real ones and others! (Cardinal, 1994). This term first appeared in 1985 as a result of rigid positions adopted by the Canadian French Association of Ontario. This ethnocentric vision is reflected in traditions and pedagogical practices that immobilize history and inhibit changes, particularly didactic and social ones, with respect to a more heterogeneous population.

Larouche (2018) points out that, in 2009, the Office of the French Language Services Commissioner of Ontario (2013) adopted a new, inclusive definition of Francophones, which allows for 50,000 more francophones to be counted in a census than the initial definition had allowed. This new definition allows for the inclusion of French speakers who are familiar with the language because it is the language of administration in their country of origin (e.g., Algeria, a former French colony). At the same time, it significantly changes the representation of this group and the school environment (Cavanagh, Cammarata, & Blain, 2016). Attracting more Francophones to ensure the vitality of schools and their maintenance is one thing, but there is still a clear distinction between the recognition of francophone diversity and an inclusive perspective.

1.7. The Ontario school macro-context

As we have pointed out, all these policies for preserving French are operationalized in the context of the school as the school's mission, which has remained historically focused since its inception, that is, on the Franco-Ontarian population. This is also reflected in the school's programs and teaching choices. In the same vein, teachers use a central document as part of their pedagogy – A cultural approach of teaching for the appropriation of culture in French language schools of Ontario (Ontario Ministry of Education, 2009, henceforth MOE). This approach guarantees the transmission of certain knowledge and "values" to be taught. It has three main objectives (p. 3):

- "for students, the increased ability to acquire oral communication skills to maximize learning and identity building.
- for school staff, increased capacity to work in a minority setting in order to support the academic learning and identity development of each student.
- for the school board, the increased capacity to maintain and increase enrollment in order to contribute to the vitality of French-language schools and the francophone community.

Although the definition of a Francophone speaker has changed, the documents that accompany teachers in their teaching have remained the same, as can be seen in the objectives stated above. In fact, becoming a francophone in Ontario means contributing to the community, but which one? There is still a vagueness around the concept of Francophonie that could suggest the idea of plural Francophonie, but nothing is clearly established. It must be said that the identity debate that persists within French Canada (see Cardinal, 2012) underscores its complexity, and that it cannot be reduced to a Manichean vision of belonging or not belonging to a group.

Within the framework of the aforementioned document, diversity is recognized, as can be seen in the following passage:

> In the context of globalization in which Ontario's francophone community is evolving, French-language schools must also encourage multilingualism in a way that an attachment to French is able to coexist with listening to and considering the needs of people who are culturally different due to their first language or ethnic origin. Believing that the traditions and practices of one's own culture, including continuing to speak one's own language, are superior to those of others is ethnocentrism. (MOE, 2009, p. 19)

We can note the political side of such a statement, but its transposition is not very present in pedagogical actions or can even be totally absent. On the one hand, there is a desire to include, but at the same time French remains the only language legitimized in the school environment, as well as the culture of the host society. This legitimacy leads to what Bourdieu (1972) calls symbolic violence, which aims "to impose meanings as legitimate by concealing the power relations that are the basis of its strength" (p. 18). In other words, this macro-context strongly influences pedagogical practices and teachers' actions, since knowledge, know-how and interpersonal skills must correspond to the culture of the school in question.

In short, whether we are talking about Cameroon or French Ontario, we can see the historical overtones of the dominant groups on the dominated groups, or of the dominant languages and cultures on other languages that convey other cultures. However, it is recognized that, for optimal learning of the language of schooling, it is essential to consider linguistic and cultural plurality (Castellotti, Coste and Duverger, 2008), which guarantees social integration and academic success.

2. Multilingualism and conceptual foundations

Our reflection is based on Candelier's (2008) plural approaches:1) joint comprehension between parent languages, which aims to infer meaning in a new language from the one(s) we know; 2) the intercultural approach, which takes into account, in an intersubjective space, the meeting of cultures; 3) linguistic awareness, which aims to develop a "meta" consciousness of how languages function by observing different dialects (the focus is on meaning, but also on the social dimensions of language), and integrated language teaching, which brings languages into contact with each other according to learning contexts and school subjects.

> These so-called plural approaches thus refer to classroom situations where more than one language is taken into account ("several" which indicates "plural") as opposed to "singular" approaches to a language, which do not consider the other languages in the learner's repertoire. (Fleuret and Auger, 2019, p.114).

The primary role of these approaches is to deconstruct the explicit vision of the language of schooling as the only 'legitimate' one (Cuq, 2003). Today, it is recognized that there is a major psycho-cognitive impact on learning when a speaker does not feel like a legitimate speaker of their language, which can lead to linguistic insecurity (Lory and Prasad, 2020). In addition, in Ontario, many new immigrants come from sub-Saharan Africa, and because their discursive practices are conducted more in the oral tradition, as is the case in Cameroon, the entry into the language of schooling represents a major break from their habits. Indeed, the family environment is the cornerstone that shapes the young child (Lahire, 2008). However, the construction of discourse, which is based on a process of co-construction through the intervention of socialization, does not necessarily have written culture as a reference point (Ochs and Shiefflin, 1987). The different ways in which writing is appropriated by different ethnolinguistic groups require pedagogical adjustments, which is why Lahire (2001) considers writing to be polymorphous. To promote better socialization in writing, it is necessary to consider the multiliterate repertoires of learners.

2.1. Pluriliterate repertoires

In her article, Dagenais (2012) properly illustrates the emergence of a consideration for pluriliterate repertoires. Broadly speaking, what she mentions is that, following the work of the New London group, the relationship to writing was considered from a perspective other than that of learning to read and write. This group of researchers criticized the traditional view, highly centered on script, which did not consider the heterogeneity of school populations or the various forms of graphic representations; they coined the term 'multiliteracies' or multiple literacies. In line with their work, Street (2003) and New Literacy Studies argue that writing is not a socially neutral tool but is intrinsically linked to social standing. In these definitory proposals, the research of Martin-Jones and Jones (2000) has also marked this conceptual field. The work they conducted in Great Britain with linguistic minorities reinforces the importance of considering the position and uniqueness of different groups. They also added that it is necessary to consider the social practices in which language repertoires are updated. They coined the term Multilingual Literacies.

Following Martin-Jones and Jones (2000), a number of researchers (Dagenais, 2020; Dagenais and Moore, 2008; Moore, 2006; Moore and Sabatier, 2014, Fleuret and Auger, 2019; Fleuret, 2020) in light of their own projects have chosen the term multiliteracy or multiliterate repertoires to legitimize children's language repertoires according to the contexts in which they are operationalized and according to the different "written" forms they adopt.

2.2. Towards a forward-looking perspective

Today, if we want to promote equal opportunities for all students, it is necessary to rethink educational policies, which will, in turn, promote academic success. Learning the language of schooling must not be done to the detriment of the students' language repertoires but rather in collaboration with the latter in order to promote cognitive shifts between languages. To do this, a didactic renewal is necessary to rethink the way of teaching the languages and cultures of the students in the classroom, through a bottom-up didactic approach, which echoes a co-construction of learning. In other words, the teacher is not the only language expert, because most students are experts in their own language, so learning is co-constructed in an intercultural perspective where everyone has a legitimate place.

By legitimizing the native languages of students in the classroom, we leave behind the traditional framework in which only French/English had the right to be used. Giving equal status to all languages present allows for a more fruitful study of the language of schooling, because it favors the development of metalinguistic reflection due to the dialects present - we speak the languages, and we speak about the languages. Beyond the obvious cognitive advantages, this legitimacy makes it possible to move away from the dominated-dominant dichotomy by granting each student a position of choice, which will give rise to confidence and the feeling of finally being included.

Conclusion

Learning to read and write in the language of schooling, in Cameroon and Canada, respects a global dynamic of integration of indigenous languages and cultures into teaching practices. The learner, as a speaker and carrier of a culture, bases his or her learning on existing knowledge from their family and socio-cultural environment. Biculturalism and bilingualism, and even multilingualism, are becoming some of the key elements of the multilingual literacies that are redesigning teaching methods.

6. Our languages in school, that's like a bar of African gold': Parents' and teachers' visions for multilingual education in Côte d'Ivoire

Michelle L. SOLORIO
Michigan State University

"In my day," began Seka, a father of six in the rural village of Konvi in Côte d'Ivoire, "when we went to school, it was only in French." I met Seka in 2018, while I was doing dissertation research about language of instruction and conflict. I quickly learned that Seka had three children attending one of the two public primary schools in the village. The public primary school his three youngest sons attended was a traditional, French-only school.

This is not the school Seka wanted his sons to attend. He would have preferred the other public primary school, which shared buildings and a school yard with the traditional school, but parents don't get to choose which school their children attend. "Choice is not something we hear along, it's not done like that yet," he explains.

This other school, funded and run by the government just like the traditional school, is a local-language school under the Programme des Écoles Intégrées (PEI), or the Integrated Schools Program. Briefly, there are rural public primary schools in 26 communities that use one of 10 local languages (out of the 60+ local languages in Côte d'Ivoire) as the medium of instruction for the first three years, during which time students also learn French as a second language. French is increasingly used as a co-language of instruction during those three years, before becoming the sole language of instruction in year four and after. (For more information on the PEI model of education, see Brou-Diallo, 2011; Solorio, 2020a; 2020b)

In my day, when we went to school, it was only in French. We started in French. It was disorienting, in fact! There was not this culture that we have now in my village, with this primary school where the kids learn in Brafé. When I was in school, it was like the lessons were a trickster - I couldn't catch on. It felt like my bag was reduced, as if my brain was empty, because I did not understand. We were lost in this history at the time when people and our base was missing from school. It is necessary to return to our culture, or to know how to bend to the cultures. That is why I support this Brafé school. With this school, we are already learning more! We are not losing children anymore. This new way is not disorienting for our kids. Because I am Brafé, and living in a Brafé area, I want Brafé in schools. If you were Senoufo, then of course you must have Senoufo in schools. Because to me, this new way becomes a vehicle for kids to learn at school. Because you know, culture comes in the head. I mean this is your roots. And language roots you in your culture, which you already know. If schooling is based on your roots, then you have a foundation, you have a place to start, and we can push forward. This is what I mean when I say that this new way, with school in Brafé, makes it so we don't lose any children. - Seka

He painted this picture about how unsettling it was for him to arrive at school for the first time and be expected to understand French. To him, it sounded like gibberish - he had never encountered French before, and suddenly he was expected to obey commands and learn math in this language. To use his words, he found it disorienting.

But that was not all - Seka told this story not to elicit pity or demand immediate change. Instead, he wanted me to know how things have gotten better for his children. They get to go to a school where they learn in their language, Brafé, and because of this they do not find themselves in the same disorienting state of mind. Not only that, but this means that school itself is more aligned with their culture - it is rooted in something that makes sense, which allows for a different kind of growth.

This phenomenon presented by Seka is not unusual, at least not among the 18 parents with whom I spoke during this project. As I demonstrate in other works (Solorio, 2020a; 2020b), most parents in both urban and rural settings in Côte d'Ivoire would prefer that their children attend a school in which a local language is used as the medium of instruction. Of course, this is not all the parents' preferences; there are some who prefer French-only schools. However, the parents who prefer a French-only school are among the minority within this group of 18 parents. In fact, while I originally expected that there might be variation based upon the parents' immigration status, I found that even among parents who are not originally from Côte d'Ivoire, it is only a minority who prefer a French-only school (Solorio, 2020b). While these findings are elaborated in my other publications related to these interviews, it is worth noting that most parents interviewed prefer local language schools.

It is also worth noting that among the three teachers I interviewed, it was only the teacher with experience teaching in a local language who preferred using a local language as the medium of instruction: Mr. Baako. Both the other teachers, Mme. Djere, a new teacher who taught in a French-only rural classroom, and Elodie, an experienced teacher who taught in a French-only urban classroom, preferred French-only instruction. The difference between teacher preferences and parent preferences are hard to compare, given the disparate sample sizes and backgrounds, but it is still important considering that, while parents will send their children to school and would like to choose what language is used in the classroom based upon how they think this language use will impact their own children, it is the teachers who will be making the choices about what languages are used in the classroom to teach these same children.

For those who are interested, in Solorio (2020a), I go into great details about the teachers' preferences and how they may have developed over time and policy implications (it was a dissertation, after all, in which detail in the minutiae is expected), while in Solorio (2020b) I explore in detail the actual language practices used within their classrooms by both teachers and students. A key takeaway that I would like to highlight here is that there are two issues the teachers wanted to make known when speaking with me. First is the issue of resources, which includes teacher training, teaching materials, textbooks, and so on; the second is the vast diversity of languages in the country contrasted against the languages that the teachers themselves speak. To the former, my interviews with teachers as well as classroom observations and reviews of teaching materials uncovered that regardless of the language used as the medium of instruction in the classroom, all materials provided to teach with and all training for teachers is centered around French. For example, in M. Baako's Brafé classroom, he was teaching in Brafé while reading from a French textbook. His on-the-spot translation from French to Brafé was not unusual - he explained to me that none of the materials he received were in Brafé. To the latter, new teachers do not get to choose where they teach. Mme. Djere told me a story about her very first school assignment in a remote location where the community spoke a language that was not only not her own but was not related to her native language and as such, she had no idea what the students and parents were saying to her unless they used French. Of course, just as it seems obvious that students should not be expected to learn in a language they do not understand, it seems obvious that a teacher cannot teach in a language that they do not understand.

This provides a nice segue into the purpose of this essay, which is to explore some of the different ideas that parents and teachers had about the possibility of multilingual classrooms in Côte d'Ivoire, keeping in mind the challenges on the ground (lack of local language materials, language mismatch between teachers and communities, teacher training, teacher preferences), as these challenges are important to contextualize and provide nuance to how some of these parent and teacher ideas may be put into place - or the constraints they may face in reality.

Their ideas are unsurprisingly diverse and complex, ultimately highlighting a desire for a new, innovative way of using languages in the classroom. Their ideas point to a desire to create learning environments that more closely mirror students' lives outside the classroom and in their multilingual communities. As such, since French remains a part of Ivorian life, all parents made it clear that French should remain part of their child's education, even if it is not the main language used in instruction. Throughout much of the rest of this essay, I will share ideas proposed by parents and teachers as well as the challenges to implementing these ideas that they brought up. I will not be sharing 18 proposals (or one proposal from every parent), as not all parents shared a specific idea or elaborated beyond why they felt it is important to have multilingual education; rather, I will share the four main ideas proposed by parents and one teacher: using a regional approach to selecting languages as the medium of instruction; teaching more African languages as subjects; expanding the existing PEI model; and transforming the PEI model from a bilingual model to a multilingual model.

Regional approach

The first idea I will present was not a parent's idea, but rather a teacher's idea. M. Baako, a teacher in rural Konvi who teaches in the local Brafé language at the PEI school, spent a lot of time extolling the virtues of the PEI school, praising it for allowing parents to understand what their children are learning and connecting the language of school to the language of home, community, and life. He did not mince his words about the challenges of the program, either, as I will briefly mention in later sections and as I go into great detail elsewhere (Solorio, 2020a; 2020b), yet his support for the program was strong enough that not only did he end our conversation by telling me that this is the way education should be, I could observe his dedication to teaching in Brafé (Solorio, 2020b).

When I asked him how local languages could be used in classrooms throughout the country, he responded that "choosing languages, that is a Chinese task. It is very difficult. But it is necessary that the people understand." He further went on to think aloud and came up with a proposal for a regional model of local language education, "We could choose one language for the north, one for the south, one for the west, and one for the east. Because, for example, in the north everyone at least understands Djula, so to teach in four languages would not be too hard. We can learn to teach in four languages."

Sabu, an urban father, had a similar suggestion, initially proposing that all schools teach in Djula before expanding to suggest that schools use "other languages, not just French but languages that are common in large areas. I prefer Djula because I speak it and everyone speaks it, but they can include the big languages". Nsia, an urban mother, shared a similar sentiment, suggesting that "we can pick, for example, the two most spoken languages in Côte d'Ivoire - besides French - and impose those languages in the classroom. It is more than two languages, more than two ethnicities, but something like that could work."

In some ways, this suggestion is a reduction of the existing bilingual local language-French PEI model of education. However, for Sabu, a father in an urban area where local languages are banned from the classroom and the only type of public education available to his child is exclusively in French, this proposal appears to be an expansion in bilingual education. In his opinion, teaching in both Djula and French "would be good, because then the parents can understand [what happens in school] and the children can understand their own ethnicity." The idea that language use in school can connect students to their roots and their communities is a shared notion among 17 of the 18 parents I spoke to, as was the hope that this would help parents to understand what happens in their child's classroom.

Mr Baako, on the other hand, proposed four regional languages because he has firsthand experience with the challenges of the PEI model of education, and he was actively trying to find a way to expand it into more locations without adding further strain on limited resources. Interestingly, though, he also suggested that each of the four regional languages could also be taught as subjects to all students in the country. Although he acknowledged the burden this would place on teachers, he was incredibly optimistic about the outcome: "the student can surmount it, he/she can learn four languages easily. They should not only learn French. They only need to put in a little effort, but they are young, and it is easy for them."

Teaching more languages as subjects

M. Baako's suggestion that students can be taught these regional languages ties nicely into the next proposal: teaching more languages as subjects in order to actively support multilingualism outside the classroom. Nsia, a mother in an urban area of Côte d'Ivoire, provides a good example of this type of proposal. "Everyone", she said, "should have the opportunity to learn the languages of their neighbor or their parent or colleague. They should be at school too, I think that's it, because if the children start to speak the language of their classmates, then they won't see each other's differences."

Nsia told me about the importance of local languages in the classroom frequently, mirroring the thoughts of other parents about how language is closely connected to culture, roots, and comprehension. But she also gave the inspiration for the title of this essay, by noting that "our languages are like a bar of African gold". Her desire to not only have local languages as medium of instruction but to also include the teaching of other local languages as subjects is rooted in the notion that the multiplicity of African languages is a wealth. This is not an uncommon belief among the 18 parents - in fact, other parents from both urban and rural areas called their language and the diversity of languages in the country as a "richness" and a "wealth." Seka went so far as to say that local languages must be "valorized", which can only be done by their inclusion in the classroom. The wealth being referenced by the parents is the diversity of culture and history contained in the languages, though the reason that some parents and M. Baako proposed teaching to students' languages besides their own language is to increase social awareness rather than increase cultural awareness. This difference is interesting, and especially in that it reinforces the importance that parents place on building multilingual classrooms in a way that is more reminiscent of the Ivorian linguistic landscape.

Expanding PEI

The "languages as wealth" motivation for including multiple Ivorian languages as subjects at school mirrors the motivation for teaching in local languages while continuing to teach French as a language, thus building a bilingual school that allows students to learn how to communicate in their communities as well as in formal Ivorian circles. The predominant suggestion for implementing local language instruction was to significantly broaden the current PEI model by increasing the range of available languages and expanding access to PEI schools across various locations. Importantly, most parents believed this most basic model of schooling should be available everywhere in the country, including in urban areas. The parents felt that there was no reason for PEI schools to be limited to 10 languages in only a select few (26) rural communities.

What I found most compelling was the rural parents' insistence that their children attending the PEI schools were better off than their urban counterparts because their education is steeped in their culture. By connecting education to culture via language of instruction, children, these parents believe, are better able to connect what they learn in school to their own realities. Recall Seka's story of his own education, which he termed "disorienting" due to the language mismatch, and this argument makes sense. This almost mirrors the "comprehension" argument made in support of various bilingual education programs (Bambgbose, 2009; Brock-Utne, 2001; Yohannes, 2009) but extends beyond the common argument that language comprehension leads to academic development. As rural mother, Ama, explained, "when they learn in their own language, they know more", while Afia, another rural mother, said, "it's good that there is this kind of school because when children are told something in their native languages, they can easily find a way to explain it."

These types of proposals are especially nuanced in their motivations, as the parents' thought behind the PEI model extends beyond the policy motivations. While PEI policy is focused on bolstering French language acquisition without hindering students' academic subject knowledge gain and cognitive development (Albaugh, 2014; Solorio, 2020a), parents are concerned about the academic benefits as well as the holistic benefits of local language instruction: cultural respect, community connections, and the tangible connection of life inside the classroom with life in the community. "Why don't children even understand a word of their own language," asked rural mother, Sopie. "It's dangerous when they don't, because then they don't know their parents. They cannot differentiate between their mother and their father, their roots." Sopie expressed a sentiment shared by 17 of the 18 parents, that when children are not exposed to their native languages outside the home they will lose them, and with it they will lose their roots. This, she fears, is dangerous. As the father of our introduction, Seka, says,

> It is necessary that our schools return to our roots. With the PEI school, we are returning to our culture, and we are learning more. When we use local languages in schools, it is not disorienting [for the students] because culture is in our heads. [...] We must

valorize our languages, build a campaign to share this model of education with everyone. We stand ready, or I stand ready, as a parent, to help make this campaign.

This proposal is likely the most feasible of all four I present in this essay, as it requires nominal modifications to an existing and resourced (albeit under-resourced) program; PEI already exists and uses the national curriculum. The main requirements for expansion are linguistic: identifying languages whose orthographic standardization could use further development for written materials, developing more materials in more local languages, matching teacher language backgrounds to their school assignments, and training teachers to teach in local languages. All of the needs, by the way, are the same needs of the current PEI program. It seems that the process of expanding the PEI will require effort on the part of policy makers, colleges of education, and resource developers, but it also seems per Mr. Baako's experience as if these are steps required simply to maintain the current PEI model. As M. Baako explained, "teachers are trained in French, and to teach in French. And the materials are in French, the resources for Brafé don't exist. We just have to make do". My own observations of M. Baako's classroom confirmed the lack of materials, notably his use of a textbook in French that he read from while speaking in Brafé (Solorio, 2020b). Teachers Elodie and Mme. Djere also shared these concerns, citing the lack of training for teaching in local languages as well as their own experiences being assigned to teach in rural schools where they do not speak the language. In my previous work, I outline some key policy recommendations to address these teaching needs (Solorio, 2020a; 2020b). Ultimately, there is more work to be done by policy makers, teacher training colleges, and the Ministry of Education to adequately provide for the existing PEI program as well as to expand the program so that it is available to all Ivorian students in all Ivorian languages. Yet my observation of M. Baako's classroom which demonstrated his willingness to overcome the mismatch between material language and teaching language, coupled with his very strong support for the PEI model, suggests that the teachers who have bought-in to the PEI model are willing to adapt even without the training or resources. What remains to be seen, then, is to what extent teacher can buy-in be increased?

Mme Djere's experience is an important one to understanding this question. As she helps us understand, buy-in is partly hindered by the process of teacher assignment - an area that would need to be closely attended to by the Ministry of Education should they continue to expand the program as it stands that teachers who cannot understand the local language could not reasonably be expected to teach (let alone teach well) in that language, just as students who do not understand the language of instruction cannot be expected to learn in that language.

In spite of the existing challenges facing the program and its expansion, the 17 parents out of the 18 I spoke with made it clear that using local languages in the classroom without eliminating French is important, and of those 17, 13 felt that there is no reason that the existing PEI program could not be expanded to include more languages in more locations.

From a bilingual to a multilingual model

Along with expanding the PEI model of local language-French bilingual education, some parents proposed transforming the nature of language use in education to be even more multilingual. One mother, Zuma, who is an immigrant from Burkina Faso living in an urban area of Côte d'Ivoire, suggested offering a variety of languages as language of instruction in a single school, so that in urban areas children could be in a classroom whose language matches home but not necessarily their neighboring classroom. Interestingly, Zuma also wavered between supporting multilingual education and preferring a French-only education, as she wanted to make sure that her children learn French.

Zuma's hesitancy also led her to propose classrooms that are multilingual. This proposal was not the most popular among parents by a longshot. However, it is an interesting proposal that most mirrors life in Côte d'Ivoire, especially but not exclusively in the urban centers. For example, in conversation with a friend and his mother, neither of whom were participants of the study but were gracious enough to consent to the inclusion of this story in my essay, the mother told stories about people she knew who fled the North during the first civil war circa 2002. One story in particular stood out: a young mother and her children en route to the southern part of the country were regularly stopped by soldiers - both northern "rebel" soldiers and southern government soldiers. When stopped by the "rebel" soldiers, she would use her native language to communicate as it was easily identifiable as a northern language. When stopped by the government soldiers, she would speak in a southern language to trick these soldiers into believing she was trying to return to her home in the south, not a "rebel". Her choice of language in both cases was intentional, with her and her children's survival at stake. I asked how she knew a southern language and was met with laughter. These languages, it was explained, are heard in communities throughout the country due to population mobility, and it is common for Ivorians to pick up phrases here and there in many languages as well as to understand the meaning of what people are saying even when you may not speak the same language.

> I'm going to bring up the neighborhood again. You need to include French because it is in the neighborhood. You also need to be around someone who can speak your own language. Or maybe someone who speaks Djula, since it is commonly understood. It's better to understand so that you can follow along, so you can understand. We need to talk so everyone understands. The problem is that... It is not just about the different languages to include in school, but it also considers not being able to explain, or whether you can understand. - Zuma

This is a very complicated idea for a classroom, as it faces greater resource, training, and linguistic challenges. It also faces sociopolitical challenges, which cannot be overstated. Returning to my interaction with my friend and his mother, we were sharing all the ways we could say "thank you" different languages. I said "i ni cɛ", or "thank" you in Malinkekan/Djula, and instantly the tone of the room changed from lighthearted to serious. My friend's mother turned to me and very sternly said, "we do not say that in this house".

This is certainly a hangover from the conflicts, where I had used a northern language to say "thank you" to a southern woman who distinctly remembers both civil wars. It is also a strong reminder that language, ethnic identity, and in some cases civil war affiliations remain linked in complex ways as the country continues to move toward a peaceful, fully post-conflict state. However, just as Nsia and other parents suggested that the teaching of other Ivorian languages could support social and cultural awareness, teaching in multiple languages could support building awareness and respect of those whose backgrounds differ in a way that more directly mirrors life in Ivorian communities.

Conclusion

In this essay, I intended to share the ideas proposed by parents and one teacher as well as the challenges brought up by teachers and parents about the possibility of multilingual education in Côte d'Ivoire. I did not share the ideas of all 18 parents as not all parents brought up a specific idea or elaborated beyond why they felt teaching in (and the teaching of) local languages is important. However, by sharing the ideas presented alongside the motivations behind these ideas and the real constraints faced by the teachers who would ultimately build these types of classrooms, I intended to provide space for these 21 individuals' voices to be heard. In this way, perhaps the dialogue between parents, teachers, communities, and policy makers can continue to incorporate more of these locally-grown ideas - not only in Côte d'Ivoire but in other countries in the continent and even off the continent - as we continue to navigate multilingual realities and continue to seek ways to make our diverse classrooms match what is occurring outside the classroom in the students' lived linguistic realities.

While I provided some examples of possible multilingual classroom settings in Côte d'Ivoire, using the ideas of parents and teachers in rural and urban areas in the country, I realize that there are many more ideas to be explored. What stands out to me is (1) the desire to have multilingual classroom settings that more closely mirror life outside the classroom, and (2) the value that Ivorian parents place on their languages which they are keen to share with their children. It is not just that parents want their children to learn their own culture and language, it's that they want formal spaces such as education to include the wealth of languages as well. Yes, parents recognize the academic value - namely that children who are taught in their own language are better able to learn academic subjects such as mathematics and other languages such as French; but the parents recognize other values as well, such as the potential that they could be better equipped to understand what happens inside their child's classroom, the potential that their child could better understand and respect other Ivorians who do not share the same ethnolinguistic roots, and the not-so-simple pride that comes with your language being recognized as "worthy" of inclusion in formal spaces such as education.

The challenges the teachers shared with me in teaching in multilingual classrooms and the lack of resources available for the current, limited bilingual education program make it clear that there is no easy answer to expanding multilingual education. However, the Ministry of Education has a history of successful sensitization for the PEI project, evidenced by the widespread support of the program. I hope that teachers can also be part of future sensitization efforts to increase their buy-in to multilingual education, just as I hope that more resources, training, and support will be granted to maintain and expand the existing bilingual PEI model of education in a way that incorporates the proposals I shared in this essay.

7. Translanguaging in indigenous Kenyan languages: Include all learners no silencing

Brenda Aromu Wawire
African Population and Health Research Center

The language situation in Kenya

Kenya is a multilingual and multiethnic country in East Africa where 68 living languages are spoken (Eberhard et al., 2021). Majority of the languages spoken in Kenya belong to the Niger-Congo, Cushitic, and Nilotic families. School going children typically speak an average of three languages. English and Kiswahili, which are official languages, are the medium of instruction in schools and indigenous language (i.e. Kikuyu, Dhuluo) are used at home. Kiswahili is the dominant indigenous language used by many Kenyans outside their homes, in media, public offices, trade and is a common language for diverse communities. The indigenous Kenyan languages are typically used for basic interpersonal communication in homes and communities. Moreover, Sheng - a mixed language code that is based on the syntactic structure and grammar of Kiswahili and draws its lexicon from Kiswahili, English, and other indigenous Kenyan languages is widely used in many rural and urban communities (Githiora, 2018; Mutiga, 2013). The language of instruction policy in Kenya stipulates that children in grades 1 - 3 be taught in mother tongue whereas English and Kiswahili are taught as subjects. However, from grade 4 onwards English is the main medium of instruction whereas Kiswahili is taught as a subject. Language of instruction recommendations have been a key component in education reforms in Kenya since independence. In 2010, the Kenyan constitution reaffirmed support for the use of mother tongue as the language of instruction. The policy has been reaffirmed in the most recent educational white paper and the educational sector plan of 2014 (the Republic of Kenya, 2015; MoE, 2014).

Language is a core component of formal education attainment as it is the medium of instruction, curriculum design and assessment, communication, and engagement in learning activities. Therefore, it is one of the main determinants of academic achievement and influences learners' socio-emotional well-being. Since independence, the Kenyan government (Ministry of Education) has constantly faced several challenges including the difficulty of developing, strengthening, and utilizing indigenous African languages as the medium of instruction particularly in the early grades, despite the language policy encouraging the use of local indigenous languages. Due to the unresolved challenges, many African countries including Kenya have opted to continue with the pre-colonial language policies that are grounded in monoglossic orientations which values monolingualism where language is seen as an autonomous skill that functions independently from the context in which it is used. For instance, schools in Kenya ignore how students use indigenous African languages in their day-to-day interactions. After independence, many African nations only made minor modifications on the language policies through education commissions, language-rationalization policies, and declarations (Chumbow, 2005; Makalela, 2015). This is contrary to research evidence that widely demonstrates the importance of using home languages in classrooms in connecting classroom content to the familiar linguistic and cultural world and to make curriculum content more accessible to students (Cummins, 2008; Garcia, 2009; Piper & Miksic, 2011; Vuzo, 2018). Learning in local languages can effectively connect individuals to their social environment which in turn influences their world view (Mazrui, 2002).

Common language use practices in rural homogeneous or urban heterogeneous communities and the media in Kenya entail the use of multiple languages simultaneously characterized by code-mixing/switching practices (Ogechi, 2005; Mazrui, 1995). These are indicators of typical bi/multilinguals - individuals who have knowledge and capacity of using two or more languages. Bilingualism is a dynamic process that draws from complex and interrelated linguistic practices of bilingual individuals and utilizes an integrated linguistic system - human beings have only one language system (García, 2009). Bilingual individuals typically use all languages in their linguistic repertoire as an integrated system to navigate their bilingual world (Cenoz & Gorter, 2013; Makalela, 2015). These multilingual practices involve shuttling between languages during the process of making/negotiating meaning, to shape experiences, to gain understanding and knowledge, and to manipulate the domains of social interactions in order to make sense of their bilingual world (Baker, 2011). This is referred to as translanguaging defined as the practice of multilingual speakers alternating between languages using the diverse languages that form their linguistic repertoire as an integrated system (Wei, 2011a, Canagarajah, 2011a). Kiramba 2016 (b) further elaborates that translanguaging in learning involves mixing, crossing, and hybridizing one or more languages in the classrooms. Translanguaging is characterized by creativity which entails following or flouting the norms of language as well as criticality, which is the ability to utilize available evidence to question, problematize, or express views adequately through reasons, responses, and situations (Wei, 2011a, b).

Learning whether in or out of school takes place through social interactions (discourse) hence classroom discourse affects and facilitates learning. Research evidence widely supports the importance of instruction in a language that students are familiar with (used in their immediate environment) as it enables students to participate and interact effectively in learning activities, promotes acquisition of literacy and cognitive skills resulting in high learning outcomes (August & Shanahan, 2006; Dubeck et al., 2012) Researchers further denote that human languages have distinct surface features i.e. sentence structure, writing system, speech sounds but beyond these, are common underlying proficiencies - the basis for L1 and L2 development. Therefore, more cognitively demanding tasks such as literacy, numeracy, content learning, abstract thinking, and problem-solving-are skills common across languages; hence, when they are learned in one language, they transfer to another (Cummins, 1979; 2000). Typically, if the language of instruction used in schools differs from the languages students use at home this can be a hindrance to students' learning and development of required competencies.

Language of instruction policy implementation

In Kenya, research reports indicate that effective implementation of the language of instruction policy over the years has failed, as English is the dominant language of instruction in lower and upper primary as well as in secondary schools (Muthwii, 2004; Piper et al., 2015). Moreover, majority of schools enact school language policies where students are expected to speak English for four days in a week whereas Kiswahili is allocated only one day. Mother tongues are not permitted in the school compounds and students speaking in the mother tongue languages at schools may be punished heavily. The monolinguistic orientation adapted by the education system in Kenya where languages are separated ignores the daily linguistic realities and localities of learners. According to Ruiz (1994), the view of home language as a problem creates multiple problems for emerging bi/multilingual individuals. These include tensions around the use of official languages and ignoring the multilingual realities of students inside and outside classrooms, subtractive bilingualism, loss of identity and culture, controversies around language testing and assessment (Kiramba, 2017a, 2018; McGlynn & Martin, 2009; Taylor & Snoddon, 2013).

The use of English as the dominant language of instruction is attributed to English being the language of high-stakes school leaving examinations such as the Kenya Certificate of Primary/Secondary Education [K.C.P.E; K.C.S.E]; English being an indicator of prestige associated with economic prosperity and global citizenship, it is a language that enables an increased ability for interethnic communication, entrenched colonial legacies, and it is the language of technological tools, teachers beliefs on the importance of English for academic success, pressure from teachers, parents and students to learn English (Muthwii, 2004; Dhillon & Wanjiru, 2013; Piper et al, 2015). The implementation of a language of instruction policy that fails to recognize the plural lingual practices of bi/multilingual speakers is a major contributor to poor learning outcomes in primary and secondary schools and post-secondary in Kenya. Many learners in primary and secondary schools fail to acquire the minimum competencies in numeracy and literacy which consequently affects their performance in other academic content areas such as social studies, science among others. Moreover, the persistent use of English as the medium of instruction in foundational grades in Kenya constrains student participation in knowledge production due to anxiety to engage in learning using a language where they have limited proficiency, reluctance to participate and lack of confidence due to developing oral language proficiency skills (Ackers & Hardman, 2001; Bunyi, 2001, 2008; Kembo-Sure & Ogechi, 2016; Kiramba, 2016a, 2018). Furthermore, the dominant use of English is spearheaded by teachers, parents, community and societal beliefs of English as an important language for learning.

Limited oral and written proficiency in the main LOI and banishing of home languages in schools could be a contributor to the teacher centered classroom discourses exhibited in many classrooms in Kenya. Whereby the teacher asserts control of the classroom interactions during learning as students do not have confidence to express/share knowledge due to limited language skills. In this case teacher-student interactions are characterized by recitation of questions by teachers and responses given by individual students or whole class, memorization, rote repetition by students, recall of facts, and minimal student input (Abd-Kadir & Hardman, 2007; Ackers & Hardman, 2001; Pontefract & Hardman, 2005). Students and teachers utilize safe talk practices - limited language use by teachers and students to avoid violating the language expectations i.e., use of mother tongue in classrooms - during learning which consequently silences students and renders their home language resources invisible and unnecessary to facilitate learning. The disconnection between the language policy, its implementation and failure to incorporate theoretical frameworks on multilingualism and lack of pedagogical training on effective multilingual pedagogical practices among others are critical contributors to poor learning outcomes and excludes many learners participating in knowledge production (see Dubeck, et al., 2011; Kiramba & Oloo, 2019; Piper & Zuilkowski, 2015; Piper et al., 2018).

Translanguaging for inclusiveness and equitability in learning

Contrary to the monolinguistic practices implemented in education settings, studies on classroom discourse in multilingual contexts demonstrate the prevalence of plural language practices such as code-switching/mixing in speaking and code meshing in writing (Heller & Martin-Jones, 2001; Merrit et al., 1992). The persistent use of English as the dominant medium of instruction contrary to the language of instruction policy that includes indigenous languages is typically not sustainable as during the learning process. Consequently, it is critical for education stakeholders to ensure equity and fair access to learning through implementing a non-discriminatory language of instruction policy. Otherwise, unfavorable language policies that promulgate language in educational settings perpetuate the denial of linguistic human rights. Linguistic human rights involve ensuring that language is not a hindrance to effective enjoyment of rights and experiences with a linguistic dimension or to meaningful participation in public institutions and democratic processes, enjoyment of social and economic opportunities that require linguistic skills (Rubio-Marín, 2003).

Translanguaging is the typical way that bilingual families and communities communicate on a day-to-day basis in formal and informal spaces to make meaning of their bilingual world and to formulate their identity. It is paramount for education stakeholders including teachers, policymakers, actors, implementers, and parents to strive to rethink ways of making learning spaces more inclusive and equitable. The education stakeholders should be on the forefront to provide sensitization and awareness on the importance of learning in familiar languages. They should seek to institutionalize education models that encourage dynamic bilingualism which will encourage the use of African indigenous languages in classrooms. Promoting pedagogical practices in which learners, use linguistic practices that mirror plural lingual practices of multilinguals could be an optimal solution to mitigating the persistent learning crisis. The typical models of bilingual programs implemented in Kenya is two-way immersion or bilingual immersion where two languages - English and Kiswahili - are used for instruction and the two language systems are treated autonomously. The language division model noted in most bilingual education programs are set up to enhance parallel monolingualism as students are forced to work solely in the target language of instruction (Heller, 1999; Orellana & Reynolds, 2008).

In the multilingual contexts, students and teachers constantly violate the principle of language separation as they utilize plural lingual practices during learning (Orellana & Reynolds, 2008). Unfortunately, education stakeholders fail to acknowledge, support, and implement flexible bilingual pedagogy that goes beyond the use of two separate languages. A paradigm shift to policies and practices that encourage the utilization of the entire linguistic repertoire of bilingual individuals through pedagogical practices (teaching and assessment) that encourage students to perform bilingually in classrooms while reading, writing, taking notes, discussing, and signing rather than the traditional conceptions of autonomous languages is urgent in Kenya.

In the education settings translanguaging as a teaching practice encompasses deliberate changing of language input and output whereby one language is used to reinforce the other to increase processing and understanding of content and relaying of meaning (Williams, 2002). Additionally, translanguaging may facilitate home-school links and cooperation as caregivers and parents can participate and support children's learning. Translanguaging enhances the integration of fluent speakers with early learners (Baker, 2001). The inclusion of multiple language practices in the classrooms promotes inclusivity and promotes social justice (García, 2009). It also promotes a high sense of self-efficacy, since students are able to self-regulate their learning (Velasco & García, 2013).

Teachers use inclusive language practices for purposes of teaching, to differentiate instruction to involve and give voice, clarity, reinforce, manage classrooms, to extend and ask questions among socially, educationally, and linguistically diverse learners (García, 2009). These inclusive practices reduce the risk of alienation of bilingual students. Teachers use translanguaging as a scaffolding approach to support emergent bilinguals to engage with rigorous content, access difficult texts and produce new language practices and new knowledge. To promote student-centered learning, teachers use translanguaging to facilitate learning through setting up project-based and collaborative groupings in which students use plural lingual practices to engage and complete learning tasks. Rigorous instruction that maximizes students' interactions supports the expansion of students' language repertoire, and academic language (García, 2009).

Students use plural lingual practices for purposes of learning as it enables them to construct and modify their sociocultural identities in response to historical and social conditions critically and creatively and to participate, elaborate ideas, and raise questions (García, 2009). According to García (2011) early grade learners use translanguaging for several meta functions including mediating understanding among each other, co-construct meaning within themselves and others, to include or exclude others and to demonstrate knowledge. Creese and Blackledge (2010) noted that student's translanguage to keep the tasks moving by using both languages simultaneously to convey information. It is also widely used in writing for writers to make sense of themselves and their audiences as evidenced in modern day technologies that have enabled the production of fluid texts in digital genres such as emails, online discussion forums, blogging, and instant messaging (Sebba, 2012; Hinrichs, 2006; Montes-Alcalá, 2007). Schools are tasked with the responsibility of creating translanguaging spaces where children are given the agency to act linguistically by being creative and critical and teachers being supportive and encouraging those actions. Bi/multilingual teachers and students continually violate the language of instruction policy that encourages separation of languages when students engage in learning tasks.

Translanguaging practices in schools in Kenya

In Kenya, evidence shows the teachers use multilingual and multimodal linguistic practices in science lessons to make content more comprehensible to students (Kiramba, 2016 b; Cleghorn, 1992). Translanguaging validates home languages and promotes identity formation - the way individuals develop a unique view of themselves shared by other people and the society at large (Martin-Jone & Jones,

2000). Translanguaging as a pedagogical strategy allows students' voices to be heard and enables them to draw on multiple communicative resources to enhance participation and creativity (Bakhtin, 1981; Kiramba, 2017 b). To illustrate further, Kiramba and Harris (2019) examined discourse practices in fourth-grade classrooms in a rural primary school in Kenya. The researcher's audio recorded 35 science lessons and English lessons each 30 minutes long over a duration of 6 months. This study revealed that translanguaging was a means of creating lively interactional space for discussion of everyday knowledge in the classrooms. It was also used to give students voice, enabled students to co-create knowledge with teachers, and disrupted the typical initiation, response, evaluation pattern during instruction. When teachers persistently use English there is persistent silence in the classrooms. Students don't respond to the questions posed by the teacher and do not engage in the learning process. But the moment the teacher switches to other languages students participate. Silence during learning could be attributed to bracketing of home language or using it minimally, monologism, misunderstanding classroom content, lack of access of content presented, incapability to negotiate meaning in an unfamiliar language. The rigid language separation in classrooms should not be enhanced as this practice is inconsistent with how bi/multilingual use language in real life which encompasses drawing on their multiple linguistic resources for effective communication (Abiria et al., 2013; Kiramba & Harris, 2019; Makalela, 2015).

The emphasis on English as the main medium of instruction and for access to the curriculum is a model that does not support equity and inclusivity in learning. These practices consequently present barriers to the realization of optimal economic growth and develop human capital within Africa's multilingual environments. In order for teachers in Kenya to use translanguaging effectively as a pedagogical strategy, training on the theoretical background on translanguaging and effective pedagogical best practices should be embedded in the pre-service programs as well as professional development training sessions for in service teachers. Teachers should be trained and encouraged to facilitate the development of multilingual spaces and be allowed to balance policy constraints with the actual students' needs and realities. Furthermore, there should be extensive mobilization and sensitization efforts in education settings and communities to diffuse the negative attitudes directed at African languages and leverage the multilingualism of Kenyan students as a learning resource.

Kenya has a great potential to provide a foundation for lifelong learning and civic engagement through implementing educational frameworks that promote inclusiveness and equitability. This can be achieved through supporting the use of African indigenous languages as a medium for learning in and outside schools. Teachers and school administrators should encourage and support classroom interactions in students' indigenous languages. For teachers to implement translanguaging as a pedagogical approach effectively, the ministry of education and other relevant stakeholders should support professional development training on this for in-service teachers. This component should be embedded in the pre-service teacher-training curriculum to equip pre-service teacher with theoretical knowledge and practical skill sets to meet the linguistic realities in the classrooms. School policies that bar home languages use in school premises should be banned through media campaigns to sensitize and create awareness in communities on the importance of using all languages that students are familiar with for learning thus eradicating the lingering colonial legacy. These efforts will contribute to bolstering Kenya's self-reliance, long-term recovery from the prodigious effects of the COVID-19 pandemic and for future transformation and participation in the global arena.

8. Improving the quality of education in Africa using African languages for teaching

Maria J. AARON
Obolo Bilingual Education Centre

Bilingual education has the potential to transform education in Africa, raising the standard, and making it authentically African. Using African mother tongues, schools can raise confident young people, with knowledge grounded in their language and cultural heritage, and well-prepared to move forward into their globalized environment. Bilingual education offers deeper understanding of all the subjects taught, while also facilitating better communication skills in the mother tongue and English and affirming the cultural knowledge and wisdom of the African community to which the students belong. At the same time, it offers higher success rates in acquiring permanent literacy skills in primary education, even in English (or French or Portuguese respectively as the official, former colonial, languages of Africa).

The situation in Nigeria, with basically English-Medium instruction: Every lesson in school teaches English, while the contents of the lesson is only partially understood.

Though the official National Policy on Education prescribes the use of the "language of the immediate environment" for instruction in initial education, and only in primary 4 a gradual switch to English, all instructional materials are written in English only: textbooks and readers for the students, teachers' guides and curricula. Moreover, all tests and examinations are written in English. Yet most of the children hardly speak English at home. Teachers, who try to communicate, and so explain using the language of the environment, can only explain new concepts partially because they themselves do not understand the English terms or the concepts well enough to come up with suitable equivalents. It is normal for them to constantly revert to the use of English terms. Besides this, knowing that ultimately, they must prepare their students to take the exams in English, most effort is spent on drilling these English terms and their definitions, rather than on explaining and understanding the concepts.

The Obolo Bilingual Education Centre

The Obolo Bilingual Education Centre (OBEC) is a model school for mother tongue-based bilingual education, situated in Andoni LGA, Rivers State, Nigeria. The Obolo Language and Bible Translation Organization (OLBTO), representing the Obolo community, are the owners of the OBEC. It is a low fee-paying private school, seeking to be an example to be emulated by Government as well as private enterprise. It was started in 2014, with only primary 1, and has now reached Junior Secondary School 1 (7th grade). Previously, the complete Bible was translated in Obolo (launched in 2014), and there was literature for leisure, as well as a series of Obolo readers for the teaching of reading in primary schools, and other literature for secondary schools. In preparation for the OBEC primary 1 class, textbooks for all the subjects were translated/adapted into Obolo. Every following year, the translation team again translated/adapted the books for the next class that was reached.

In the OBEC which has no nursery section, from primary 1 to 4, all subjects are taught in Obolo. Meanwhile, English is taught only as a subject. Obolo is also taught as a subject. From primary 5 onward, English is used as an additional language for teaching. The school intends to continue teaching bilingually up to the end of Basic Education in Junior Secondary 3 (ninth grade). All teachers are fully qualified holders of NCE (National Certificate of Education).

Illustrations demonstrating higher quality of teaching and learning through mother tongue-based bilingual education

From memorization of meaningless terms for new concepts, to understanding terms with meaningful elements

As in the OBEC, the textbooks for all the content subjects were written/translated in Obolo, the English terms used for many concepts are also re-expressed in Obolo. Some of the effects of this are a deepening of understanding, and better retention of the concepts learned. This is best illustrated through description of observations as follows:

The father of an OBEC student in primary 1, a motorcyclist, told my husband about a discussion between her and her elder brother, a primary 3 student in another school. She asked the brother, "What is zero?" The brother answered, "Zero is zero!" But the younger sister, not satisfied, insisted, "No, what is zero? "The boy, exasperated, just repeated, "Zero is zero; zero is zero!" Then she told him, "No, zero is 'ofok' (empty/empty space). There is nothing in it!" The father was so impressed with the understanding his daughter had acquired in primary 1, that he wanted to transfer all his other children too to the OBEC!

In the above illustration, the Obolo word for "zero" by itself had communicated the meaning of the concept to this girl. When meaningful terms are used instead of English terms, which often don't communicate any meaning to Nigerian students, they easily understand, and easily remember the new concepts. This is even the case at the level of tertiary education. As teachers need to use statistics to analyze class results, the words "mean", "median", and "mode" were translated for them into Obolo. They were translated with "Ikike ifuk" (Literally: the equal number), "Ifuk-etete" (the middle number), and "Uwa/Owa ifuk" (the most common number) respectively. Some teachers in the workshop where these terms were translated, then exclaimed, "Oh, now we understand it better! Before now we couldn't really get it. This makes it very clear!" While mother tongue speakers of European languages could get meaningful clues from some of these English words, these clues are lost on African learners. But when they are translated, the meaning of the very words used to label the new concepts can help students to understand the concepts, and to retain them.

Improved teaching and learning: From memorization to active thinking and learning

The mode of teaching used most frequently in Nigeria is teacher- rather than learner-oriented. It involves a rather passive form of learning, with a lot of memorizations, rather than active learning.

Even though currently in teacher education, student teachers learn that it is better to involve their students more actively in the learning process, in practice this is hard to do when the language of communication in school is English. Apart from the elite, commonly, primary school children can hardly communicate in English, and even teachers cannot express themselves fluently. The use of English limits the options. Teachers feel more secure relying on the wordings in the textbooks and so they teach from the front of the class, without having contributions from the children, who cannot answer questions in English. The children only speak when asked to repeat something, or to reproduce what the teacher has said earlier.

Observing nursery 3 in a private English-medium school in a rural area, the teacher was teaching about "transportation", saying loudly and vigorously, "Transportation is the movement of people to go...", and the class repeating rhythmically after her, over the period of several minutes. Then the teacher asked: "Transportation is what?", and the class answered, "Transportation is the movement..." Then she said, "Transportation is the movement of what?", and they answered, "Transportation is the movement of people..."

In the OBEC, using Obolo, teachers initially tended to continue similarly, telling the pupils everything directly from the textbook, while the children listened, repeated what the teacher said, and then copied the notes from the blackboard. However, in a lesson in primary 2 on transportation, I interrupted the teacher after she started to "lecture" the children on various modes of transportation as listed in the book and urged her to first ask the pupils what they knew about modes of travelling. Then the children perked up and were all struggling for a chance to contribute from their own experience. They talked about motorcycles, "Keke" (motorized tricycles), "moto" (cars), "flying boats" (fast engine boats), "market boats" (large wooden boats with a small engine), canoes, and barges, and what each of them could transport, and how they were operated, and the kind of people driving them. Both teacher and pupils were elated! The children also mentioned "uji inyọn̄ "air boat/aero plane" and described two types, "the one that is like a cross", and "the type that has something like a fan on top", which some had seen landing. So, the teacher ended up, asking the students to sort the vehicles into the categories of land-, water-, and air-transportation, and wrote these in their categories as summarizing notes on the blackboard. Having contributed these items themselves, the pupils easily learned to read the notes on the board together. Then they copied it into their exercise books, and all visibly felt satisfied.

Through the group discussion in Obolo, children learned more details from the experience and observations of their classmates. This affirmed them, seeing that they already knew something about the things taught in school, and that they could be successful in education.

From disregard for cultural and environmental learning, to integrating new knowledge into the prior knowledge of the children

After the lesson described above, the teacher expressed surprise and delight that the children knew so much about the topic already! In fact, they knew much more detail than what was taught in the textbook! There was hardly anything added to what the children already knew. It appears that, with the pervading use of English and the students' consequent inability to communicate in class, teachers and educators generally mistakenly assume that children don't have any previous knowledge about the subjects taught in school. So then, the teacher thinks she needs to supply all the information, and the children only listen and then re-produce the memorized information in tests and exams. However, when teachers learn to make better use of the communicative resource of their mother tongue, students are able to interact on the topic and express what they know for the teacher and the whole class to hear. In the case described above, the teacher was able to access the previous knowledge the children had acquired in their home environment, affirm it, and then build on it. Thus, using their own language interacting in class, the children connect their outside-school experience with the concepts being taught in school. They are processing what they have known and integrating the new concepts. They are thinking and not merely memorizing, and the gap between their African environment and the world of school is reduced.

From knowledge of theory to knowing for life improvement

One of the outcomes of this kind of learning in their own language, where the students are encouraged to talk in school about things they have observed and learned in their homes and their cultural environment is that they start to apply their knowledge to their lives. One father of a boy in primary 1 reported that the boy surprised him one day, because it had appeared that he wasn't performing well at school. Then, at home, when the boy saw him cleaning his ear with the pointed shaft of a feather, he said, "Daddy, our teacher told us that we should not use anything that is thin and pointed to clean our ear, but only our little finger, so that we don't damage the inside of the ear. The father was shocked to hear this from his little boy who he said, "didn't even know anything in school". It has been recognized that application of "knowledge" acquired in formal education is sorely lacking in Nigerian society, even the knowledge acquired in institutes of higher education. It appears that this is at least partly due to the low-communicative and basically foreign language that has been used for instruction, hindering the students' thinking and connecting of things offered in school with what they know from their life outside school. Using the mother tongue for teaching changes this and enables the children to bring all their understanding to bear.

Improved teaching methodology: From unclear- or non-communication to finetuning of communication for supportive teaching

In a group interview of Obolo parents of school children, one parent described what happened when he himself reached primary 4, after the first three years when his mother tongue had been used to teach as well as English. He reported that in primary 4 the teacher announced that he would only tolerate speaking in English. Describing what happened from then on, he said, "When they would ask a question and you would know the answer, you would quickly swallow it, because the teacher would say, 'Speak in English!

Because of the language obstacle, students are unable to express what they understand or to ask a question for clarification. As they keep quiet, they leave the teacher less aware how much (or how little) she has been able to communicate to them. In contrast, when their own language is used for instruction, there is no obstruction to communication, and children normally understand what the teacher is saying. They will be responding visibly, or with exclamations, laughter, interjections, questions, or comments. The teacher can also see from their faces when they are or are not understanding. Typically, bilingual classrooms are lively, with the children following along, and responding. Through their response, teachers then can immediately correct any misunderstandings, re-expressing what was said in a different way. Children can also be encouraged to ask for clarification, and frequently do so. Moreover, teachers too can ask questions to evaluate the children's understanding during their teaching. This contrasts with English-medium education, as we have seen in the above illustration.

More authentic evaluation of learning with examinations in the mother tongue

As English is used for all tests and examinations, in primary 1 in a government school, I saw many students were baffled and marking just any of the answers in the Multiple-Choice exam papers. Obviously, with large numbers of advanced English vocabularies which are hardly appropriate for beginning learners of English, the children are overwhelmed. The teachers read out the questions and the Multiple-Choice answers to the students (which is practiced throughout primary school) because the students could not yet read these by themselves. Even though the teachers also translated the questions in Obolo, upon hearing some of the lengthy instructions and questions in English, some children already put their heads down and started sleeping! Some nearby me were struggling to recognize the number of the question the teacher was reading, and then marked the answer for the wrong question. No doubt, the results of such tests cannot provide much insight into the level of the students' understanding and learning.

In contrast, the children in the OBEC primary 1 had been taught in Obolo and their exams were also not written in English, but in Obolo. (Here, because these children in primary 1 couldn't read or recognize numbers sufficiently yet, it was also decided that they should be asked the questions orally and individually, while the teacher would tick their answers on the paper.) With this, except for two who refused to talk (out of 38 students), they were able to do well, demonstrating what they had learned. During meetings of the staff at the end of the year, the class teacher reported that he had not thought that his students would be learning as well as this. He exclaimed, "Even little X, who is always playing, stood there quite confidently and answered every question correctly!" There was no confusion for the students themselves, neither for the teachers, as to what they had learned, and what was not learned well. Instead, the students were happy and proud that they were able to perform well in the exam and were succeeding in school.

Improved oral communication skills in both languages
A group of researchers who came to visit the OBEC told us that our students, even in primary 1, were exceptionally good communicators and well composed - much better than what they had found in the other schools they visited in all the Geo-Political zones of Nigeria. As they had a researcher in each class (except primary 2) they interviewed each child individually, using English, with translation by the class teacher if needed. In primaries 1 to 4 where Obolo was used for teaching, the children mostly answered in Obolo, while in primaries 5 and 6, where English also had been used for teaching, they were able to answer part of the questions in English too. The quality of language used, and the comportment of the students in communication (with an adult) clearly impressed and pleased the researchers.

Using mother tongue to teach Reading and Writing yields higher literacy rates in primary education, and better performance in English
Mother Tongue-Based Bilingual education is more inclusive: during the Obolo Pilot Project in the 1980s and 90s, the subject of Reading using Obolo was added to the curriculum in all Government schools in the Local Government Area. In the junior classes of primary school, four out of seven periods for language were then assigned to Obolo (Reading), while only three were left to teach English. Through testing in 1990-91, these rural schools were found to have

higher literacy rates than better-resourced urban Government schools (Aaron, M. 1998). The testing was done through English essay writing in primary 6. The schools in Obolo area that were tested had 68.75 and 60 percent of literate students respectively, while the "schools of the urban poor" had only 51.6 and 48 percent literate students respectively. All other rural schools had much lower literacy rates, the highest of which was by a rural school located near the metropolitan area, with 36.6 percent literate students (Afiesimama, A.F. 1991). Therefore, the Obolo schools clearly outperformed the ones in the capital city of the state. Since they had had fewer periods for English, and more for reading in Obolo, it was also clear that the students used the same competencies acquired in Obolo also for English (See also Cummins, J. 1980 and 2016).

Later, this was also confirmed in the OBEC, which achieves even higher literacy rates. Of the first two student-intakes, a total of 79 students, those who stayed in OBEC till the end of primary 5, there were only two students who didn't succeed in reading, both with severe learning problems.

Their performance in both reading and writing was by primary 6 also of a higher standard than the standard Obolo schools achieved during the Obolo Pilot Project, and apparently comparable to the standard of the best-resourced schools of the elite in the cities. The researchers who came to the OBEC tested reading in OBEC's primaries five and six. Already two consecutive teachers of primary 5 had reported that their students could read any book in Obolo well. Consequently, the researchers tested by opening any book they found in the classroom for a student to read. All students were tested this way. In primary 6, in the same way, the students were presented with any book written in English, and they did equally well (though in the rare instance of meeting unknown vocabulary, the teacher would quickly pronounce this for the student to continue reading uninterruptedly). The researchers were visibly impressed by their ability to read well, with comprehension, and good expression, in either language.

Earlier informational uses of reading, and communication skills in writing

Through the use of the mother tongue, students can start early to read their textbooks and the notes written on the blackboard. In schools where the mother tongue is not used to teach reading, generally in rural areas such as Obolo, by primary 6, only less than 20 percent of school children manage to read with understanding, while the rest only copy and attempt to memorize for reproduction in exams, without much understanding.

I observed that in Nigeria, the teachers always write extensive notes on the blackboard to be copied by the students into their exercise books. This is understandable, as most children don't own any textbooks except an English reader. However, children are drilled in extensive copying right from the first weeks of their schooling, so they copy a lot of materials which they cannot read yet. Parents of students in primary 1 want to see a lot of "writing" in their children's exercise books. Even teachers find it important that the children can do this "writing" well early on. As a result, however, many children tend not to know that writing is meant for communication. In English, they cannot write creatively early on, because they lack the vocabularies. Using the mother tongue however, in OBEC, the children in primary 4 were able to write welcome letters to a staff who returned from a prolonged leave of absence. Some also started to write folk stories, cartoons, poems, and they love it. Some wrote shopping lists, and by primary 5, students wrote the answers to exam questions in their own words. Also, by primary 5, the teachers observed that their students started to be able to write short stories in English too (though they preferred writing in Obolo, since their English vocabulary was still more limited), but by primary 6, more children wanted to write in English too.

As they can read independently earlier, OBEC students also read their notes with understanding (from the end of primary 1, about one quarter of the students start to read independently), and by primary 2, teachers can use short notes to practice reading with them. In primary 5, I saw that the students used the notes in their exercise books to check up details during revision week. OBEC students also love library time, where they can be reading whatsoever they like.

The more they read, the more their reading improves and their speed increases. Comparing this with most other schools, which use English as medium of instruction, it is clear that the use of mother tongue affords a head-start in sound literacy, a foundational requirement for further life-long education.

Conclusion

Given the undeniable evidence that without incorporation of local African languages, education cannot yield the expected benefits for the majority of African children and instead remains shallow and stunted, it is clear that every effort must be made to facilitate the use of these languages in education.

III. MULTILINGUALISM / LANGUAGE EQUITY

9. The urgent need for reorientation with regards to multilingual education advocacy in Africa

Daniel NDUBUISI OBAH
VARDIAFRICA

Multilingual education advocacy is so vital and urgently needed in Africa. My interest is shaped by the fact that Africa is a continent endowed with different diversity in culture and languages. Education in that perspective will help preserve the rich African culture, make learning easy and engender development and peaceful coexistence. There is so much benefit as it relates to multilingual education. My research in value reorientation advocacy as a key to development and peaceful coexistence in Africa to a great extent will be adequately understood with multilingual education where mother tongue is reintroduced in schools.

Any level of education that cannot help to advance individuals and the society is meaningless and of no impact. Imparting knowledge via local African language to a great extent will be of positive impacts with regards to economic development, peaceful coexistence and help eradicate crimes/social vices. To have a full understanding of multilingual education advocacy with regards to adequate reorientation, there is the need to explain some basic terms such as multilingual education, reorientation, the essence of reorientation in advocating multilingual education in Africa and the urgent need for multilingual education advocacy.

Multilingual education

Multilingual education refers to 'first language - first education' that schooling which begins in the mother tongue and transits to additional languages. Multilingual Education programs are situated mostly in developing countries where speakers of minority languages tend to be disadvantaged in the mainstream education system. Multilingual education helps learning not just in mother tongue but other languages that will help advance the course of learning and better understanding of situations. Multilingualism also refers to being fluent in multiple languages. It is normative in many countries for children to be raised multilingual. Being multilingual has the obvious benefit of being able to communicate with more people from different cultural background. It also has the benefit of protecting the brain from dementia. According to UNESCO (2003:17) Multilingual education refers to the use of two or more languages as medium of instruction.

Multilingual learning environment is a growing phenomenon around the world because of rapid increase in global mobility and migration. In most of the learning environment students have different linguistic and cultural backgrounds, speaking probably a language at school and a different language at home. Students with knowledge of various languages are at more advantage, understand situations better and are better positioned to solving societal challenges. One key benefit of multilingual education is solving the increasing societal challenges with regards to crime and social vices in Africa.

Multilingual children are exposed to more diverse social experiences, as a result multilingual child often become adept at considering other people's perspective making them effective communicators. Being multilingual also helps you to monitor your environment, proffer solutions to critical societal problems, gives you the needed edge and positions you as a great leader. Africa is in dire need of leaders and problem solvers, which multilingual education can greatly solve if its advocacy is properly and adequately driven. Albert Costa a researcher from the University of Pompeu Fabra in Spain stated "Bilinguals have to switch languages quite often - you may have to talk to your father in one language and your mother in another language. It requires keeping track of changes around you in the same way that we monitor our surroundings when driving".

Reorientation

As defined by the dictionary, reorientation refers to "the act of changing the emphasis or direction of something," and can also refer to becoming reacquainted with something. For the purpose of this book, reorientation is the process of impacting values that are geared towards better living standard and peaceful coexistence. It involves changing of attitudes, standards to meet a particular desired result. It is the act of figuring out again where you are in a relationship to your environment or changing the direction. For reorientation to be effective, major attitudinal change towards a better society and peaceful coexistence is required. People and organizations have to undergo a process of enlightenment and training to achieve the desired result. The major purpose of reorientation in this book is changing of set of attitudes and beliefs which adversely has affected our society in respect of development, obedience to rule of law, responsibility of leaders to citizens, and general peaceful coexistence. Our concern is to x-ray processes and methods to aid adequate reorientation in order to guarantee development and peaceful coexistence in African countries. It is key to know that through adequate reorientation, the younger generation can be positively influenced towards love for one another, fight against social vices and crime, development of our society, peaceful coexistence amongst all. The responsibility of reorientation should be all-encompassing, both in child parenting, school training, religious setting, workplaces, marriage, international transactions, community social responsibility, business organizations, leadership settings, security. It is worthy to note that the role of value reorientation in driving peace and development in Africa cannot be overemphasized. It also involves a total re-engineering of the economic settings geared towards economic development and prosperity. For reorientation to be result oriented, it has to include all parties in the desired system. A successful reorientation program will include, children / educational reorientation, leadership reorientation, business/private sector reorientation, political reorientation, security reorientation, environmental reorientation, customer relationship / services reorientation.

Reorientation is an essential component of advocating for multilingual education, as promoting the learning of both mother tongue and other languages can foster not only a value-driven education, but also value-driven leadership. This can in turn help address the increasing societal challenges faced in Africa. Given the importance of multilingual education, it is crucial to provide teachers with the necessary training and retraining to effectively impart this knowledge. It is important to note that reorientation must occur first among the teachers, and subsequently among the children taught by these trained educators. Without adequate reorientation, the impact of multilingual education advocacy in Africa may not be fully realized.

The essence of reorientation in advocating multilingual education in Africa

Having explained the terms multilingual education and reorientation, it is important to highlight the major benefits of reorientation in multilingual education advocacy. To properly drive home the multilingual education advocacy, reorientation is necessary. In my book, *The Key to a Great Africa,* I strongly advocated for value reorientation as a necessary element if the continent is going to achieve sound leadership and peaceful coexistence. Reorientation should be a vital part of multilingual education advocacy, as it involves campaign and advocacy for the inherent benefits of this type of education, to help children have full control of their environment, mental capacity and needed confidence in handling major challenges of life.

I would say value reorientation combined with multilingual education will be effective and impacting as people are better enlightened with their mother tongue and other language. Now the essence of reorientation in advocating Multilingual Education as highlighted below.

- Multilingual education advocacy will not be readily accepted by majority if adequate reorientation amongst Africans is not carried out. People need to be properly informed about its

huge benefits through reorientation for it to be widely accepted.
- Education done with different languages especially with that of mother language is value driven and imparting. There is a great demand for good leadership in Africa, which can be best advocated through reorientation with multilingual education for a far-reaching impact.
- The rate of crime and social vices is on the increase in most African countries. How can you reach more people to inform them that despite the rise in crime and social vices, seeing crime as a way of life is not the best way? Value reorientation can be best delivered with multilingual education.
- Adequate reorientation in multiple languages will enhance a child's level of knowledge both in English and other languages and positions them in handling issues better.
- Adequate reorientation will help the teachers and children to build great confidence and they become more comprehensible in the language they speak.
- Reorientation plays a vital role in addressing the challenges of inequality and inferiority complex in advocating for multilingual education. With proper awareness, individuals can better position themselves to avoid being subject to such issues.
- Enhanced efforts to promote multilingual education in Africa through appropriate reorientation could facilitate crucial awareness and support for advocacies towards providing quality education for all.
- Multilingual education has the potential to bring about numerous accomplishments in Africa through a value reorientation approach, particularly in promoting effective governance, improving public health, eliminating crime and social misconduct, nurturing young African leaders, fostering peaceful coexistence, and more.

It is crucial to recognize that for multilingual education advocacy to be successful, reorientation must be an integral component, given the diverse cultural backgrounds present in Africa. Given the ever-changing nature of the African continent, reorientation is key to promoting this kind of education. Continuous learning is necessary to achieve excellence in education, and effective advocacy plays a crucial role in this regard. It is with this in mind that I have contributed to this work.

The urgent need for multilingual education

Multilingual education advocacy cannot be overstated, given the tremendous benefits it offers in driving value reorientation. Education forms the foundation of development, as being well-informed enables individuals to make better decisions that can positively impact society. Urgent action is therefore required to promote multilingual education advocacy, especially in ending crime and social misconduct, promoting sound leadership, increasing awareness on safeguarding against various viruses and diseases, fostering peaceful coexistence, and nurturing young African leaders who value the rich African cultures.

To achieve reorientation in advocating for multilingual education, it is crucial to establish platforms in various African countries to first reorient children on the need for this type of education. Additionally, the use of mother languages should be encouraged to educate children on sound leadership and peaceful coexistence, while discouraging them from embracing crime and social misconduct. The benefits of multilingual education are far-reaching and driving advocacy through reorientation is the most effective approach to take.

Conclusion

Much has been said about multilingual education advocacy in Africa through adequate reorientation for effective enlightenment amongst children. I am fully interested in reorientation with regards to multilingual education advocacy across countries in Africa. My interest is shaped by the fact that Africa is a continent endowed with different diversity in culture and languages, and education in that perspective will help to preserve the rich African culture, make learning easy, engender development and peaceful coexistence. My past research especially in value reorientation advocacy as the key to development and peaceful coexistence in Africa, which was captured in my book, *The Key To A Great Africa,* to a great extent, will be better delivered and properly understood with multilingual education where the mother tongue is reintroduced in schools with many other numerous benefits.

This work offers a comprehensive understanding of the distinct characteristics and advantages of multilingual education that have been previously overlooked. Drawing on my extensive experience advocating for value reorientation in schools across 28 institutions in Nigeria and South Africa, this paper also showcases successful practices using these countries as a case study. Despite the challenges, the benefits of multilingual education are too significant to ignore, and it is imperative for all stakeholders to support its advocacy, with a focus on urgent reorientation efforts.

10. Multilingual teachers for the multilingual classroom

Pierre DE GALBERT
Brown University

Cornelius GULERE
Uganda Christian University

"Monolingualism is the carbon dioxide of culture. Multilingualism is the oxygen of cultures. I hope we choose oxygen." Ngũgĩ wa Thiong'o, April 17, 2018

Teachers form the central part the student experience in schools. Policies are designed to organize the education system, and curricula are written to create a scaffolded pedagogical structure, but teachers make the final decision crafting the classroom experience for their students. Once the bell has rung and the door has shut, the teacher can decide aspects of what material to cover, how students will engage, and indeed, what language(s) she will use to conduct the lesson. These decisions are based on the resources made available, support she has received in pre-service training and professional development, and importantly their beliefs and knowledge of the needs of their students.

As this book makes clear, the majority of classrooms on the continent are multilingual as a result of the rich linguistic diversity of its students and teachers, or because educational systems make use of languages rarely spoken in the community. In these classrooms, teachers are faced with a constant choice of what language(s) to use, mediating official policies. If the official policy requires a fourth-grade teacher in Uganda to use English, this requires him to feel comfortable using that language and confident that his students will understand. Conversely, a first-grade Senegalese teacher required to use Pulaar in the classroom may not feel adequately prepared. She may have gone through school and teacher training in classrooms that use French or may have grown-up in a Wolof-speaking environment, and thus feel her linguistic skills are not adequate. The language(s) these teachers choose to use in the classroom will depend not only on the official policy, but also on teacher resources and beliefs.

In this chapter, we center the conversation on a bilingual revolution around teachers, specifically on the factors that lead teachers to choose one or more languages in their classroom and the systems that enable or hinder their choices. We start with describing a conceptual framework of the teacher's place in the decision-making process. We then examine the lived experiences of teachers in two contexts: Senegal and Uganda. In Senegal, the government recently introduced three local languages as the medium of instruction in the first two years of school and implemented a literacy program to accompany the shift. We explore how this new program affected teacher support for the policy and their self-efficacy. In Uganda, we review how local actors have supported the development of Lusoga in the formal education system, including teacher development, and the introduction of the language in higher education institutions. Finally, we discuss the implications of these two case studies for the region.

Teachers as language-choice mediators

Teachers are the street-level bureaucrats of the education system (Lipsky, 1969). As the actors in the system responsible for engaging students daily, they are the ultimate deciders of what language(s) to use. As such, they are mediators in the language in education policies designed at higher levels of the bureaucracy. Figure 1 illustrates the context in which teachers make their decisions, and three important factors that influence how teachers make their decision. The context in which teachers must make these decisions include the official language policy, and the beliefs held by school officials, specifically the director or other members of the school hierarchy. Teacher beliefs about language and the policy, their understanding of their students' needs, and their own linguistic skills mediate the process of choosing what language(s) to use.

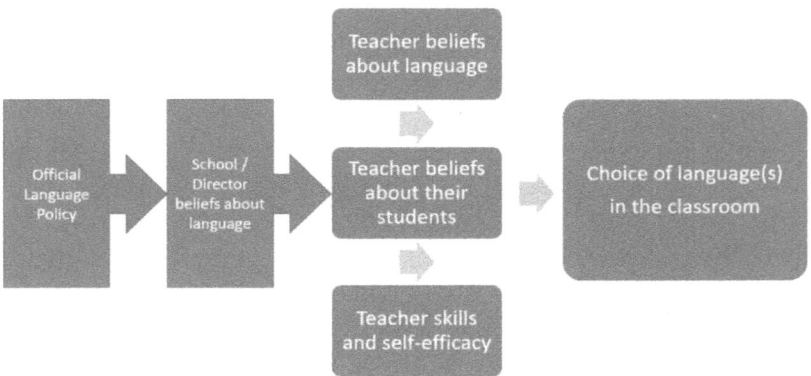

Figure 1: Factors influencing the choice of language(s) teachers use in the classroom

One of the main factors influencing teachers' decision about language use is their own beliefs about the role language has in the classroom. This is exemplified in how three teachers in Laos responded differently to the official language policy prescribing exclusive use of Lao in communities where most children were Kmhmu speakers. All three teachers were fluent in Kmhmu but responded differently to the official policy. One teacher used Lao nearly exclusively in their lesson, explaining "If they want to speak [Kmhmu], they can speak it as they wish, then when we're studying, they speak the official language with the teacher". (Cincotta-Segi, 2011, p. 200). The second teacher used the two languages in equal measure, using Kmhmu to explain the text students were reading in Lao. This teacher justified the use of the children's language from a pedagogical stance: "If I say things in Lao, the children might not know. If I can say it in Kmhmu, I have to use Kmhmu with them" (ibid). The third teacher made nearly exclusive use of Kmhmu to teach the lesson, using Lao only when introducing words and letters to their first-grade students. In addition to pedagogy, the third teacher justified using their language from as social perspective: "If I use Lao, they'll say I'm stuck-up (...) Most of the time, if they're Kmhmu too then speaking Lao doesn't seem right". (Cincotta-Segi, 2011, p.206). These three teachers expressed different beliefs about the role language should play in the classroom and community, and thus made different decisions despite the same policy and linguistic context.

In addition to beliefs about language use, teachers use their knowledge of their students to influence their choices. Other than caregivers, teachers are the adults in the community who know young children the best. This knowledge allows teachers to adapt instruction to student needs. There clearly is no single approach that fits the needs of all classrooms in the implementation of language-in-education policies. An understanding of the linguistic diversity of the classroom and the skill level of their students influences teacher choices. The use of a local language in some settings might help some students while simultaneously alienating others. Joyce, a refugee student in a diverse urban school in central Uganda, feels excluded when her teacher uses the local language in the classroom even though the school only sanctions the use of English: "It's not good because also us, we don't understand Luganda". (Reddick & Chopra, 2021, p.10). Of course, the ability, or perceived ability of the teacher's own language skills in Luganda and Joyce's home language will enable or prevent the use of some languages.

Believing in the positive impact of using a child's language in the classroom and understanding students' linguistic skills and needs is not sufficient for teachers to make use of the local lingua franca. Teachers also need to have linguistic skills and beliefs in their ability to use the language effectively. Ensuring teachers have the requisite skills is mainly the result of recruiting and training teachers from linguistic communities they will teach in. However, there remains a gap between a teacher's language skills and their belief that they have the requisite linguistic skills. Non-dominant languages have been diminished and derided through decades of colonial rule and post-colonial policies considering European languages and those available in higher education as superior. This leads some individuals, though fluent in their first language, to doubt their ability to "properly" use their language in a formal context such as schools.

Teachers can and do make choices to use multiple languages in their classrooms every day in a variety of policy and linguistic contexts. These choices are partly influenced by teacher beliefs about language, their students, and their language skills. If a multilingual revolution is to occur in African classrooms, it will require official policies to promote it, such as has been the case in Senegal. However, it will also need grassroots efforts such as those taking place in the Lusoga-speaking region of Uganda. The next two sections describe how top-down, and bottom-up approaches can support teachers to make choices toward a multilingual revolution.

Scaling-up the use of local languages in Senegal

In Senegal, French is the official more than 60 years after its independence, and it remains the main language used in the formal education system. In addition, the 2001 constitution recognized six national languages and provided an avenue for languages to be recognized if an orthography was developed and approved. Numerous initiatives have been led by community-based organizations and the government to use national languages in schools, many with great success. Until 2017, when the government introduced a new policy to make three Senegalese languages the medium of instruction for two years, these programs were limited in scale. Lecture Pour Tous has introduced one of three languages - Wolof, Seereer, and Pulaar - in 7 regions of the country in the Cours d'Initiation (Grade 1) and Cours Préparatoire (Grade 2). Collectively, these three languages are spoken at home by more than three-quarters of the population (Leclerc, 2013). Nevertheless, ensuring that teachers included the literacy skills, confidence, and desire to use these languages as the medium in their classrooms remained to be seen.

As part of the evaluation of the program, teachers were surveyed at three time points: in 2017, before the new program started, in 2019, after two years of school with the new program, and in 2021, after four years. Two questions teachers answered that are relevant to the framework presented in this chapter include support for the use of local languages and a self-evaluation of linguistic skills in French and the local language used in the school through the program. In 2017, teachers already overwhelmingly supported this policy, with only 5% who stated disagreeing. After two years, this proportion fell to 1%, before rising again to 4% in 2021. School directors were slightly less supportive at first, with 11% in disagreement in 2017. After two and four years, this proportion fell to 1% and 3% respectively. While the slight increase between 2019 and 2021 is disheartening, it came after two school years heavily disrupted by the global pandemic. Overall, these figures indicate that teachers and school directors were generally in favor of the use of local languages in the early years of schooling and became even more so after the policy was implemented.

In addition to support for the policy, it is important to understand how teachers evaluated their linguistic skills over time. Figure 2 displays the average score teachers gave themselves on a scale from one to ten across four skills and three timepoints. These data reveal several important trends. First, teachers generally indicated they were more skilled in French, which is not surprising given their own formal education took place in the colonial language. These scores were consistently close to nine out of ten across skills and time. In the three local languages, teachers reported much lower scores in 2017, before the program started, especially in reading and writing. However, teachers expressed much more confidence after having worked in schools using these languages for two and four years. For example, teachers in Wolof-speaking areas reported an average of 5.3 and 4.6 in reading and writing in 2017, but this increased to 8.6 and 7.8 in 2019. The trends were less pronounced, but similar in oral skills. Finally, teachers reported slightly lower skills in 2021, after two years of disrupted teaching.

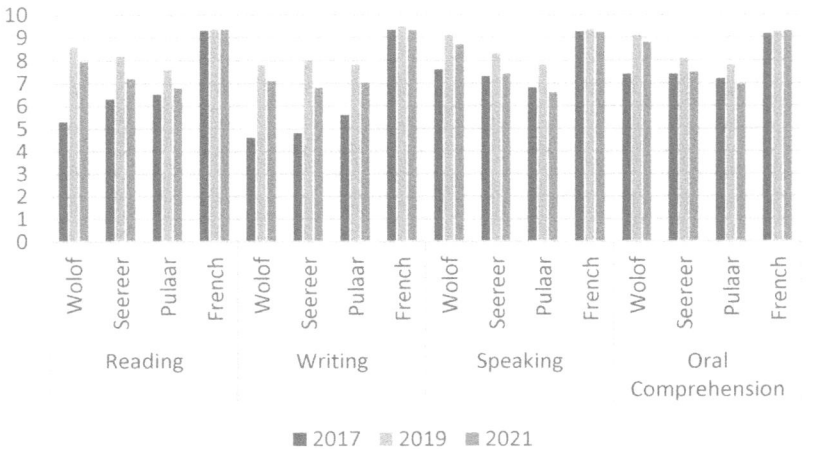

Figure 2: Teachers self-reported skills in reading, writing, speaking, and oral comprehension across three time points in Senegal.

Building a Lusoga teacher workforce in Uganda

The 2005 constitution of Uganda recognized over fifty "indigenous communities", and there are currently more than forty living languages in the country (Eberhard et al., 2019; Republic of Uganda, 2005). While English remains the official language of the country, and the main language used in the formal education system, the language-in-education policy adopted in 2007 promoted the use of local languages in the first three years of school. The implementation of this policy was made uneven across contexts because of differences in the development of languages themselves, availability of teaching materials, community support, and, indeed, the availability of teachers trained to teach in local languages (de Galbert, 2021; Namyalo & Nakayiza, 2014; Ssentanda, 2014; Tembe & Norton, 2008). While the policy encouraged the use of local languages, decentralized education leaders were given the choice to use English, or a local language based on local needs, resources, and preferences. Communities speaking non-dominant languages and wishing their children to learn in their own language have thus had to engage with the development or standardization of the language's orthography, teaching resources, or teacher training. The Lusoga speaking community exemplifies the efforts that grassroots organizations make to support official language policies.

Lusoga is spoken as a first language by approximately three million Ugandans in the Eastern part of the country (Eberhard et al., 2019). Because of its linguistic and geographical proximity with the dominant Luganda language, Lusoga was not promoted by institutions of power for much of the country's history. Local organizations such as the Lusoga Language Development Academy, the Basoga Cultural Research Centre, and the Lusoga Language Academic Board have worked to promote the language in the region. One of the important works done was to support the use of Lusoga in primary schools starting with the new policy in 2007 and introduce the teaching of the language as a subject in secondary schools and university. At the intersection of all this work, a primary goal has been to develop a Lusoga teaching workforce.

Most teachers working in primary schools in Uganda have been trained in a Primary Teaching Center (PTC) after finishing four or six years of secondary school. As part of their training, student-teachers spend some time working in schools. As the following testimonials highlight, these young people are working to change minds and habits where the use of Lusoga was not always valued:

- "I had never imagined that I would need to read, write and teach in Lusoga. Teachers used to punish us for speaking Lusoga."
- "I love teaching children in Lusoga because it makes learning easy. I also use Ateso to relate experiences. They love it. They feel it is fun to study."
- "In fact, the school doesn't like it that teacher trainees are using Lusoga as language of instruction. [...] But this is the policy and we have to obey."
- "The challenge is when it comes to exams, some find difficulty writing in English. They use both Lusoga and English. For me, I mark that as long as it is correct."

While some school officials were reticent to adopt Lusoga as the language of instruction, there has been a positive shift in attitudes in recent years. Lusoga is now being taught in A-levels and the language is part of a program called UNITE aiming to introduce more Ugandan languages in universities. The number of students taking Lusoga in O-levels increased from 13,000 in 2018 to 18,000 in 2020, and approximately 500 sat for A-levels in 2020. Lusoga should be available as courses to study at Busoga, UNITE, Kyambogo and Makerere universities starting in 2022/23. This progress will lead to more Lusoga-speaking educators in PTCs and in schools, ultimately pushing forward the multilingual revolution in classrooms.

Conclusion: A multilingual teacher workforce

A multilingual revolution in the school system requires the development and support of a multilingual teaching workforce. Developing a cadre of multilingual teachers willing and able to use multiple languages in the classroom to support their students cannot happen fast, but certainly can happen. Teachers are a key ingredient of the education system, but they are also the product of the system they are part of as students and student-teachers. In order to create this multilingual teaching workforce, we must work at different levels of change.

First, countries should support the use of non-dominant languages in the school system. Equally important, official language-in-education policies must be written to explicitly promote the use of these languages in specific grades and curricula. In Uganda, while the constitution in 1956 and the education white paper of 1990 promoted the use of Ugandan languages in education, it was only in 2007 that the Ministry of Education officially rolled out the current early-exit model. Without this official support, teachers willing to use the community's language must first expend energy fighting against the grain of an unsupportive official policy.

Second, teacher training should include important conversations about language. The extent to which teachers use multiple languages in their classrooms will depend on their understanding of the benefits and support for multilingual pedagogical approaches. The data from Senegal shows that most teachers and principals were supportive of the use local languages. This is positive but some teachers and community members still believe in a false choice between a dominant and non-dominant language when it is possible to develop both. Student-teachers in Uganda shared that they sometimes had to work against their principal's preference to use Lusoga despite the support of the official policy.

Third, teachers must believe in their own ability to use multiple languages. The data in Senegal shows part of that will come from experiencing multilingual policies, but that it is not enough. Teachers need the support to the develop the literacy skills in the languages used in schools. Time will help with this in places like Uganda where the work is being done to support instruction in Lusoga in secondary schools and teacher colleges. These efforts must come from top-down policies as well as grassroots support.

11. Multilingual glossaries for teaching and learning: an initiative at the University of South Africa

Feziwe SHOBA and Koliswa MOROPA
University of South Africa

This chapter starts by giving background information about the Language Policy for Higher Education (LPHE) (2002 / 2020), the University of South Africa's Language Policy (2010 / 2016) and its implementation plan before providing a brief overview of the compilation of multilingual glossaries at the University of South Africa (Unisa). Since 1994, language development has been one of the key priorities of democratic South Africa. The Constitution of the Republic of South Africa, Act 108 of 1996, brought about major change regarding the status of indigenous African languages, declaring nine of them to be official. Section 6 (1) of the Constitution stipulates that "the official languages of the Republic of South Africa are Sepedi, Sesotho, Setswana, Tshivenda, Xitsonga, Afrikaans, English, siSwati, isiNdebele, isiXhosa and isiZulu." The education policies of the apartheid regime marginalized the indigenous languages, recognizing only Afrikaans and English as official. The release of the National Plan for Higher Education in 2001 resulted in the radical transformation of the higher education system. After the merger of universities and technikons, the demographic profile of student populations demonstrated a multilingual and multicultural society. This new, linguistically diverse environment had major implications for languages of teaching and learning. Before 1994, the education system in higher education was dominated by the use of English and Afrikaans as languages of science and academic research. The colonial bilingual education system did not recognize any of the African indigenous languages, and therefore the technical/scientific registers of these languages remained underdeveloped (Moropa & Shoba 2017).

Language Policy for Higher Education (LPHE)

A landmark in the commitment to language development and promotion of multilingualism in institutions of higher learning was the Language Policy for Higher Education (LPHE) (2002: cf. § 6) which states:

> The challenge facing higher education is to ensure the simultaneous development of a multilingual environment in which all our languages are developed as academic/scientific languages while at the same time ensuring that the existing languages of instruction do not serve as a barrier to access and success.

The Language Policy Framework for Public Higher Education Institutions (2020) is a review of the 2002 Language Policy for Higher Education (LPHE) and thus "seeks to address the challenge of underdevelopment and underutilization of indigenous official South African languages in higher education and at the same time sustaining the standard and utilization of languages that have already progressed" [Preamble]. This policy framework declares that, since the proclamation of the Language Policy for Higher Education, little progress has been made in exploring and exploiting the potential role of indigenous African languages in facilitating access and success as well as the development of these languages for academic purposes. The Language Policy for Higher Education requires higher education institutions (HEIs) to develop language policies together with implementation plans. The next section outlines the current situation at the University of South Africa with reference to its language policy and its implementation.

Implementation of the Unisa Language Policy – a brief overview

The Unisa Senate Language Committee (SLC), chaired by the Vice Principal (Teaching and Learning, Community Engagement, and Student Support), oversees language activities. The functions of the committee are to:

- maintain and implement the language policy of the University

- monitor the phased-in implementation of the language policy
- advise Senate and Council on language-related policy matters.

In compliance with the Language Policy for Higher Education (2002), the University adopted a language policy in 2006 and revised it in 2010, formulating a plan with activities and timeframes. A phase-in approach was adopted in the implementation plan, informed by factors such as costs and availability of resources. The policy required the Directorate of Language Services and academic departments across colleges to facilitate the development of multilingual glossaries and terminology lists in collaboration with terminologists and the Pan South African Language Board (PanSALB). The main objective of the policy was to promote functional multilingualism. This meant that the purpose and context of communication, the availability of resources, and the target audience would determine the choice of languages. In order to accommodate linguistic diversity, the functional approach to language development at the University resulted in the multilingual glossary survey that was commissioned by the Senate Language Committee in 2010 and conducted by the then Department of Information and Strategic Analysis (DISA). The survey focussed on two pertinent issues, namely:

(i) the language preferences of students
(ii) the usefulness of multilingual glossaries, which were included in particular modules.

Questionnaires were used as research techniques, and purposive sampling determined the population of participants. The findings showed that the majority of students favored a continued and improved compilation of glossaries for those students whose first language was not English.

Two other projects that were steered by the 2010 revised Unisa Language Policy comprised:

(i) Students' Language Attitudes (SLA) (2013 - 2016)
(ii) African Languages in Teaching and Learning (2014 - 2016).

The Senate Language Committee (SLC) commissioned the strategic project of Students' Language Attitudes (SLA) (2013 - 2016). The specific aims of the project were threefold:

(i) to investigate which languages were preferred by Unisa students for communication and as media of instruction (Unisa Language Policy 2010: § 4.1.3, 4.2.3 (b) and § 4.2.7)

(ii) to investigate how and why students were making particular choices regarding media of instruction (Unisa Language Policy 2010: § 4.1.5)

(iii) to make recommendations for the implementation of an informed, successful language policy at Unisa.

Some of the recommendations which emerged from the findings of the qualitative research on the language attitudes and language preferences of Unisa students included the following:

- Languages should be developed for academic purposes, and a parallel medium of instruction should be encouraged where possible.
- A phase-in approach to language policy implementation should be used.
- African languages should be used to facilitate and support learning.
- The use of African languages in the education system should be normalized in learner support.

The project African Languages in Teaching and Learning (2014 - 2016) derived its mandate from the decision of the Senate Language Committee (SLC) to have a number of first-year modules (NQF level 5) translated into all official South African languages to support students in their learning. The first author was the researcher in the project, and she designed a workflow chart to monitor the translation and the quality process of the translated product. Out of eight ABET modules that were translated in the project, one example, 'Planning and administering ABET classes and projects,' was translated from English into nine official indigenous South African languages. The total size of the corpus comprising the source text (ST) and target texts (TTs) is 418,427 words or tokens. The tokens in each of the Nguni languages (isiZulu, isiNdebele, siSwati, and isiXhosa) are fewer compared to the Sesotho, Sepedi, Xitsonga, and Tshivenda. The reason for this is that the Nguni languages write conjunctively while the other indigenous African languages write disjunctively, and this leads to a large difference in the size of the target texts. For example, isiZulu is 30,282 words, and Sesotho is 52,913 words.

SOURCE TEXT (ST)	TARGET TEXTS (TT)	SIZE
CEDU: ABT1515 Planning & administering ABET classes and projects. Word count: 43 334)	**IsiZulu** Ukuphatha nokulawula Amakilasi namaprojekthi e-ABET	30,282 words
	IsiNdebele Ukuhlela Nokulawula Amatlasi Namaphrojekthi We-ABET	27,874 words
	Sesotho Ho rera le ho tsamaisa Dithuto le diprojeke tsa ABET (Thuto ya batho ba baholo)	52,913 words
	Siswati Kuhlela nekulawula emaklasi nemiklamo ye-ABET)	28,848 words
	Sepedi Go beakanya le go sepediša dithuto le diprotšeke tša ABET	55,296 words
	IsiXhosa Ukucwangcisa nokuqhuba Iiklasi neeprojekthi ze-ABET	31,538 words
	Afrikaans Beplanning en administrasie van BOOV-klasse en –projekte	42,269 words
	Xitsonga Makunguhatelo na mafambiselo ya titlilasi na tiphurojeke ta ABET	56,281 words
	Tshivenda U pulana na ndaulo ya Kilasi na thandela dza ABET	49,792 words
ST Word count: 43 334		**Sub-total-TTs 375,093**
TOTAL (no. of tokens/ words)		**ST+ TTs 418,427**

Table 1: ABET Module in ten official South African languages

The three projects discussed above were implemented in order to promote multilingualism and develop South African languages. The Language Policy for Higher Education (LPHE) (2002: § 15.2.1 / 2020 § 37) states that the promotion of South African languages for use in higher education requires, amongst others, the development through the translation of subject-specific texts, terminologies, glossaries, dictionaries, and other teaching and learning materials. The Department of Higher Education has to work closely with "relevant government departments and entities to create or strengthen existing open-source multidisciplinary terminology banks to be accessed and used as a teaching and learning resource by all higher education institutions."

The transformation of Higher Education, entailing the merging of public higher education institutions in South Africa in 1997, brought about fundamental changes such as a linguistically diverse student population in universities and colleges. Following these changes, higher education institutions were required, amongst other things, to develop South African languages as media of instruction alongside English and Afrikaans (LPHE 2002 / 2020), as already mentioned. However, "the promotion of South African languages for use in instruction in higher education required, amongst others, the development of dictionaries and other teaching and learning materials" (LPHE 2002: § 6 / LPHE 2020: § 37). This is because terminology development is a prerequisite to language development and use.

In response to the mandate set by the Department of Higher Education of using African languages as languages of instruction alongside English and Afrikaans, the University adopted a multilingual approach of producing glossaries as learning aids that could assist students who are not proficient in English to access specialized subject fields in their mother tongue. Since this study deals with the collection of terms for glossary development and how they are described and presented in multilingual glossaries, it falls within the framework of terminology development. Terminology as a science and practice is very complex in nature and requires a clear understanding of what is involved; hence the necessity to define terminology as a key concept in this study.

Terminology defined

Reviewed literature on terminology shows divergent views and perceptions of the concept of 'terminology.' Some theorists view terminology strongly as a scientific discipline, whilst others see it as an art or practice. Sager (1990:2) defines terminology as "the study of and the field of activity concerned with the collection, description, processing, and presentation of terms, i.e., lexical items belonging to specialized areas of usage of one or more languages." Sager (1990) goes on to argue that terminology as a field of activity involves several practices that start with the creation of terms and their collection and presentation in various printed and electronic media. The above view demonstrates that Sager does not view terminology as an independent scientific discipline but rather as a practice and an aspect of the methodology. Terminology has also been defined as the science of terms, the art of analyzing terms in context, and the systematic study of naming or labeling concepts. This discipline or practice is closely related to various fields and disciplines, including lexicography, linguistics and translation, and information sciences, from which it borrows some concepts and methods. The subsequent section provides a brief background of the development of terminology.

The development of terminology: from the prescriptive to the descriptive approach

Terminology, as it is understood today, began to develop in the 1930s. The prominent figure associated with the study of terminology is an Austrian scholar, Eugen Wuster. He realized that unified standards and guidelines are necessary for the solution of terminological problems and developed the General Theory of Terminology (GTT) based on the significance of concepts and their delineation from each other. The main objectives of Wuster's work were intended to:

- eliminate ambiguity from technical language by means of standardization.

- convince all users of the technical language of the benefits of standardized terminology
- establish terminology as a discipline for all purposes and give it the status of a science.

In the 20th century, the traditional theory of terminology received various criticisms from many terminologists and scholars, such as Sager (1990) and Temmerman (2000). The critique of the traditional theory comes from three sides: cognitive science, language sciences, and communication sciences. Criticism of the above principles is based on the purpose, and the new demands of terminology in modern science and technology since language is dynamic and changes over time.

Subsequently, numerous theories of terminology were formulated in light of these perspectives. It is apparent that the theories that arose in reaction to the General Theory of Terminology are descriptive and show an increasing tendency to incorporate premises from cognitive linguistics since they focus on the social, communicative, and cognitive aspects of terminology. They analyze terms as they are actually used and behave in texts. Sager (1990) asserts that "the recognition that terms may occur in various linguistic contexts and that they have variants which are frequently context-conditioned shatters the idealized view that there can or should be only one designation for a concept and vice versa." These scholars agree that a 'term' as the basic unit of terminology is cognitive, linguistic, and communicative. The move from a prescriptive to a descriptive approach has resulted in new methods of managing the development of terminology. The section below discusses the descriptive, user-oriented approach adopted to guide the current research and the reasons for selecting it.

User-oriented approach to terminology

This research is based on the user-oriented approach, a modern approach to terminology that emerged in the 20th century because of the criticism of traditional methods. This approach focuses on determining the user's needs and expectations during terminology development. The application of this approach is defended by Sager

(1990:131), who states that "the concept of user-oriented terminology has been taken a stage further with the terminologists pre-empting the user's requests and ensuring that the majority of queries concerning a particular text are satisfied." The relevance of the user-oriented approach to the current study is strengthened by the assumptions that any activities that are concerned with the representation and transfer of specialized vocabulary should satisfy the needs of the users, in this case, students.

Having discussed the theories and methods applicable to modern terminology, the next section presents a brief overview of what has been done at selected institutions of higher learning in South Africa with regard to the development of terminology.

Terminology development in selected South African institutions of higher education

Terminology development at institutions of higher learning is handled differently due to various institutional needs, student profiles, and available resources. The Language Policy for Higher Education (2002/ 2020) requires that higher education institutions develop language policies together with implementation plans. In compliance with this policy, HEIs formulated language policies with multilingualism as their main objective. Several projects were started in order to promote multilingualism and develop indigenous languages, including compiling multilingual glossaries to aid students in technical subjects. For example, the University of Stellenbosch responded to the demands of multilingualism by establishing a unit for isiXhosa and developed a number of glossaries with isiXhosa as one of the target languages. To cite an example, it developed subject-specific terminology lists in the following fields: sociology, social work, psychology, and law. Sibula (2007:398) reports that the unit for isiXhosa has the special task of contributing to the promotion of isiXhosa as an academic language and creating opportunities to further the use of isiXhosa in general. According to Sibula, these multilingual glossaries were developed with first-year students, whose first language is isiXhosa, in mind. The aim was to help them understand Afrikaans and English terms in the selected fields of study. The multilingual glossaries are also intended to broaden the scope of understanding by affording the students the opportunity to learn the technical terms through their mother tongue (Moropa 2013:242).

The University of Cape Town also initiated a Multilingual Concept Literacy Glossaries Project in 2007 as part of the implementation of the University's Language Policy (1999, revised in 2003) and the Language Plan adopted in 2003 (Nkomo & Madiba 2011:154). The lexicographical function approach used in the compilation of multilingual glossaries in the project not only demonstrates new trends in terminology development but indicates how modern lexicography can improve terminology outcomes.

Many reasons have been forwarded as to why glossaries are the point of departure in introducing African languages as languages of instruction at the university level. Developing teaching material in the form of multilingual glossaries is a way not only to support students but also to illustrate that these languages can be developed for academic use in higher education. Although there are hurdles in this endeavor for various reasons, the progress made so far in terminology development and promotion of multilingualism is promising.

Compilation of multilingual glossaries at Unisa

This study utilized the tools and principles of the qualitative research methodology with the aim of gaining an in-depth understanding of the subject under review. Document analysis was used as the central data collection method. Bowen (2009:27) defines document analysis as "a systematic procedure for reviewing or evaluating documents – both printed and electronic material." The relevant documents were selected in order to provide information and knowledge about what has been done.

In transforming teaching and learning, Unisa takes into consideration how the majority of students learn with regard to epistemological access and is aware that language continues to be a "barrier to access and success in higher education" LPHE 2020), hence the adoption of a multilingual approach to produce glossaries as learning aids that can assist students who are not proficient in English to access specialized subject fields in their preferred language. The Senate Language Committee is responsible for the implementation of the language policy, whilst terminology working groups monitor the implementation in various departments and specific domains. Prior to the dawn of a democratic South Africa, the Directorate of Language Services at Unisa built its capacity around English and Afrikaans. Anticipating transformation, two African language specialists (one for isiZulu and the other for Sesotho sa Leboa / Sepedi) were recruited in 2007 when the Department of African Languages was restructured. However, the capacity did not expand because the demand for translation into these languages was minimal. The situation improved slightly when Senate took the decision that academic departments should develop multilingual glossaries. As mentioned earlier, the glossaries are intended to broaden the scope of understanding by affording students the opportunity to learn technical/scientific terms through their mother tongue. The various stages in the process are outlined below:

- The process starts with the subject field experts (academics) who identify the subject from which the key concepts are extracted.
- After selecting the key concepts, definitions are provided in English as the source language.
- The end product is a monolingual glossary with an equivalent and concept description, which is later submitted to the Directorate of Language Services.
- The key concepts and the definitions are then translated into the selected languages, which were mainly Afrikaans, isiZulu, and Sepedi.
- The glossaries are either appended to the relevant study guide for access by students or uploaded to *MyUnisa* as additional resources.

The figure below represents a multilingual glossary for the discipline of *Ornamental Horticulture* in four official South African languages, i.e., English, Afrikaans, isiZulu, and Sepedi.

Ornamental Horticulture Glossary:

Source module	English	Afrikaans	isiZulu	Northern Sotho
PSO1501	**Abaxial side**: the side furthest away from the central axis, ie the (dorsal) underside of the leaf	**Abaksiale kant**: die verste kant van die sentrale as, dws die (dorsale) onderkant van die blaar	**Icele**: Lena yileyo ngxenye ekude neqhelile kwiphakathi, noma kwingaphansi leqabunga.	**Bokatlase bja letlakala**: lehlakore leo le sego kgauswi le bogare bja letlakala, ke go re, bokatlase bja letlakala
CEC1501	**Abiotic component**: the component of an ecosystem comprising the inactive or dead organic material, dissolved organic matter and nutrients in the water and soil	**Abiotiese bestanddeel**: die bestanddeel van 'n ekosisteem wat bestaan uit onaktiewe of dooie organiese materiaal, opgeloste organiese materiaal en voedingstowwe in die water en grond	**Ingxenye engaphili**: Ingxenye ethile yezsintyo eziphilayo enokuthile okungasebenzi noma okufile nokungumsoco emanzini noma emhlabathini.	**Ditho tša tikologo tšeo di se nago bophelo ka gare**: setho sa tikologo seo e ka bago dibolang tše di se nago le mohola goba tšeo di hwilego, dibolang le difepi tšeo di tologetšego ka meetseng le mmung
CEC1501	**Abiotic**: non-living	**Abioties**: nie-lewend	**Okungaphili**: Okungenampilo	**Setlhokabophelo**: selo seo se sa phelego
PSO2601	**Abscisic acid**: plant hormone that promotes senescence	**Absisiesuur**: planthormoon wat veroudering induseer	**I-abscisic acid**: Lolu wuhlobo oluthile lwehomoni olukhuthaza ukuguga.	**Esiti ya apsesiki: homone ya dimeleng** yeo e bakago go hlagala
HOR2602	**Abscission**: natural separation of flowers, fruit or leaves from plants at a special separation layer	**Afspening**: natuurlike skeiding van blomme, vrugte of blare van plante by 'n spesiale skeidingslaag	**Ukwehlukanisa**: Lokhu kusho ukwehlukaniswa ngokwemvelo kwezimbali, kwesithelo noma kwamaqabunga ezitshalweni kunqenqema oluyisipesheli olwehlukanisayo.	**Apsišene**: kgaoganyo ya tlhago ya matšoba, dienywa goba matlakala go dibjalo llageng ye e ikgethilego ya kgaoganyo
PSO2601	**Abscission**: the separation of parts, leaf fall	**Afspening**: die skeiding van dele, blaarval	**Isehlukaniso**: Lena yindawo lapho kwehlukana khona izingxenye zeqabunga.	**Apsišene**: kgaoganyo ya dikarolo, matlakala a a wa
EMG2601	**Absenteeism**: absence, skiving; non-attendance	**Absenteïsme**: afwesigheid, wegbly, niebywoning	**Ukulova**: Ukungabibikho, ukushabalala, ukwenqena ukwenza into okufanele uyenze.	**Tlhokagalo**: tlhokego, go thiša go se be gona.

Figure 1: Ornamental Horticulture multilingual glossary in four official South African languages

The above example illustrates a four-column glossary. The first column is the Source Language (SL), English, followed by the Target Languages (TTs), Afrikaans, isiZulu, and Northern Sotho/ Sepedi. The translation of terms is usually handled by in-house or freelance translators. The translated texts are then reviewed by professionals to ensure quality translations. The key role-players in the process comprise translators, revisers or quality assurers, subject field experts, typesetters, and study guide developers.

The working languages prior to the 2016 Language Policy were mainly English, Afrikaans, isiZulu, and Sepedi / Northern Sotho. In 2016 the Unisa, in line with its vision, amended its language policy and, in 2017, adopted the implementation plan entailing that, as a national university, it:

- acknowledges that there are eleven official languages in South Africa and ensures that, together with South African Sign Language, they enjoy parity of esteem and equitable treatment (§ 4.1.1)
- endeavors to support **all** the official languages of South Africa (§ 4.1.6).

This led to the initiative by the first author to develop a terminology list of assessment terms (verbs/phrases) that are commonly used in assessment practices, i.e., assignments, examinations, and any other forms of assessment. Developing such a term list not only assists students in understanding the terms in their preferred languages during the assessment but also promotes the standardization of terminologies. The following stages of the development process are set out below.

- The Web was used as the main source of harvesting the source language terms across subject fields or disciplines.
- The verbs and verb phrases that occurred commonly in all sources were selected.

After consolidating the data, a monolingual English list of 143 terms was compiled and sorted in alphabetical order and then sent for translation into all official South African languages. Two language practitioners for each of the ten official languages were appointed (one translator and one quality assurer). The majority of translators were Unisa staff members from the Departments of African languages, English Studies, Linguistics, and Modern Languages and Study Material Production and Delivery. The translator worked on the English term list and provided equivalents in a relevant target language. After checking the translation, a bilingual terminology list was sent to a quality assurer. The responsibility of the quality assurer was to read and perfect the target language. All the translated lists were submitted to the Language Unit.

A verification workshop was held because a verification process is a very important phase of terminology development and a requirement of PanSALB. It is a consultative and collaborative process that involves a variety of stakeholders/partners in language and terminology development. The purpose of the workshop was to involve the target language experts in the verification of the term list developed so that they could discuss and agree on the standard or preferred terms in their respective languages. Amongst the external stakeholders were the representatives from PanSALB and STATS South Africa.

The finalization phase involved updating information, formatting, and final checking. The corrections made during the verifications were affected by the Language Unit team. A terminology list of assessment terms is provided below in the eleven official languages of South Africa for use by students and academic staff across colleges at the University of South Africa.

ENGLISH	AFRIKAANS	ISIZULU	ISIXHOSA	SEPEDI	SESOTHO	ISINDEBELE	SISWATI	TSHIVENDA	XITSONGA	SETSWANA
Account for	Verklaar	Beka izizathu	Nika ingxelo	Maikarabelo	Hlalosa, arabela	Ziphendulela	Bika nge-	Fhindulani nga ha	Tihlamulele	Tlhalosa, tsaya boikarabelo
Adapt	Verwerk	Jwayeza	Lungisa	Tlwaetša	Fetola, kgema	Jayela	Jwayela	Shumisani sa	Fambelanisa	Tlwaela, fetola tiriso
Advise	Aanbeveel	Eluleka	Cebisa	Eletša	Eletsa	Yeleliša	Yeluleka	Eeletshedzani	Tsundzuxa	Kgakololo
Analyse	Ontleed	Hlaziya	Hlalutya	Sekaseka	Sekaseka, manolla	Cozulula	Hlatiya, hluta	Sengulusani, fhendani	Xopaxopa	Lokolola, kanoka
Answer	Antwoord	Phendula	Phendula	Araba	Araba	Phendula	Phendvula	Fhindulani	Hlamula	Araba
Approximate	Benader	Sondezelela	Qikelela	Bokgaufsi	Atametsa	Tjhideza	Linganisa	Gaganyani	Pimanyeta	Lekanyetsa, tshwantshanya
Arrange	Rangskik	Hlela	Lungelelanisa, cwangcisa	Beakanya	Hlopha	Hlela	Hlela	Vhekanyani, dzudzanyani	Lulamisa	Rulaganya
Argue	Aanvoer	Chaza wesekele	Xoxa	Nganga	Nganga	Phikisana	Seka-, phikisa, seka umbono	Talani	Nhekanjhekisa	Nganga, ganetsa
Apply	Toepas	Sebenzisa	Sebenzisa	Kgopela, diriša	sebedisa	Faka isibawo	Sebentisa	Shumisani	Tirhisa	Kopa, tshasa, ama
Assess	Bepaal	Hlola	Hlola, vavanya	Lekola	Lekola	Hlola	Vivinya	Lingani, Iolani	Hlahluwa	Sekaseka, lekola, keleka, atihola, lekanya
Balance	Vergelyk	Linganisa	Cingisisa, lungelelanisa	Lekanyetša	Se setseng masala	Linganisa	Linganisa	Linganyisani	Ringanisa	Lekanya, tekatekano, itsetsep
Calculate	Bereken	Bala	Bala	Hlakantšha	Sebetsa palo	Balisisa	Bala	Rekenyani, vhalelani	Khakhuleta	Bala, balela, ikaelela
Carry out	Uitvoer	Qhuba, feza	Yenza	Tšwetša pele	Phethisa	Khipha, veza	Yenta	Shumani, itani	Endla	Diragatsa
Categorise	Kategoriseer	Hlukanisa ngezigaba	Hlela ngokweendidi	Aroganya	Hlopholla	Ngokwengaba	Hlela	Khethekanyani	Avanyisa	Arologanya, rulaganya
Change	Verander	Guqula, Shintsha	Guqula, tshintsha	Fetola	Fetola	Tjhugulula	Ntjintja	Shandukisani	Cinca	Fetola, fetoga, refosanya
Choose	Kies	Khetha	Khetha	Kgetha	Kgetha	Khetha	Khetsa	Nangani, khethani	Hlawula	Tlhopha
Clarify	Verduidelik	Cacisa	Cacisisa	Hlatholla	Hlakisa	Cacisa	Cacisa	Talutshedzani, bviselani khagala	Basisa	Tlhalosa
Classify	Klassifiseer	Hlela ngononina	Hlela	Hlopha	Hlophisa	Hlukanisa	Hlela, hlunga	Khethekanyani	Hlengeleta	Ntlawahata
Collect	Versamel	Qoqa	Qokelela, landa	Kgobokeša	Bokella	Buthelela	Butsisa, coca	Kuvhanganyani	Hlengeleta	Kgobokanya, phutha, tsaya
Combine	Verbind	Hlanganisa	Dibanisa, hlanganisa	Kopanya	Kopanya	Hlanganisa	Hlanganisa	Tanganyani	Katsa	Tlhakanya, kopanya
Comment on	Lewer kommentaar	Phawula	Caphula nge-, phawula	Swayaswaya	Tshwaela	Beka umbono, fakaza	Nika umbono ku-	Bulani muhumbulo	Nyika mieheketo	Tshwaela, akgela

Figure 2: Assessment terminology list in eleven official South African languages

In the above figure, it is observed that in some instances, African languages translators provided more than one equivalent of the source term, for example:

(i) Analyze

Sesotho: *sekaseka, manolla*
siSwati: *hlatiya, hluta*

(ii) Assess

isiXhosa: *hlola/ vavanya*
Setswana: *sekaseka, lekola, keleka, lekanya, athlola*

(iii) Carry out

IsiZulu: *Qhuba, feza*
IsiNdebele: *Khipha, veza*
Tshivenda: *shumani, itani*

This shows that the indigenous African languages are capable of drawing on their own resources and creating the necessary terms from their own vocabularies.

The research findings of the current study show that the compilation of multilingual glossaries in higher education is a result of a national policy directive that emphasizes the development and use of African languages as languages of teaching and learning. Most language policies adopted by most universities place emphasis on the implementation of multilingualism. The implementation of functional multilingualism at the University of South Africa, where the focus is placed on the users, the function, and the message, aligns well with the notion of a user-oriented approach to terminology. The student profile and expectations were not the only determining factors for the type of glossaries but also contributed to their content and presentation.

The choice of languages is directed by the language policy and needs assessment. The design and the presentation of terminological data are very simple and user-friendly for undergraduate-level students. The types of glossaries differ according to the needs of the target users and the purpose for which they are designed. Cabre (2003:183) maintains that "a terminological application must be oriented towards the solution of specific needs and therefore, it must take into account its recipients and the activities they plan to carry out by means of such application." This view is further supported by Nkomo (2011:157) who states that "glossaries are conceived as multilingual pedagogical resources which facilitate communication and learning in the context of special subject fields." The communicative and cognitive role in solving students' queries strengthens and justifies the continued development and improvement of glossaries for pedagogic reasons. If the ultimate goal of terminology development is teaching in these languages, it is essential that we persist in our efforts to develop different types of multilingual glossaries as determined by the users' needs.

Conclusion

The transformation of higher education in South Africa brought changes in the development and use of African languages, which necessitated the development of language resources, including teaching and learning material in higher education institutions. The aim of this study was to give a brief outline of current trends at selected institutions of higher learning and particularly the compilation of multilingual glossaries at Unisa. Its recommendations are intended to encourage the continual improvement of this significant exercise. The appropriateness of the support material should be in line with the success rate of students in the most at-risk modules, i.e., modules in which students perform poorly. However, the current study did not review the impact of the glossaries on the success and pass rate of students, so there is a need for further research on this issue in order to test the appropriateness of the student support material for continual improvement. In view of the discussion above, this study recommends the following:

- A continued compilation of multilingual glossaries in line with the needs and expectations of the users, that is, students
- An assessment of the effects of the glossaries on the pass rate
- The introduction of computer technology in the collection of terms, retrieval, and dissemination of information

- A strengthening of active involvement of domain experts in the identification of key concepts and validation
- The inclusion of databases and corpus development in the language policy implementation plan in order to improve the speed and cost-effectiveness of developing these glossaries.

The promotion of multilingualism is feasible only when there is a plan and resources available to attain the set goals. The progress made by the University of South Africa in compiling glossaries is a step forward in the use of African languages as languages of learning and teaching. Given that the Language Policy for Higher Education (2020) requires universities as centers of scholarship to play a critical role in the development of indigenous African languages, African language departments, as primary custodians of scholarship in these languages, should be supported in terms of funding, infrastructure, and personnel. It is the role of higher education to train language teachers, interpreters, translators, and other language practitioners to serve the needs of our multilingual society and facilitate success for tertiary-level students.

12. Multilingual education for improved foreign language acquisition: The importance of using students' native languages for learning foreign languages

Tony VUVU MUZAU
University of Bonn

As the previous chapters showed, multilingualism in Africa and bilingual education present many opportunities for personal development, for the enhancement of education systems and for sustainable development as a whole on the African continent. We are now living in a globalized world that increasingly requires Africans not only to master their own official languages but also other world languages, most importantly English, French, Spanish and Chinese. Proficiency in these languages provide important career prospects and can, thus, help elevating families and communities out of poverty. Those who are unable to communicate in European

> The term **Foreign Language**, as used in this chapter, refers to a language other than a native or official language of this country (Richards et al., 1992). For example, English in francophone countries and French in anglophone countries are considered foreign languages.
>
> The term Foreign Language is used in contrast to **Second Language**, which refers to a language that is not the speaker's native language but is among the languages spoken in the country (Richards et al, 1992). For example, French is a Second Language in francophone Africa for those people who speak African languages at home.

languages are ultimately left behind, often condemned to make a living in the informal sector.

But the proficiency in foreign languages is not only an economic concern in Africa. It is a matter of regional political and social integration and a prerequisite for the long-desired goal of African unity. In fact, colonialism and the infamous Berlin Conference of 1884/1885 did not only result in the political fragmentation of the continent, but also led to a deep linguistic divide. In an effort to facilitate the communication with and between the different ethnicities in their colonies, European colonial powers introduced their own languages as official languages, bringing along a linguistic rift through Sub-Saharan Africa. This rift becomes most apparent in the political, economic, and cultural divide between anglophone and francophone Africa. We therefore argue that, apart from the valorization of African languages and the improvement of proficiency in official European languages, foreign language learning (especially of English in francophone Africa and French in anglophone Africa) are vital as linguistic contributions to regional integration and sustainable development on the continent. However, foreign language proficiency in Africa remains low (see, for example, Coleman, 2013; Adetuyi-Olu-Francis & Opara, 2018; and Egwujioha et al., 2021). Additional to the overall challenges of formal education in African countries, low foreign language proficiency is the result of the neglect of the role of first languages for foreign language acquisition in African education policies and practice. In simpler terms, it comes to no surprise that a Congolese student, for example, is not able to adequately communicate in English after completing secondary school, given the fact that the student was introduced to English through French as the language of instruction and that the curriculum and materials for learning English that are used, are developed for students, whose first language is French. The Congolese student's first language, however, is Lingala and he/she is not even sufficiently fluent in French by the time English is introduced to the curriculum.

In order to improve foreign language proficiency in Africa (especially of English and French), the current chapter suggests making use of learners' first languages. This recommendation is based on scientific knowledge that the chapter will present in a condensed and comprehensible way. Moreover, drawing on real-life examples, the chapter will discuss challenges of such an approach and make suggestions to how these might be overcome. The examples used in this chapter will also draw on the author's own experience of promoting English as a foreign language in the education system of the Democratic Republic of the Congo (DRC) through a joint academic-civil society initiative. The findings of the chapter aim to provide important insights for policymakers and education practitioners and encourage further discussion on language policy in education in Africa.

The Anglophone-Francophone rift in Sub-Saharan Africa

Twenty-one countries in Sub-Saharan Africa use English as an official language, twenty countries use French (Eberhard et al., 2021). Of these, four countries use both English and French as official languages (Cameroon, Mauritius, Rwanda and Seychelles). However, bilingualism in European languages in these countries does not always go without conflict (see, for example, Fon, 2019 on Cameroon; and Sibomana, 2018 on the case of Rwanda).

Despite the fact that there are also other official languages in use in Sub-Saharan Africa (i.e., Arabic, Portuguese, Spanish, African languages), it is particularly the rift between anglophone and francophone countries that is most apparent. This rift is not only a linguistic phenomenon, but it has large-scale geo-political and economic impacts and affects regional cooperation in science, culture and other spheres that are crucial for sustainable development.

At first glance, it is francophone Africa that seems particularly marginalized. From an economic perspective, Anglophone Africa is much better integrated into the global economy and in trade with middle- and high-income countries than Francophone Africa (Pacific, 2015). On average, francophone African countries score lower than anglophone Africa on the Human-Development-Index, which compares indicators on health, education, poverty, security, and environmental and socio-economic development (UNDP, 2021). Moreover, French speaking African countries seem to be worse off at the international negotiation tables for matters of global concern. As the media outlet *Jeune Afrique* revealed while covering the 2021 climate negotiations in Glasgow, francophone Africa receives considerably less international climate funding than its English-speaking neighbors, despite being more vulnerable to the adverse impacts of climate change (Toulemonde, 2021). Certainly, concluding that the marginalization of francophone Africa is due to the use of French as an official language in diplomacy and business, would be an utter misperception of the complexity and multitude of the historic and present political, economic, social, environmental, and cultural factors influencing francophone Africa. However, promoting English as a foreign language in these countries, while continuing to value French and the region's African languages, could certainly contribute to increasing the regional and global integration of francophone African countries.

Similarly, it can be argued that promoting French as a foreign language in anglophone Africa could contribute to enhance Pan-African and cross-border trade (especially on a small and medium-business scale) (see, for example, Djité, 2008) and to facilitate knowledge exchange and cooperation in science and culture. In fact, Pan-Africanism through African unity and integration in economics, finance, trade, sciences, education, security and the valorization of Africa's common heritage and shared values are corner stones of the African Union's Agenda 2063 (African Union, 2015). Already the conferences of African ministers of education in Yaoundé (1961) and Addis Ababa (1963) recommended that anglophone African countries adopt French foreign language education and that francophone African countries likewise teach English in their schools (Adetuyi-Olu-Francis and Opara, 2018). Furthermore, Umukoro (2015) explains, based on the example of the Calabar Christmas Festival in Nigeria, how the promotion of French as a foreign language could provide an additional boost to tourism in anglophone African countries. Additionally, French language proficiency in anglophone countries also contributes to economic growth in other business sectors. The Nigerian Ambassador in France, Modupe Irele, stated in 2018 that there are around 120 French enterprises based in Nigeria (Irele, 2018 as cited in Adetuyi-Olu-Francis and Opara,

2018), providing jobs particularly to those Nigerians that master the French language. In Ghana, French businesses created around 20,000 jobs (Adetuyi-Olu-Francis and Opara, 2018).

Current foreign language education in Sub-Sahara Africa

The knowledge of both English and French is vital for the regional integration and sustainable development in Africa. Promoting English and French as foreign languages will break the communication barrier that exists among the African people, who are striving to be united and to cooperate in different domains such as research and business. There is, hence, a need for African French-speaking countries to learn English in the same way that African English-speaking countries should learn French. This is reflected in the African countries education policies that all include English and French foreign language teaching in formal education (Coleman, 2013 and Adetuyi-Olu-Francis and Opara, 2018).

Yet, as studies show, foreign language proficiency of English and French in Sub-Saharan Africa is still generally very poor (see, for example Coleman, 2013; Adetuyi-Olu-Francis & Opara, 2018; and Egwujioha et al, 2021). Foreign language teaching is affected by the same institutional and social challenges as education in Africa in general. Lack of access to education, inadequately equipped schools, too large class sizes, inadequate training, and absenteeism of teachers, the application of inappropriate pedagogic methods and student nonattendance (Coleman, 2013) are all factors undermining the success of formal school education in general as well as the outcomes of foreign language teaching. In many Sub-Sahara African countries, English or French as foreign languages are introduced at late primary school level or at the beginning of secondary school, at a time when even countries with a bi-lingual education policy already switched to their respective European official languages as language of instruction (see for example Coleman, 2013 for English in francophone West Africa and Adetuyi-Olu-Francis and Opara, 2018 for French in Nigeria). In fact, most Sub-Sahara African countries either employ only their colonial language as language of instruction or use African languages in the early years of primary education before switching to the official European language as language of instruction in later years (Fehrler & Michaelowa, 2009). Despite the relevance of the official European language in education in Sub-Sahara Africa, the proficiency of the language of instruction of students remains inadequate. A 2014 and a 2019 study, both conducted under the authority of the Conference of francophone Ministers of Education, revealed that in 10, and 14 francophone African countries respectively, the knowledge of French of students at the end of primary school was unsatisfactory (PASEC, 2020). Entering secondary school, students are introduced to English through French as a language of instruction, even though students were still struggling with French. A similar situation persists in many Anglophone African countries where French is introduced through English as language of instruction (Fehrler & Michaelowa, 2009). A more concrete example helps us to understand the impacts of this practice. In the DRC, as in most francophone African countries, English is introduced as a foreign language at secondary school level. The language of instruction at the very beginning of English language education remains French even though it is continually replaced by English. However, explanations by the teacher, for example on vocabulary or grammar, continue to be provided in French. Lists of vocabulary that are provided on the blackboard or in textbooks exclusively present English to French translations. Exercises and school exams often require translations of words or phrases from French to English. For a child that is not yet sufficiently proficient in French, the acquisition of English through French presents a major challenge. Indeed, the introduction of English as a foreign language through French as language of instruction was identified as one of the many challenges of English language education in Francophone West Africa in a study of the British Council in eight countries (Benin, Burkina Faso, Côte d'Ivoire, Guinea, Mali, Mauritania, Senegal and Togo) (Coleman, 2013).

Moreover, the design of curricula, textbooks and other teaching materials for foreign languages used in Sub-Saharan Africa does currently not take into account the first languages of learners. Either the curricula and books are designed to the needs of speakers of the colonial language (i.e., French textbooks used in anglophone countries are based on learners with English as their first language and English textbooks in francophone countries are based on learners with French as their first language) or they follow a standard design that disregards first languages entirely. The latter is based on a rather outdated scientific assumption that foreign languages, like English and French, are acquired in the same way for all learners, no matter what their first language is. However, today there is overwhelming linguistic evidence that this is not the case and that first languages do indeed influence the acquisition of second and foreign languages (see, for example, Fathman, 1975; Andersen, 1978; Kwon, 2005; Murakami & Alexopoulou, 2016; Shatz, 2017; Muroya, 2019; and Slabakova, 2018).

Importance of First Languages in foreign language acquisition

The First language (L1) is the language a child acquires first. In multilingual settings in Africa, the term can also refer to the language a person is most confident in expressing herself (Richards et al, 1993). In many cases, First Languages in francophone and anglophone Africa are African languages or Creole languages. However, especially in middle-class and affluent urban families, English and French can also serve as First languages (Fehrler and Michaelowa, 2009).

The L1 is the biggest asset but also challenge that a learner has for understanding how another language works. In formal education, learners, subconsciously, aim to understand a new language through the languages that they already know, particularly through their first language. As a result, the L1 of a learner strongly influences the acquisition of another language (see for example, Murakami and Alexopoulou, 2016 and Muroya, 2019). Similar grammatical features between the First and the foreign language, facilitate the acquisition of the foreign language. This is referred to as positive L1 transfer (Shatz, 2017). Going back to our example of a Congolese child learning English, whose first language is Lingala, we can see that the position of objects in Lingala is similar to English but not to French (the language of instruction):

English: I see **him**.
Lingala: Nazomona **ye**.
French: Je **le** vois.

We can see that in both English and Lingala, the indirect object is placed behind the verb, while it is placed in front of the verb in French. There is, thus, the opportunity for positive L1 transfer (i.e., the transfer of a known grammatical principle from the learner's first language to the foreign language) from Lingala to English, while this is not the case for French to English. The advantages that positive L1 transfers provide for learning a foreign language are lost if these foreign languages are learnt through a third language (in this case French) that does not exhibit the same grammatical features.

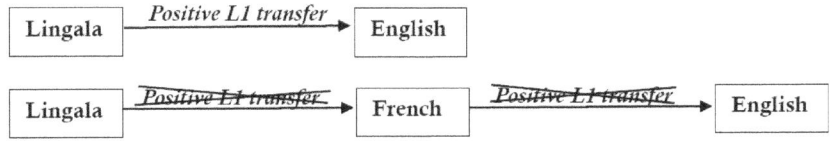

On the other hand, grammatical features of the foreign language that differ or do not exist in the learner's First language make the acquisition of the foreign language more difficult. These features need more time and effort to learn and to master them. These negative influences of a learner's First language on foreign Language acquisition are referred to as negative L1 transfer (Shatz, 2017). In the case of our Congolese student, we can find negative L1 transfer in the use of third person singular pronouns:

English: **He** is cooking the meal. **She** is cooking the meal.
French: **Il** prépare la nourriture. **Elle** prépare la nourriture.
Lingala: **A**zolamba biloko ya kolia. **A**zolamba biloko ya kolia.

In fact, in Lingala (as in many Bantu languages) there is no distinction between male and female third person singular pronouns or verb prefixes. There is a positive L1 transfer from French to English, where the use of third person singular pronouns is similar. For that matter, English curricula and textbooks that are based on French as a First language do not provide much focus on the correct acquisition and use of third person singular pronouns in English, since it is not a difficult issue for French speakers. However, from Lingala to French as well as from Lingala to English there is a negative L1 transfer, which means that learners would need more repetition, targeted exercises and more time to acquire the correct use of third person singular pronouns. In fact, also in the author's own experiences, even those Lingala L1 speakers that are fluent in French and English often confuse *il* and *elle* or *he* and *she* respectively. These mistakes are evidence for negative L1 transfer.

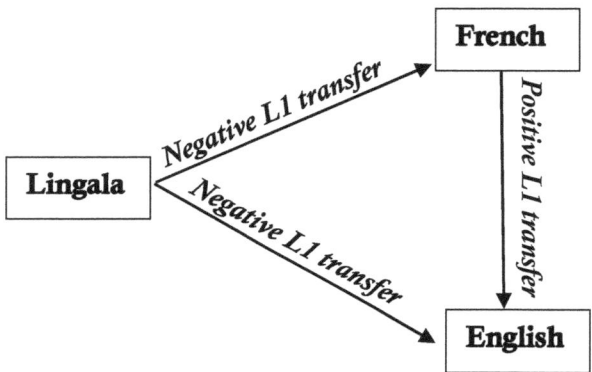

These findings from linguistic research show that failing to take into account the learners' First languages in the design of foreign language education curricula and teaching materials ultimately leads to foreign language education that does not address the needs of the learners and undermines learning outcomes. A thorough analysis of similarities and differences in both the learns' L1 and the foreign language would help to identify the features that can be easily acquired and those that will need more time, and subsequently will need more practice by the learner. English and French curricula and teaching materials should be designed according to these similarities and differences in order to make use of positive L1 transfers and overcome negative L1 transfers.

Moreover, given the fact that most African students are not adequately fluent in their European language of instruction at the end of primary school (see available studies on anglophone and francophone Africa by Fehler and Michaelowa, 2009; and PASEC, 2020), lists of vocabulary, translation exercises and exam questions as well as necessary non-foreign language communication in class should be in the learners' first language. Switching to learners' First languages as a medium to introduce and acquire foreign languages will help to overcome the challenges of students' insufficient knowledge of the official language of instruction and will significantly improve learning outcomes for foreign language education. To support this point, a study of learners of French and Spanish showed that those learners who were allowed to use their first language during pair and group exercises on grammar questions worked more collaboratively and achieved better learning outcomes than students that were prohibited from using their first language in class (Scott & DeLaFuente, 2008). The findings of this study demonstrate that at least for foreign language classes, popular regulations in African schools that prohibit the use of local languages in class, should be reconsidered.

From the above evidence, we can conclude that current education policies should opt to base foreign language teaching (especially French in anglophone Africa and English in francophone Africa) on learners' First languages, while continuing to promote the acquisition of the official European language and language of instruction through other subjects and targeted measures that set in well before foreign language education starts. Thus, the Congolese student from our example would acquire English more easily while continuing to improve their proficiency in French through other school subjects.

Challenges

The linguistic evidence presented above and the policy recommendations that derive from it seem relatively straight forward. However, Sub-Saharan Africa is far from reaching the Sustainable Development Goal on Education of the 2030 Agenda (see the outcomes of the global stocktaking for the 2019 United Nations High-Level Political Forum, 2019) and implementing educational policies remain an extremely difficult task.

As the president of a joint academic-civil society initiative to promote English language education in the DRC, the author experienced firsthand the challenges of improving English language acquisition through First language-based curriculum and textbook design. Nonetheless, the initiative, which is called *Projet d'Appui au Programme d'Anglais en RDC (PAPA CONGO)*, gained experience with over 50 pilot schools since 2012 which helped to identify major challenges and develop adequate strategies to overcome these.

A multitude of First Languages

Most African countries are home to a multitude of local languages. This means that within one country there many different First languages. In the DRC, for example, there are around 215 languages spoken (Eberhard et al, 2021). It is not uncommon to find speakers of different languages within one school. How can we then base foreign language teaching on First languages if there is a multitude of local languages?

A solution to this question is the focus on major lingua francas of the country. Through increasing urbanization and mobility in African countries, these lingua francas are increasingly changing into First languages. In the context of the DRC, there are four national languages serving as lingua franca: Lingala, Kikongo, Ciluba and Kiswahili. In terms of identification and consideration of positive and negative L1 transfers between these four languages and English as a foreign language for curriculum design and the development of teaching material, the languages provide one great advantage: they are Bantu languages and carry similar grammatical features. As an illustration, verbs in infinitive are formed with the prefix "ko/u" + the stem. This structure is similar to the infinitive form in English, which is formed with the prefix "to" + the stem. In simple present tense, the prefixes in English disappear in the same way it does in all the four national languages. In contrast, verbs in infinitive in French are marked with the endings "-er, ir, -oir or -re". Many learners fail to acquire these endings even after learning this notion for many years until completing their high school program. By looking at the structures of the cases, i.e., the infinitive forms in English, in Bantu languages and in French, we can clearly see that the infinitive structure of Bantu languages is closer to the English compared to the French. With these findings, we can draw assumptions that explanations based on how the infinitive form works in the learners' first languages would be understood better than providing any other explanations based on the French language grammar.

Also in other African countries, foreign language teaching could be based on the official national African languages, serving as lingua francas and as First Languages to most inhabitants. Nonetheless, the variety of local dialects in these languages should not be underestimated. In the DRC, for example, Kiswahili vocabulary can differ tremendously between speakers from Kisangani and Lubumbashi. The already existing promotion of standardized national languages (in this case Standard Kiswahili) in pre-schools and primary schools is extremely helpful to ensure that lists of vocabulary for Kiswahili to English or Kiswahili phrases for translation exercises into English are understood by all students.

Moreover, it is important to note that French in francophone Africa and English in anglophone Africa do indeed also serve as First languages, especially in middle-class and affluent urban households. Fehrler and Michaelowa (2009) emphasize, for instance, the importance of French as a First language in parts of Côte d'Ivoire. Foreign language teaching that considers First Language influence should, therefore, avoid underestimating the roles of official European languages as First Languages. This also underlines the importance of education policies and practices to be able to adapt to and accommodate possible changes in the number of First language speakers of a given language in a certain region or nationwide over the course of time. These changes can be a result, among others, of improved education, increased urbanization or forced migration and internal displacement of population groups.

Due to the challenges of multilingualism listed above, it is important to test this new approach to foreign language teaching first in a few pilot schools in different regions of a country and to compare teaching outcomes to non-pilot schools or to a baseline from before the new program was introduced. The influence of other factors, such as an overall improvement or decline of public education, should be considered when evaluating the success of a new First language-based approach to foreign language teaching. As for other education policies, also the implementation of new foreign language programs needs to be continuously monitored (best within a wider education policy monitoring scheme), evaluated and, if necessary, adapted (Adetuyi-Olu-Francis and Opara, 2018).

Motivation of learners

As Umukoro and Ohanyere (2020) demonstrate in their study on French language acquisition in Anglophone Africa, motivation and the immediate study environment are key to the success in foreign language acquisition of a learner. Teachers and students alike should be aware of the objectives of foreign language teaching as well as the future opportunities that foreign language proficiency will provide to learners (Coleman, 2013). Nevertheless, it should be acknowledged that there is an urban-rural divide in the motivation for foreign language acquisition as the study of the British Council on English in francophone West Africa shows (Coleman, 2013). Francophone urban students are much more often in contact with English, for instance through media, and have much clearer career prospects through English language acquisition than their rural peers. Also, francophone learners in regions bordering anglophone countries may have a higher motivation to learn English than school kids elsewhere (Coleman, 2013).

Moreover, Umukoro and Ohanyere (2020) found out that francophone African learners are generally more motivated to learn English than anglophone African students to learn French. This is not at least due to the lack of awareness of the benefits of French proficiency in Anglophone Africa and a low attractiveness of the French language to these learners.

The author's own experiences in English language teaching in the DRC underline the importance of the learning environment and pedagogic approaches for increasing the motivation of students to learn foreign languages. Conventional teacher-centered pedagogical approaches that limit students' class interventions to learning and reciting vocabulary and grammar by heart, leave no room for students' creativity and independent learning processes. The PAPA CONGO English teaching program therefore includes alternative pedagogic approaches that place the students and their learning experiences in the foreground, for example through physical tasks and games that train language competencies, peer, and group work as well as visually attractive and age-appropriate text and exercise books and audio materials. Sonck (2005) comes to a similar conclusion for improving English language teaching in Mauritius.

Moreover, English and French language teaching should take into account the living realities of students in order to make language learning more attractive. References to local food, landmarks of the region and its cities as well as popular culture will provide students with vocabulary that they might deem useful to express themselves in the foreign language on topics that are of interest to them. It is, however, important to keep in mind that references to popular culture, in particular, should be updated every few years to avoid appearing outdated.

Inadequately trained teachers

Understanding the importance of First languages in foreign language education, working with reformed curricula and applying new pedagogical approaches require adequately trained English and French teachers. Unfortunately, insufficient capacities of teachers remain a major problem for education in Sub-Sahara Africa in general (UNESCO, 2019). The British Council found out that many English teachers in francophone West Africa are not sufficiently proficient in English themselves and therefore lack confidence in teaching and engaging with their students in English (Coleman, 2013). Further problems are inadequate pedagogical training and insufficient renumeration of teachers (Coleman, 2013). Egwujioha et al (2021) made similar observations on French teachers in Nigeria.

Given the difficulties that teachers in pilot schools in the DRC were facing in applying the PAPA CONGO program, the initiative decided to broaden its scope and to offer free and regular training to teachers in order to increase their English proficiency and acquire additional knowledge on pedagogical approaches. This training was key in enabling the adequate application of the PAPA CONGO English program. Despite these positive results, improving the capacities of English and French teachers respectively, cannot be part of civil society engagement in the long run, but rather need to be integrated into overall reform measures of the education sector. Recruitment criteria for teachers need to be reviewed, the quality of training in teaching colleges and universities enhanced and the funding for teachers and school infrastructure and equipment appropriately increased (see for example Coleman, 2013; UNESCO, 2019 and Egwujioha et al, 2021).

Financial constraints and institutional weakness

The above-mentioned challenges show that switching foreign language teaching in Sub-Sahara Africa to a First language-based approach cannot be realized independently from the overarching efforts of education sector reform in each country. Changing approaches to foreign language teaching need to be considered and planned against the backdrop of overall language planning in education in order to ensure the valorization of African languages and the best possible learning outcomes in all subjects, including French and English as second and foreign languages. Questions that need to be addressed are, for example, when to introduce which language, how to use these languages in education and how much time to provide for which language in the weekly curriculum (Snock, 2005).

Following a new approach to foreign language education is costly and will require necessary funding for the development, printing and regular update of teaching materials, for better training of teachers and for adequate equipment in schools. At the same time, schools as well as education authorities at the decentralized and at the national level need to be capable to run pilot projects, evaluate them, plan foreign language teaching at a country-wide level and continuously monitor teaching outcomes and adapt programming if necessary. This requires institutional capacities that many African countries do currently not possess (see UNESCO, 2019). Integrating new First language-based foreign language programs into overall education policies and strategies, will decrease the financial burden of the former through the creation of synergies with similar approaches in other domains of education.

Conclusion

The promotion of English as a foreign language in francophone Africa and French language education in anglophone Africa are vital for enhancing regional integration in Sub-Sahara Africa and for political, economic, scientific and cultural cooperation on the continent and with the rest of the world. However, foreign language proficiency in Sub-Sahara Africa is still low, which can be explained, among other things, by the lack of consideration of learners' First languages in foreign language teaching. In fact, first languages strongly influence the acquisition of new languages positively (through positive L1 transfer) and negatively (through negative L1 transfer). In Africa, the use of French as a medium to learn English as well as the use of English to learn French disregards the importance of positive and negative L1 transfer and significantly undermine learning outcomes. A First language-based approach to foreign language teaching is therefore necessary. Implementing such an approach, however, comes with many challenges, such as the multitude of first languages in most African countries, the lack of motivation of foreign language learners, inadequate teacher training as well as overall financial constraints and institutional weaknesses for the implementation of education policies. The chapter highlights that only coherent and inclusive education sector planning that takes into account foreign language education against the backdrop of overarching language policy will ensure the best possible education outcomes and a cost-efficient use of public education funding and external assistance.

V. BILINGUAL EDUCATION: MOTHER TONGUE / FRENCH, MOTHER TONGUE / ENGLISH

13. The need for bilingual education for the promotion of regional integration of communities in the eastern part of the Democratic Republic of Congo

Félicien MASANGA MAISHA
University of Florida

The education system in the DRC exists thanks to the legacy of the Belgian colonial administration, which favored French as the language of education and administration. Today, more than 60 years after the departure of the Belgian colonists, French remains the language of knowledge, through which children learn what they need to flourish. French is the standard language used from nursery school to university.

Although the use of a foreign language as a driving force in the education system of an independent country seems to be a perpetuation in itself of the influence of the former colonizing country, it must be said that this still provides advantages for African learners in general and specifically for those in the DRC, a country which has a mosaic of languages (Makita, 2013). Indeed, it is difficult to decide which language to privilege to the detriment of others for fear of generating endless conflicts and creating a technologization (see Ouane & Glanz, 2010) capable of weakening communities that are already fragile due to endless armed conflicts such as those experienced in the East of the country for over two decades.

French, English and other European languages, although associated with colonization (N'Guessan, 2007; Iveković, 2007; Senghor, 2003), seemed to be a solution to the problem posed by African languages in which it was difficult to find a common denominator. However, this solution was only valid at the national level where one language could be adopted, but, at the regional level, the existence of one or more other 'national' or 'local' languages used in teaching created an obstacle to regional integration by making educational exchanges between teachers and especially learners difficult. In order to solve this problem, the initiation of a bi- or multilingual system in education has become an unavoidable solution that can bring together these populations, optimize linguistic exchanges and even facilitate the human development of young learners (Lavoie, 2009).

It should be noted that other advantages of bilingual education are based on the use of a mother tongue coupled with a foreign language such as French or English (Faso, 2009; Ouane & Glanz, 2010), meaning that, in addition to the foreign language used in education, the student also learns in the mother tongue they have mastered from a young age. The utility of this system is that the student (child or adult) learns, for example, how to read and write in their own language, and this exercise does not require much effort on the part of the student. Nevertheless, this requires learning tools to be prepared in advance by the education system and to be in line with or identical to those used in other countries. However, if we take the example of a country like the DRC, which has a multitude of local languages, there are several that have not yet been sufficiently studied to give teachers the necessary tools to teach them. Also, at an advanced level of learning, such as secondary school, teaching in the local language will have limitations in integrating learners who do not speak it because they come from other backgrounds and have received basic education in another mother tongue.

In this chapter, I discuss the limits of a monolingual education using only French, as well as the need to resort to bilingualism through the integration of a second language and a foreign language as Braslavskym (1999) demonstrates in his article 'Bilingualism or multilingualism. Human rights and foreign languages.' I will refer here to the concurrent use of French and English language teaching, for which the influence and expansion in several Central and East African countries is no longer in question. This expansion is unfortunately anarchic in the sense that it imposes itself on communities and populations that are not prepared for it beforehand and thus have difficulty conforming to its requirements. Eastern DRC, for example, is dominated by the humanitarian agencies of the United Nations system and several Anglo-Saxon non-governmental organizations (NGOs). These actors dominate nearly all critical aspects of life, including health, education, agriculture, livestock, and more. When it comes to recruiting, individuals with knowledge of English are the most privileged compared to those who only know French and local languages. However, the majority of young graduates do not know English, and those who do are the few who attended bilingual private schools or who had the chance to study abroad, mainly in the English-speaking countries of East Africa. As a result, many graduates in eastern DRC are unemployed because they are unable to meet the language requirements of international NGOs which are practically the only available employers in the region (James, 2021).

This chapter is organized as follows: first, I present a general overview of the Congolese education system with French as the standard language of instruction. I will then discuss the challenges facing the Congolese education system before turning to the problems associated with monolingual education in the DRC. Before concluding with a plea for the establishment of bilingualism in the region, I will discuss the eastern region of the DRC and its isolation from the capital Kinshasa, as well as its close contact with English-speaking East Africa.

The Congolese education system and its challenges inherited from the Belgian colonization

The Congolese educational system is the work of the Belgian colonial administration which forged it by providing the framework that it has had for more than 6 decades. Although there have been some attempts at reform, the bulk of the system remains largely as originally defined. French, although a foreign language, is the language of instruction everywhere in the country, from kindergarten to university. The Belgian colonial administration had conferred a superior status, a prestige to the French language and an ideal behind which the entire indigenous population would have to work in order to be able to be requalified as 'evolved' and thus able to acquire civilization (a western value absent among the local indigenous peoples).

The few Congolese who, at the time, had the privilege of attending the missionary school of the colonial administration were de facto separated from the rest of their community in order to be called elite indigenous, or evolved, therefore capable of being subordinate to the whites in the administration of the immense territory of Congo (Kadima-Tshimanga, 1982).

At the beginning, the evolved were not intellectuals in the true sense of the word but were individuals who had basic notions of arithmetic and above all basic linguistic knowledge enabling them to express themselves in French. In addition, they were able to internalize and disseminate the colonial ideology acquired in missionary schools (Xiberras, 1992).

If French has been able to have a great value in the Congolese educational system, it is, among other things, because of the superiority granted to it during the first contact between the Europeans and the local indigenous populations. Black individuals who could speak French were easily assimilated as whites by their black colleagues, and a wall of separation was consequently created between them.

This wall persisted throughout the post-colonial period in the sense that it was the ability to use French that determined who was an intellectual and which skills were better than others. One sent one's child to school primarily so that he would be able to express himself in French, and in this case, the community evaluated the success of a school education based on mastery (or non-mastery) of the French language. Even when the value of the French language is required to establish an equilibrium within the school, it is observed that this course is, if not the most important, then the second-most important compared to the rest of the courses offered in school. The French language has maintained a special position within the Congolese education system, ensuring that no local language can be suggested to be taught or used in schools throughout the country.

The DRC, a monolingual education based on French in a particular geographical and sociolinguistic context

In the DRC, knowledge is acquired through the use of the French language, which is not only a foreign language but also, and above all, a language descended from colonization, as mentioned above. Belgian colonization conferred upon French a value and a grandeur behind which the indigenous or native populations came running with vehemence and fervor. The establishment of the advanced class based on language skills is an important cause of this. French is given the privilege of conveying linguistic knowledge (learners are equipped to master the language) and non-linguistic knowledge (students have no choice other than to learn other subjects using French). Thus, didactic and sociological issues (Gajo, 2009) are pursued solely by manipulating one singular language.

The enthronement of French and its coronation as the language of administration - or official language - has not failed to have harmful consequences on the many local languages spoken by the indigenous people. These languages, accused of being unfit for civilization and unworthy of being taught in modern schools, were pressured into being relegated to the background. Many of these indigenous languages have disappeared today, especially those that had few speakers because they belonged to small tribal or ethnic groups. Other indigenous languages are disappearing because they have not pushed back against the linguistic competition, especially in urban areas where French is the preferred language not only in the educational system but also in the households of wealthy families. In these households, in order to be recruited as a child's nanny, one must pass a spoken French language test, because parents are afraid to hire someone for their children who cannot speak French.

The post-colonial period had blown a slight wind of awareness toward the value of local languages during the famous period known as 'the period of recourse to authenticity' instituted by the former dictator Mobutu in the 1970s (White, 2008). As a result, some local languages considered to be in the majority were given the privilege of being taught in elementary classes - not to establish bilingualism, but for socio-political purposes to encourage fluidity of communication between pupils from different ethnic groups. This enabled students to acquire a near advanced linguistic knowledge in these languages, also known as national languages. Among these languages are Tshiluba in the Kasai regions in the center of the country, Kikongo in the extreme west, and Lingala in the capital Kinshasa and the northwest, while Swahili covers the entire eastern part bordering several countries.

The situation described above has contributed to the elevation of French above all other languages in the sense that only French was, and continues to be, the language of instruction, the language capable of communicating knowledge and transmitting other disciplines. In the current public administration in DRC, French is the language that all state officials are encouraged to use. Private companies also have the same duty, although there is an intrusion of English imported by international agents who are there and, in general, occupy positions of leadership and therefore able to influence the conduct of the organization.

English is increasingly becoming the official language of UN agencies and international NGOs, yet it is also the leading private sector language in Eastern DRC. Indeed, the world of work in the East is dominated by humanitarian agencies that offer the privileged few from the local community the opportunity to work. However, linguistic skills are very important, and the language that these organizations target today is no longer French, but rather, English, which is presented as the language of donors.

This requirement to be fluent in English excludes many young graduates who have the technical skills required for the positions available. This is why there are only few rare pearls who, after attending the few bilingual schools present in the region, end up being recruited and join the class of employees in an environment where employment is more than a luxury because of the scarcity of job opportunities due to the weakness of the Congolese state.

Bilingual schools are themselves a rare commodity in the region. For example, in the province of North Kivu, which four years ago had a total of 3,300 primary schools, only ten or so were recognized as bilingual. 1,538 secondary schools were counted and only five among them claimed to provide bilingual education. There are 111 universities and higher- education institutions, and the only one that claimed to be bilingual has just been closed by a recent instruction from the Congolese Minister of Higher and University Education for reasons of non-viability.

Apart from the fact that English has succeeded in overtaking French in its own territory, especially in the field of employment, there is also the fact that opportunities to access quality education are rare for schoolchildren and students living in eastern DRC because, unlike others who live in the center or west of the country, they are at some distance from the universities that have a great reputation in Africa, such as in Kampala, home of the famous Makerere University ranked high on the list of African universities, or in Nairobi, which also has several universities and academic institutions ranked high on this list.

Some promoters of private schools have responded to the needs of parents who come to them requesting that English be taught in their schools and that the language be granted the same privileges as those enjoyed by French. This is why only a decade ago, the first bilingual school was created in the city of Goma and, 11 years later, 4 others were added to make a total of 5 bilingual schools, one of which was at the university level. The town of Beni in the far north is the only one to have a bilingual university whose teaching qualities are praised by the students attending it. This is the Bilingual Christian University in Congo (UCBC), which teaches in French and English according to the language skills of the teachers available.

Further south, in the city of Bukavu, bilingual schools are also rare, despite the need that has been felt there recently. So-called bilingual schools in the cities of Eastern DRC are not really bilingual in the strict sense of the word. In these schools, although English is taught, it does not occupy the same place as French, and is taught only as a course that is given a bit more importance than others with the objective of seeing the learners quickly develop skills and linguistic abilities in the English language as much as they have in French. It is a form of Canadian-style immersion (Coste, 1994) with the only difference being that, in the DRC, the state is not involved in what is being done and the teaching of English is solely didactic.

Nevertheless, although bilingualism practiced in its present form in some private institutions is struggling to flourish in this region due to organizational problems, it has produced results in its facilitation of some students who easily integrate into the educational institutions of the English-speaking system that is utilized in the countries of East Africa (limited to the DRC at its eastern border). It is thanks to the training acquired in the 'bilingual' schools in the cities of eastern DRC that these Congolese schoolchildren are easily accepted and that they manage to satisfy the aptitude tests in English, which are imperatively offered before any enrollment in the schools of neighboring countries that offer high-quality training according to the standards set at the international level.

It should be noted that, apart from formal bilingual schools, there are English language training centers in all the major cities in eastern DRC. These centers are normally part of vocational education, and most of them operate informally and are not officially recognized. Therefore, as they are not regularly audited by inspectors from the Ministry of Primary, Secondary and Technical Education, the quality of the training they offer is to be taken with great reservation. Nevertheless, the majority of individuals with an interest in learning English, especially after having studied in ordinary schools in the Congolese educational system, flock to these centers because the training cost is very affordable, even though the quality of training offered there leaves much to be desired. They do so because, following the baccalaureate, for example, they feel the need to continue their studies in academic institutions in East Africa and do not have the linguistic capacity to do so. Finding themselves unable to take a step backwards to a bilingual instructional experience (for which there are only a few establishments to meet the enormous, overwhelming need), they are content to join the informal English training centers available, regardless of the quality of the training provided.

It can come to a point that a single individual may go to three separate centers in turn before acquiring a more or less acceptable level of English. However, at the end of each training course, the center attended issues its students a certificate that qualifies their level as 'satisfactory' when compared to the laureate, as the latter does not reflect any mastery of the language learned, neither orally nor in writing, because the type of evaluation conducted is not based on instructional performance. This is why, for those who are lucky enough to be trained in the so-called 'bilingual' institutions, the level of English training is fairly good compared to those who attend vocational training centers for learning English. This is because, in these private institutions, the language training program is standardized or copied from a western institution. Also, the training done by these institutions is regularly audited and validated by the state inspectorate of primary, secondary and technical education. French being a compulsory language of education in DRC, everyone who has acquired an education at the secondary or university level has, automatically, a relatively high knowledge in French - with some exceptions. This is the reason why there are, for example, almost no training or learning centers for French except in French institutes found in larger cities like Bukavu, Goma, and Kisangani.

Eastern DRC, a region isolated from the capital Kinshasa and facing the eastern part of Africa

The DRC is a large country with its capital located in the far west. Outside of the capital region, the country has a serious problem with a lack of reliable road infrastructures. As a logical consequence, the populations of the eastern parts of the country have almost no connection to the capital. Travelling to Kinshasa, and even to other cities in the center and west of the country, is a luxury that only the wealthy can afford. This trip is only possible by air and therefore very expensive. The only alternative that remains for the populations of eastern DRC is the exploration of neighboring countries for obvious reasons, especially for business or, secondarily, for educational purposes (especially for young people), as well as for cultural exchanges.

However, these countries to the east all have English as their official language, even though Swahili, a powerful African language, also comes in as a hyphen facilitating contact between people from different countries in the region. Yet Swahili also has its dialects depending on country or region. The Swahili spoken in Goma or Bukavu, for example, has many words in local languages (Mashi, Kinande, Kirega, Kihunde) and French. This is why it is not surprising that when a Mushi from Bukavu or a Nande from Goma finds himself in Dar es Salaam or Mombasa and expresses himself in Swahili he will find it difficult to be understood. This is the same case for people from East African countries when they find themselves in Eastern DRC (Swahili phone). They are always told that the Swahili they speak is very difficult, much like English. Therefore, for interregional comprehension, bilingual learning is a necessity in the East, as suggested by Daff & Buttin (2010) in other parts of Africa.

Below is a map of the DRC and an illustration of how the integration of English is more than a necessity given the influence of English-speaking countries in the eastern part of Africa (map by Kennedy Ulikuwe, January 2022).

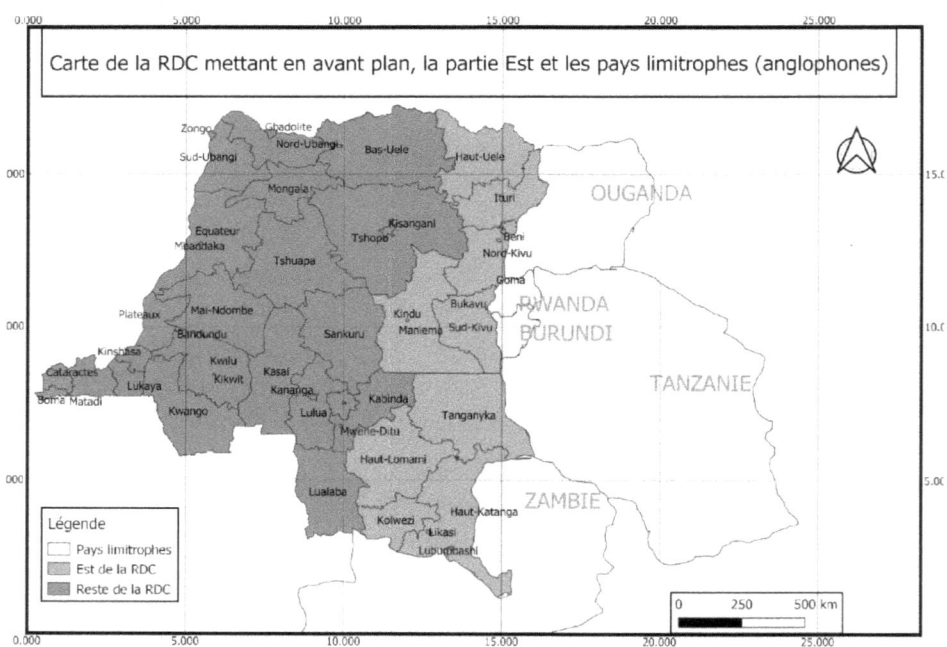

Conclusion

Given the geographical, sociolinguistic context of the eastern region of the DRC, it appears that the integration of English in education is of great necessity for its inhabitants, especially for the reasons mentioned above. The right way to teach it without harming the already functional and officialized French-speaking system is the establishment of a bilingual system that uses English as a second language of instruction.

The introduction of bilingual education from primary school onwards in the schools of Eastern DRC is beneficial not only for the young school children for purely educational reasons (opening up to the English-speaking system from neighboring countries) but also for the whole local community of this region whose acquisition of English language skills opens them up to more opportunities by connecting them to the economic, technological and cultural achievements of East Africa. In addition, for young graduates from the region, there is a better chance of being able to access the local work force (mainly in the humanitarian sector), which, as mentioned above, is increasingly dominated by experts and managers from Anglo-Saxon countries, who impose English for better communication among local and international agents.

14. Tips from the hen:
Bilingual school as a social project

Thomas BEARTH, Goh SOUPOU, Lika Sopouh LEGRAND,
Fan Monsia DIOMANDÉ, Siaba SIDIBE,
A. TOKPA GOUESSE[17]

LAGSUS Project (Follow-up)

Early on the day following the workshop comprised of about twenty participants that had gathered on April 5 and 6, 2018 in the city of Man in the West of Côte d'Ivoire to discuss the theme *School and Extracurricular Bilingualism in the Toura country*, I leave my hut to fulfill the first duty of the stranger benefitting from Toura hospitality - to thank the chief. Three of us had accepted his invitation to visit Yengbèyalé (Yeng), a site off the main roads, occupied some decades ago by his late father. A sparsely exploited area of 2 to 3 thousand hectares at the western end of the former Toura administrative district, it had been set up, according to the idea of its founder, as an innovative village with volunteers from the region, from other parts of the country and, recently, with a strong influx of cocoa planters from Burkina Faso.

At night, the chief had reflected on the two days of workshops he had spent in the city alongside public school teachers, language didactics researchers, and a delegation from the Direction Régionale de l'Education Nationale. "At school," he told me in order to illustrate the insight he had gained, "I learned to read '*The Tricks of the Chicken,*' but *without understanding what it meant or what it was about.*"

---

[17] Besides the authors, female villagers also played a key role in the establishment of the bilingual school. See page 184 below, last paragraph.

Through the Yeng school that had opened at the start of the 2014 school year, his application for a Toura-French bilingual type school had been approved by the Ministry. For the first time on the western slopes of the Toura Mountains, Toura children had taken the first steps in learning the three-step process of *reading, writing, and calculating* in a language and with words that made sense to them.

A pivotal factor in the acquisition of any skill - *acquiring new knowledge from what is known* - the cognitive resonance of the aligned letters of the alphabet opened the way for them to know how to read their language, and not only that, it served as a relay to access French through a meaning first identified and validated in Toura, the language by default to serve as a support for understanding. Understanding French with the help of Toura changes everything for them; sometimes a glimmer of light on a face, captured on video, confirms it. A tour de force at the origin of a dissuasive pedagogy now officially banned, but difficult to banish from minds (Noyau 2016), learning French through French, with spelling intricacies on top of it, turns out to be an equation with several unknowns, presages a chronic deficit in comprehension and preludes the abandonment of school careers. Instead of the happiness of knowing how to read as the result of a cyclical process of decoding clumped symbols and attributing meaning, learners, like a bird deprived of its wings, experience the broken cognitive cycle as a permanent handicap, compensated for by snatches of knowledge reproduced like a parrot or, in the event of silence, by the teacher's vociferation substituting for their guilty ignorance. Could this ritual, which can be observed in the classroom, be the cause of a cascade of academic failures rather than the trace of progressive appropriation, and an indicator of a loss of human resources, 'an enormous waste' (Mamadou Cissé, n.d.)?

Such a diagnosis will seem exaggerated to some and unfair to others. It would indeed be unfair not to acknowledge, on the one hand, the ingenuity of certain teachers and their efforts to circumvent the failure of methods to create a sense of achievement and the cases of academic success that may result. Yet we must recognize the basic error of attributing deficits of learning not otherwise explained to the innate or hereditary ineptitude of the mindset or to the interference of the native linguistic heritage. The positive effects of compensating for the deficit through a resolutely bilingual approach, on the other hand, suggest that many failures can be explained as the reverse effects of an innate linguistic intelligence (in the Chomskyan sense), in which the child makes use of a familiar language spontaneously at home or among peers, but is discouraged from using it for learning purposes at school. Hence, also, the effect of linguistic insecurity noted in monolingual regimes even among the best students (Vahou 2018).

Luc's success[18]

Luc, a gifted and sociable child, knew how to greet in the language of each one of the people with whom he shared the space of Yeng: Toura, Yacouba, Baoulé... Knowing how to address each person in his or her language or how to react intelligently to them - even Mooré, the language of Burkinabe immigrants, was no exception - was of little use at the school that young Luc attended in Biankouma, the administrative center half a day's walk from the village of Yeng where he lived with his mother. As *Joseph Baya* (2022: 117) says about SDG 4 of the 2030 Agenda: Education for All (EFA), decreed by the government, is only really within reach of everyone in disadvantaged rural areas if it "reduces the suffering of parents having to send their children to school at a distance, and is also a means of easing the pain of children being forced to evolve far from their parents". It is therefore not surprising to find Luc in the middle of the school year in an uncultivated field, sitting in a wheelbarrow playing with two of his fellow pupils who have dropped out of school like him. At the start of the 2014 school year, however, we learn that he has returned to the "bench" at the newly built school in his native village; the gamble seems to have paid off. Even more so, since he will learn in CP 2 class in Toura what he could only imperfectly retain in CP 1 class in Biankouma. As J. Baya states, access to the subject in a language already known is essential for EFA to be effectively

---

[18] Luc : name changed

accessible to all. The first class to pass the *Primary School Certificate* in 2019 will be remembered for the fact that the interview conducted in French with Luc and his peers does not reveal any trace of linguistic insecurity.[19]

Two years later, on August 19, 2021: Back in Biankouma, this time as a student at the college, Luc returned to the village for the holidays. Having joined the round of men under the *appatam*, the latter, having been able to note his understanding of Toura and his respect for the protocol privileging the word of the elders without excluding that of the young, will benefit from the added value of his competence to flesh out their debates of statistics. The relationship between school and society, which used to be alienating, is becoming complementary and productive, made more dynamic thanks to the bilingual mode of early referrals for school learning.

The challenge of ambient society

Among the challenges to be overcome in the context of a local bilingual experience, which is positive on the whole, as the chief keeps saying, is the divide between it and the sometimes less favorable perception of bilingual education by the surrounding world, including parents and sponsors. Turning a child into an adult, versed in the official language, the indispensable key to success, sums up the parents' vision - a legitimate one - of the goal of schooling, in rural as well as urban areas. But to claim to achieve this by first teaching the alphabet in the mother tongue may arouse suspicion that this is a false goal, a useless and costly 'detour', or even a deception. A cause of dropouts, as the headmaster of the Yeng school pointed out at the workshop in April 2018, this recurring reservation calls for a response commensurate with the challenge. Presented to the Workshop by *Clarisse Hager M'boua* (2022: 149), it calls for a reordering of priorities and the sequence of modules within the experimental bilingual program established under the name of PEI, in favor of simultaneous language learning with, among other things, more immediately perceptible benefits from the French component

---

[19] toura.ch/fr/projets/ecole/bonnes-nouvelles-de-l-ecole-de-yenggbeyale

of the bilingual formula. It should be noted that by the start of the 2021 school year, the number of pupils newly enrolled in CP 1 in a bilingual class had risen to 47 from 19 in the year of the Workshop. However, the adhesion of public opinion, first locally, then regionally and even nationally, to the principles of the bilingual school remains one of the objectives of the laboratory that was formed around the multilingual site of Yeng. Documentation accessible to the general public through various channels is therefore essential to convince opinion leaders not only of the need - which many scientific publications have already done - but also of the *feasibility* of a more flexible approach to the languages of instruction which, according to the World Bank (2019), has the potential to change the key indicators of school performance in rural Africa.

Curriculum development

The rest of this article will give a voice to various actors who are professionally or voluntarily involved in the realization of an ongoing bilingual education project. It is an opportunity to highlight the scientific, educational, technological, and organizational aspects necessary for its success in the context of simultaneous management of languages that are distant from each other from the point of view of the learning objects they bring into play (phonemes, letters, tones, lexico-grammatical structures, texts and cultural references).

This distance is multiplied by the distance between the places of training and implementation of the instruments: in the case of the Yengbèyalé bilingual school, the field of application is 650 km away from the administrative and scientific centers of reference. If the physical distance, by no means exceptional in Africa, poses an infrastructural, logistical, communication and organizational challenge, difficult roads and the inconsistency of a barely existing communication network pose additional coordination challenges. Nevertheless, the mostly long-distance cooperation, the organization of WhatsApp sessions and the collaboration over the internet and telephone offer a stimulating and economically interesting field of experimentation for the pioneering implementation of EFA, in order to meet the real challenge, namely that of not letting generations of children go by helplessly with the "tricks of the chicken": Learning the intricacies of a language from which they are mentally cut off by a hiatus of incomprehension and thereby deprived of the educational inclusion advocated in Agendas 2030 /2063. How can the "WhatsApp Toura Lab" help to manage this multiple challenge? This collective article, based on the ongoing experience, will propose some answers to these questions, of which motivation is the first. Chief Sidibé says it in these words: "Bilingual education in Africa means giving our children every opportunity to succeed." (4 February 2022)

Where does the bilingual school of Yengbèyalé come from?

I was privileged to introduce the alphabet into the Toura language in return for the hospitality granted to my wife and myself by its speakers which has enabled me to obtain a doctorate in linguistics at the University of Geneva (Bearth 1971). As scientific coordinator of the Language, Gender and Sustainability (LAGSUS) project commissioned by the Volkswagen Foundation[20], I took part in the closing ceremony of the Ivorian part of this research, which coincided with the end of the war (2002-2007). The war had divided the country into a southern half under government control and a northern and western half under rebel control. The absence of government and development agencies during this period had led the inhabitants of the Toura Mountains to discover their power to act and succeed through their own language. And why not try using this recipe in school as well?

The symbolic laying of the foundation stone of the bilingual school in Toura country on 15 September 2007 by the representative of the Ministry of Education, the first post-war act broadcast on national television, was coupled with a collective appeal by the women of Yengbèyalé to have a school built in their village. And as requested by the village, the Ministry gave permission to use the local language for teaching in first and second grades.

---

[20] Hannover, Germany, 2002-2007, www.lagsus.de, website in French, English, German

This wish, displayed on the screen in the Toura language, has been fulfilled since 2013 through the partnership between, on the one hand, the local association of Ilse & Thomas Bearth Institute of Language and Development (IITBLD), which is supposed to extend the achievements of LAGSUS for the development of the region, and, on the other hand, by the association of Toura Mountains Initiative (ITM), with the support of the Swiss municipality of Spreitenbach, a support which will be reiterated for the expansion of the school in 2021.[21] My commitment as a linguist in the West of Côte d'Ivoire for a school standing on two legs is furthermore motivated by the long-standing experience in my home canton in the Swiss mountains among the Retoromanic and Italian-speaking minorities, an experience whose positive effects are no longer to be demonstrated.

Textbook writing for Toura reading classes by Goh Soupou (Man)

A good number of African and even Ivorian children, and particularly Toura, have stopped going to school for many reasons. Among others, the lack of financial means of the parents, the distance of the school from the place of residence of the child and especially the fact that the courses are given in a language other than the mother tongue. The PEI (Integrated School Program) comes to correct this situation. This program encourages bilingual education. Teaching must be based on didactic material, a bilingual book.

As the name implies, a bilingual book is written in two different languages, thus with two different alphabets. The Toura alphabet uses 19 letters of the French alphabet and 5 special characters. In addition, some digraphs: association of two French letters to make a Toura letter: gb, kw, bh; association of two French letters to make a sound: un, an, in; association of French letter and a special character to make a Toura sound: ɩ + n = ɩn, ɛ + n = ɛn, ɔ + n = ɔn. Toura uses accents to mark tones.

---

[21] toura.ch/fr/projets/ecole

Lesson Design

The Government of Côte d'Ivoire wants all school-age children to attend school. A teaching system has been put in place to support this desire. The Ministry of National Education and Literacy, through its pedagogues, publishes teaching materials in French. Our job consists in producing the materials of the same kind in Toura while following the different stages of the French model. This means that if it is the letter *u, pronounced as 'ou' in French,* that is being studied, for example, we have to find a Toura word well known to the child that contains the vowel *u*, e.g., *gu* 'clay' or *tu* 'piece'. Having isolated the letter *u* in Toura, the child learns to read and write it and to recognize it I in new words that the child reads or hears, and finally to compose sentences by themselves that contain the new letter.

Each lesson should have a short reading text at the end. There should also be exercises to assess the students. The exercise will ask the child to recognize a sound or a letter by circling it, putting the letter where it is needed to obtain the correct spelling of the word. As a contribution of the manual to the knowledge of the cultural and natural environment; the choice of words and texts represents an added cultural value:

> *Tìà-à yɛɛn* Tia's creel (*traditional tool used to catch daytime termites, highly valued as a delicacy and for their social value as a gift*)
> *Tààpé tíi* the black loincloth (*female garment*).

The children thus discover their environment and the particularities of their language through the written word.

Difficulties

Writing a manual is not without its difficulties. The translation of an object name from language A (French) to language B (Toura) is not at all easy. Rendering the meaning of an exercise statement verbatim is not easy. One must therefore be experienced in this field to succeed. French and Toura have a number of letters in common. If in writing, one has no difficulty, in reading, a problem arises. If the French reads "a" *a* and the Toura reads *a*, it will be reading French in Toura. So, what can be done to distinguish French from Toura? You have to affect *a* with a tone mark so that it sounds Toura. Between a French é and a Toura é, there is no graphic difference. It is in the diction that the difference is heard. The sound emitted when pronouncing the French é will be less acute than that of the Toura, which differs because of the high, mid-high, or low tone - marked respectively by the acute (é), circumflex (ê) and low (è) accents - or mid-low (e without accent).

In addition to the difference in a few letters, it is therefore necessary in some cases to master the difference in their pronunciation. For this purpose, *a teacher's guide* should accompany the manual. Pictures and illustrations are essential in a book for children. Sometimes the object whose name is chosen to isolate the letter under study does not have a picture or illustration. In such cases, a picture or illustration must be made or found.

ICTs at the service of the bilingual school by Diomandé Fan Monsia (Abidjan)

Bilingual education brings together several actors at different levels of participation, from the writer to the printer of the teaching material and to the students and teachers. All these exchanges take place on a Whatsapp platform created by an administrator who adds each actor with a smartphone and an Android system on which is installed the African keyboard with the character set of Côte d'Ivoire. The resources are shared on this platform as well as the meetings in audio or video conference.

WhatsApp is a free mobile instant messaging app, allowing users to exchange messages in real time. It is available on various devices, including smartphones and tablets. Connected to the internet, users of these devices can interact to produce texts, images, audio, and video messages. They can create groups and participate in discussion forums. A tool for communicative use between several registered members, it is used for the co-production of teaching aids in favor of bilingual education in the Toura country.

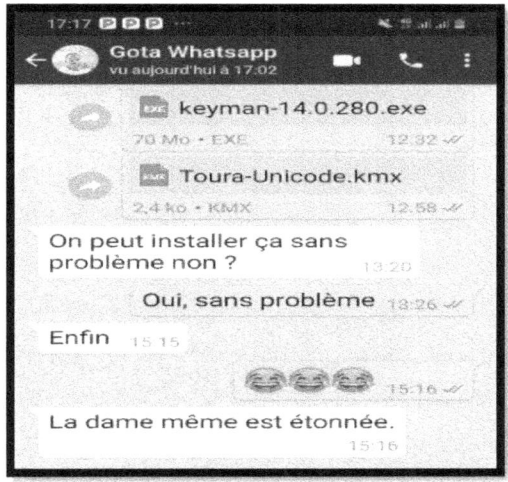

From the exchange of files and the installation of the *Keyman* software, which is essential for Toura writing, an operational interface has been set up between the computer technician in Abidjan and the printer in Biankouma. By means of distance training for the teacher and the printer, daily worksheets were designed and distributed to the pupils.

Learning with worksheets in class.

Biliteracy Learning by Lika Sopouh Legrand, PEI teacher (Dio)

First Approach to Literacy: Letter recognition
Alternation between visual recognition and auditory recognition

Visual recognition
with the help of graphics

Competence
→ Reading

→ Mental alphabet
→ Writing

Auditory recognition
using the image alone

Literacy Learning Cycle
Checklist for the Teacher

Observation/Question	Task/Question	Comment
Teaching medium	Tendency: all in French	Use a language in which the child can respond
Purpose of the exercise	Recognition of the letter/graphic symbol/grapheme	Recognized and pronounced from the image. Write and describe the new letter
Question 1	Learning to read with pictures?	We always need both, the word in writing and the image
Question 2	Not all children are Toura	Toura children help others
Question 3	Overall result	Progression: Letter, Word, Sentence, Text
Question 4	Can children write freely?	TEST: Know how to replace the image by the word in writing

Afterword. Benefits of learning the Toura language
A. Tokpa Gouessé (Man), High school teacher and
Secretary General of traditional Toura chiefs

The work undertaken over the last few decades on the Toura language has made it eligible for the Integrated School Program (PEI) today. But in addition to this significant progress, it is worth noting the role of reading and writing in one's own language, and its pervasive socializing effect. One only has to look at the admiring look of the listeners when someone reads a paper, not in French to give the explanation in Toura, but directly in the Toura language, a reading that everyone seems to follow with their eyes at the same time, like spectators of a scene that is both entertaining and instructive. And for this "inspired" reader and for his listeners/spectators, it is a great pride.

For the learner in the bilingual classroom, it is an encouragement and a relief to recognize letters in the unknown language (French) that are similar to those in his or her mother tongue. It makes it easier for him to recognize the first one through the last ones. And when he learns that his mother tongue is taught as an option in large, distant countries, this increases his enthusiasm and strength: his drive to learn.

We will be even prouder when we succeed in publishing a dictionary of the Toura language. We are working hard on it, the time has come for the consensual validation and the edition of the dictionary.

The Toura people are one of the smallest in terms of population and one of the least known. This is sometimes a handicap. But if we work better with the language, it can be an advantage when we have to teach a national language, for example. Because, geopolitically speaking, no one can imagine and therefore fear that someone would rely on this tiny ethnic group to dominate the others. So that's another motivation.

15. The power of multiliteracy in The Gambia and Ghana

Ari SHERRIS
Texas A&M University-Kingsville

Joy KREEFT PEYTON
Center for Applied Linguistics

Reading and writing remain a challenge worldwide. Globally, at least 773 million youth and adults still cannot read and write, and 250 million children are failing to acquire basic literacy skills (UNESCO, 2021). In The Gambia and Ghana, 50% of young women who are 15-24 years of age cannot read and write.[22] As the World Bank (2021) points out, "nearly 37% of students in low- and middle-income countries are taught in a language, they do not understand." The UNESCO Institute for Statistics (2021) reports that "Globally, at least 773 million youth and adults still cannot read and write, and 250 million children are failing to acquire basic literacy skills."

In this chapter, we describe two projects: The Gambia Reads Programme and the Safaliba Project. The Gambia Reads Programme was developed by the Ministry of Basic and Secondary Education in collaboration with the World Bank and Global Partnership for Education. The Safaliba Project is a small unfunded grassroots project. The aim of both projects is to develop early childhood literacy. In both cases, we argue that, when multilingualism is linked to multiliteracy, four goals are accomplished: (1) an increase in the number of *languages* an individual can read and write; (2) an increase in the number of *individuals* who can read and write; (3) a reduction or mediation of marginalizing social forces in society and a rise in the linguistic capital of marginalized languages and groups (Bourdieu, 1977, 1983); (4) affirmation of and respect and welcome for potential family, clan, and community involvement in institutions and schooling.

---

[22] http://data.3is.unesco.org

Language and literacy development in The Gambia

The Gambia Reads Programme was first developed in 2008-2013, when, in reading assessments conducted in primary schools during 2007, 2009, and 2011, it was found that children were not reading and writing well. They scored very low on the Early Grade Reading Assessment (EGRA), which was developed to measure the levels of foundational literacy skills that children have to engage in reading and writing (See Dubeck & Gove, 2015; Gove & Wettterberg, 2011, for discussion of uses of EGRA; see *Report on Early Grade Reading Ability Assessment,* 2011, for a description of the reading assessment process followed in The Gambia). After these assessments were administered, the Ministry of Basic and Secondary Education developed the Gambia Reads Programme to help children learn to read and write in the language they speak at home by using it also at school.

This focus grew out of the recognition that multilingualism is a source of strength, the ability to read and write is essential to success in the country, and when children begin to read in their mother tongue, they make important language connections, starting with the oral language that they know (Goal 2: to increase the number of individuals who can read and write). They are then able to transition to English (the official language) (Goal 1: to increase the number of languages an individual can read and write). This focus brings into the education system, and into discussions about learning and advancement, the languages that communities speak, which up to then had been ignored in education in The Gambia (Goal 3; to raise the linguistic capital of marginalized language and groups). Finally, it recognizes and engages professionals (teachers, program administrators, teacher professional developers, curriculum developers, computer-competent educators), who have the opportunity to use their language to improve education in their country. Hymes (1980) described this as "a mutual relation of interaction and adaptation" between researchers/consultants and the people they work with, "a relation that will change both" (p. 89; Goal

4; to affirm, respect, and welcome community involvement in schooling).

By 2016, when the project described here began (it had started as a pilot in 2011), instructional materials had been developed for Grades 1-3 to respond to the EGRA assessments. They supported literacy development in five Gambian languages and English. These materials, which included textbooks for children (referred to as pupils in West Africa) and teacher guides, were reviewed and revised by Gambian educators in the project described here, and materials were developed in two more Gambian languages. Curricula were prepared for Gambian language and English language development — speaking, listening, reading, and writing. New teacher guides (which describe ways to teach English and promote literacy in the Gambian languages) were written, as well as leveled readers in seven Gambian languages and English, for students in Grades 1-3, to improve their reading abilities. Teacher trainers were trained so that they could teach teachers to use these materials in their classes. The goal was that students would engage in oral and written language (reading and writing) development in their mother tongue for two hours per day in Grades 1, 2, and 3. At the same time, they would learn oral and written English for making a transition to English instruction in Grade 3. The component of the project described here is the writing, publishing, and use of the leveled readers.

The Gambia and languages chosen for materials development

The Gambia (Republic of The Gambia), shown in Figure 1, is located in West Africa, occupying 4,127 square miles, with a population of 2,486,937 (Population Pyramid, 2021). It is the smallest country on the African continent and is surrounded by Senegal, except for its opening from The Gambia River to the Pacific Ocean. In 2018, the population was 2,051,000, 11 languages were spoken, and the official language was English. The literacy rate was 56% (Simons & Fennig, 2018; citing the World Factbook, 2015).

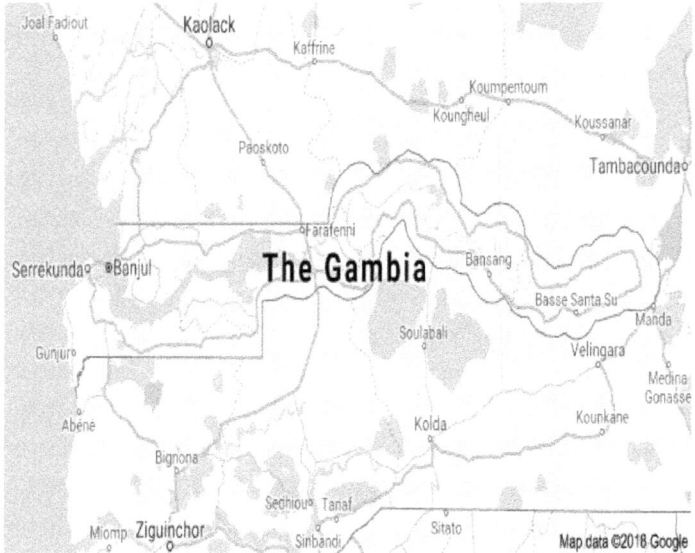
Figure 1: Republic of The Gambia

Figure 2 shows the number of speakers of each language, according to Simons and Fennig (2018), with the year the data were collected. The languages selected for materials development in *The Gambia Reads Programme* are marked with *.

> * English (official language) - 60,000 (2,000 L1 speakers, 58,000 L2 speakers) (2016)
> * Jola-Fonyi - 117,000 (2018)
>   Karon - 10,800 (2016)
> * Mandinka - 879,000 (2014)
> * Manjak (Manjaku) - 37,700 (2018)
>   Maninkakan - 4,260 (2016)
>   N'ko - No known L1 speakers in The Gambia
> * Pulaar - 377,000 (2018)
> * Serahule - 130,000 (2018)
> * Serer-Sine - 52,300 (2018)
> * Wolof - 314,000 (2018)

Figure 2. Languages spoken in
The Gambia and number of speakers.

The reasons that the eight languages marked with * were selected for materials development can be associated with the classification of the languages in the *Ethnologue* (Simons & Fennig, 2018). English is the official language. Mandinka and Wolof are Languages of Wider Communication (used in work and mass media without official status to transcend language differences across a region). Pulaar and Serahule are Developing Languages (in vigorous use, with literature in a standardized form being used by some, though this is not yet widespread or sustainable). Jola-Fonyi, Mandjak, and Serer are Vigorous Languages (used for face-to-face communication by all generations and the situation is sustainable). At the same time, the following languages were not selected for materials development. Karon is a Vigorous Language, but it is not used in schools; Maninkakan is a Threatened Language (used for face-to-face communication within all generations but losing users); and N'ko is spoken only as a second language.

Book development

Following revision of textbooks students in Grades 1, 2, and 3, the teachers, school administrators, teacher educators, and professional writers who had worked on those materials-all are native speakers of the focal languages–were brought together to develop leveled readers, which would provide opportunities for pupils to practice the literacy skills they were acquiring in instruction using the textbooks. Work began with a set of themes (Grade 1, my family; Grade 2, my community; Grade 3, our country) and a set of topics for each theme. The writers developed books in the eight languages, using Bloom software (Bloom Library: Read). In each grade, books were written at three levels, based on the curriculum, to be 1) easy, 2) moderate, and 3) hard for that grade level. This was determined from the new curriculum, which guided selection of letters used (in Grade 1), words used, length of sentences, and length of stories for each level of difficulty in each grade. The books included comprehension questions to promote thinking about the content and discussion of the content among peers and small groups. The goal was that the books would be not only readable but also highly engaging – children would be engaged with the topics; *want to* read the books; develop the ability to read and write in their mother tongue and in English; and learn about the richness and beauty of their family, their community, and their country. All of the books produced were reviewed and edited by the language teams and project leaders, using a review rubric that was developed together, before they were finalized and printed. When they were finished, there were nine books in Grade 1 (three for each level), twelve books in Grade 2 (four for each level), and nine books in Grade 3 (three books for each level). Here are some example book contents, translated to English:

- Grade 1 – My Family – A Party at Our House
- Grade 2 – My Community – My Village Shops, We Celebrate Corate, We Go to the Ocean, My Friends Go to School
- Grade 3 – Our Country – Taking Care of Our Rivers

Figure 3 shows one group of writers working together.

Figure 3. A group of writers developing leveled readers in Bloom.

Successes

The leveled readers development resulted in a set of books that could be distributed to schools, which students could read and discuss in class, on their own, or at home with parents and other family members. The working groups, composed of individuals who were considered leaders in home language materials development (Goal 4), appreciated the importance of developing this new kind of reading material and making them available. Some of them wanted to come together again, for a longer and more intense time, and write more complex stories for students in higher grades.

Did the project result in an increase in the number of languages that the students could read (Goal 1), improved reading skills of the students (Goal 2), or increased linguistic and social capital of the students in civil society, government, and business (Goal 3)? This remains to be seen. Increasingly, Gambian educators and other leaders are interested in collecting data to answer these questions.

The project leads had ideas for other activities that they could be engaged in, which included:

- Write stories in the eight languages for teachers to read to Grades 1-3 pupils, possibly including big books. The stories would reflect the school curriculum and be written by accomplished writers and experts on culture, history, and geography of The Gambia, who are native speakers of one of the languages, to bring richness to the stories.
- Write stories for grades after Grade 3, possibly into secondary school, which would become richer and more complex as they progress through the grades. What is in place now is an "early-exit bilingual education system" (Trudell, 2016).
- Continue to develop resources and professional development opportunities for teachers. Continue to develop the literacy learning skills of the master trainers who manage and provide this professional development.

Challenges

The project faced a number of challenges (see also discussion of challenges and proposed solutions, in Ancarno, Bouy, & Jeng, forthcoming).

- As shown above, one language classified as "Vigorous" was not included. We don't know why. Decisions about languages of education were made before this component of the project began. What factors weighed into the decision? To what extent does it make a difference for speakers of that language?
- For some of the languages, where were disagreements among the writers about the orthography to be used.
- It was a challenge writing books for Grade 1, when students had not yet learned all of the letters of the language, and words that could be used in the books were limited in the beginning. Sound/symbol frequency in the language had not been taken into consideration when the textbooks were written.
- Not all of the team members had story writing and book production skills. They were educators, not always professional writers.
- Developing stories that were well-formed and interesting, and writing inviting, informative story titles was hard work, involving a lot of review and revision.
- Two hours per day learning in the mother tongue is not a lot of time.
- Not all of the teachers who will be involved in teaching children in their mother tongue and using these materials read and write the language well. They need to develop that proficiency, and they need support and mentoring. Many of the teachers had not taught in their mother tongue before. They need professional development in reading their Gambian language, in teaching it overall, and in using the materials.
- It is one thing to develop the materials and another challenge to get them into schools - printing, delivery, having a place to store them in the school. For a couple of years after the materials were

developed, they were not in schools at all (there were no funds for printing and delivery), although one language group was able to pilot them. There was a hope to have them in schools by September of the following year.

There needs to be in place a plan and infrastructure for continuing to develop materials (especially leveled readers), use them in instruction, and review and evaluate their use. This goal can be difficult to accomplish because of financial and administrative challenges, even if key stakeholders support it. The World Bank (2021) argues that a policy package is needed to ensure that all children are taught in a language they understand that instruction is effective, that training for teachers is available, and that there are engaging books and other resources in the language.

Questions to ask in these projects

There are a number of questions to be asked when engaging in a project of this type for it to be successful:

- For what grades will the books be developed?
- In what languages will the books be developed, and how are those languages selected?
- What will guide selection of themes, topics, and text features in the books?
- Who will be involved in writing the stories, and how much training and resources do they need?
- In what form will the books be made available? Low-cost, black, and white, locally printed? Four-color durable paper?
- When the books are completed and available, how will they get into schools? Where will the funding come from for this delivery?
- How are the books linked to the curriculum and learning outcomes?
- How will teachers be encouraged to use the books and guided in their use?
- Can the time learning in the mother tongue be extended beyond two hours per day?

- What other preparation and support do teachers need to teach reading and writing in the community's language, in their classes?
- Will teams continue to develop books over time, for the current grade levels or for more advanced grades? What systems and procedures need to be put in place for this to be accomplished?

The grassroots Safaliba project in Ghana

Language Policy Context

Ghana has a reported 83 languages; 73 of these languages are Indigenous. However, the Ghanaian government only produces and distributes materials to teach reading and writing in nine of Ghana's Indigenous languages and in English, Ghana's only official language (Lewis et al., 2016; Sherris, 2017, 2019, 2020 a, b). These languages are three dialects of Akan (Asante Twi, Akuapem Twi, and Fante) and the languages of Dagaare, Dagbani, Dangme, Ewe, Ga, Gonja, Kasem, and Nzema. This unfortunate policy, albeit typical of many multilingual nation states, leaves 64 Indigenous Ghanaian languages without government-issued materials to teach reading and writing and with mandates to use a different Indigenous language in instruction than the language that children speak at home.

The official language education policy is problematic for an additional reason. For the nine Indigenous Ghanaian languages that do have materials to teach reading and writing, the state-mandated curriculum limits their use to a two-year kindergarten program for children ages four to six and the subsequent first three years of primary school. After that, schooling and higher education are English-only endeavors, the iron-grip legacy of colonialism.

Moreover, when youth are not schooled in reading and writing in their language through adolescence, their knowledge, experience, and skill in their language abate and their confidence, at best, often falters over time. These social-psychological phenomena have deleterious effects on ethnolinguistic identity, social cohesion, and language vitality. This brief discussion sets the policy context for the focal language of this project, Safaliba, which we turn to next.

Spatial distributions of languages

One of the languages left out of the official language education policy is Safaliba, which is spoken by an estimated 7,000-9,000 Safaliba who primarily live on their traditional tribal lands in the Savannah Region of Ghana. Eleven additional languages are situated in a 50-kilometer radius of the Safaliba lands. These include Birifor, Choruba, Dagaare, Deg, Gonja, Jula, Kamara, Lobiri, Siti, Vagla, and Waali (Figure 4). The Ghanaian government has developed and distributed materials to teach reading and writing in Dagaare and Gonja, as noted earlier, and the government provides the Safaliba, as it does other tribes in the Savannah Region, with Gonja materials. However, these materials are problematic for Safaliba speakers.

Gonja and Safaliba are morphosyntactically dissimilar, leading to difficulties for young children to learn to read and write. Perhaps this negative stimulus and the positive stimulus of the Safaliba people's pride, esteem, and love for their language and culture have kindled the grassroots Safaliba literacy activism (Sherris, 2020) that is the focus of this project, which asks: What have the Safaliba accomplished to disrupt the reproduction of the Ghanaian postcolonial language education policy status quo?

The Safaliba language dominates the first seven towns listed in Figure 4 and is a contributing, albeit non-dominant, language in the last seven towns. Figure 4 has a small map of the nation-state of Ghana in the upper left corner. On the small map, Tamale, the most populated city in northern Ghana, and the Safaliba tribal lands are marked. The large map in the center of Figure 4 indicates the spatial or geographic distribution of the towns listed on the left-hand side. The grey area marks the Safaliba tribal lands. The tribal administration of the Safaliba lands is under the Gonja tribe. The Gonja, so local history tells it, arrived in the 1500s, invading the earlier inhabitants-the Safaliba, Choruba, Deg, Siti and Vagla. Sherris (2019) explores these issues more extensively.

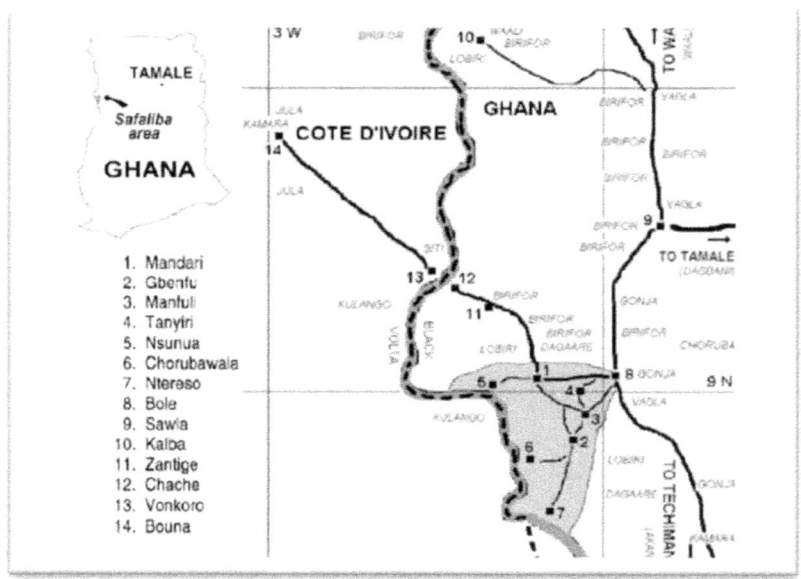

Figure 4: Nation State of Ghana (Schaefer, 2009).

Research approach

The documentation of this work is ethnographic. It is based on field notes, photographs, interviews, and video and audio recordings. Ethnography is both a reporting style and an approach that stresses learning from people rather than experimenting with them in some way.

Grassroots Safaliba Language and Literacy Activism: Disrupting the Reproduction of the Status Quo

Early grassroots Safaliba literacy activism initially stems from a letter that Safaliba storyteller, poet, and teacher Edmund Kuŋi Yakubu wrote in 1996 to the Ghana Institute of Linguistics, Literacy, and Bible Translation (GILLBT). In that letter, Yakubu shared his own Safaliba orthography and requested that GILLBT assign a linguist to conduct fieldwork in Safaliba communities to determine the viability of the Yakubu orthography (a copy of this letter is in Sherris, 2017). Two years later, in 1998, GILLBT sent Paul and Jennifer Schaefer to live among the Safaliba. Paul Schaefer made minor changes in Yakubu's Safaliba orthography based on his fieldwork, and Yakubu's orthography was in play. The Schaefers have become long-term allies of Safaliba literacy activism and continue to collaborate in solidarity with both adult- and child-focused reading and writing programs. Their publications have become a growing body of academic support (Schaefer, P., 2008 a, b, c; 2009; Schaefer, P. & Schaefer, J., 2003, 2004).

In 1999, storyteller, writer, and teacher James Zenesoŋŋa Kotobiri taught a group of Safaliba children to read, and about the same time, Safaliba teacher activist **Iddi Bayaya began teaching Safaliba adults to read their language.** However, it was not until 2011-2013 that we see multilingual efforts based on Safaliba and English. These transpired in two government primary schools and disrupted some, not all, of the government effort to teach reading and writing in Gonja and English. Two head teachers, Dramani Issahaku and Moses Gbolo, from two different schools, made separate and concerted efforts to request paraeducators and materials from the adult Safaliba program to support efforts in their schools to teach children in their Safaliba mother tongue.

It had been clear for some time that the government mandate to teach children to read in Gonja was failing most children in learning to read either Gonja or English. For many children, school was taught in two very different languages from their home language and made little if any sense. Quite simply, Gonja did not provide a linguistic or a cultural bridge to English for the successful transfer of language or customs in any meaningful way. It did not go unnoticed among teacher activists in the government schools that the Ghanaian Constitution states, under the heading of Educational Objectives, that 'The State shall foster the development of Ghanaian languages and pride in Ghanaian culture' (p. 30). Safaliba activists wondered about the apparent hypocrisy in the Gonja-English policy.

From 2015-2017, we see more sustained activism among three grassroots teacher activists, Aworo Samua Mango, Fatima Kosiaku, and Moses Gbolo and their allies, Abdulai Adams and Mohammed

Issahaku. The latter two teachers are speakers of Safaliba as an additional language and thus have the status of 'allies. The first author of this paper, as well as Paul and Jennifer Schaefer, identify as allies too.

The transformations that these activists and their allies have initiated and sustained has been remarkable. They began to create little bilingual, photocopiable bilingual materials about the lives of different Safaliba to teach reading in Safaliba and English. During this period of materials development, it was rare to see bilingual materials for children or adults. Teachers' guides for the nine official Indigenous languages were bi/multilingual and were distributed nationwide in 2010 from the National Literacy Acceleration Program (NALAP). However, the NALAP materials for students separated all the languages into separate books (Rosekrans, Sherris, & Chatry-Komarek, 2012).

Government schools are still early exit, with students transitioning into English-only schooling after a two-year kindergarten program and the first three years of Primary Schooling. By creating bilingual readers for the first two years of kindergarten and Primary Schooling through grade six, activists were breaking new ground on two fronts. Students were able to blend their knowledge of Safaliba and English as well as learn both languages for eight, instead of five years. This decision was strategic among the young teacher activists. Were there to be pushback from the government for introducing Safaliba, the argument could be made that it was an important bridge that reduced student attrition by building on local knowledge of local members of the Safaliba community and the local language.

The lead of this younger generation of activists was Teacher Samua Mango Aworo. Early in the 2015 academic year, Teacher Samua, as his students called him, began taking his Primary One students once a week on fieldtrips on foot to different community people who talked about and showed what they did. Different community members on each weekly fieldtrip shared knowledge about Ghana, drumming, mud wall art and designs, fashion design, bicycle repair, driving taxis, pumping gas, selling provisions in a kiosk, cutting hair, leading African, Christian, and Islamic religious services, wood cutting, cooking, farming, baking, and weaving-among many other Safaliba practices. During each of these fieldtrips, either Teacher Samua, a paraeducator, or the first author of this chapter would take photographs of the event with their mobile phone. Following these oral language events, students walked back to their classroom and discussed in small groups what they had learned. After group discussions, Teacher Samua elicited accounts from a member of each small group and carefully wrote the contributions on the chalkboard, in the child's words, as he repeated them aloud, further reinforcing the links between speaking, writing, and reading (Figure 5).

Figure 5: Teacher Samua writing the words of Safaliba children learning to read and write.

With his mobile phone, he would photograph the chalkboard when it was full of the words the children had shared from their weekly fieldtrip. After class, these photos were emailed to activists and allies, who keyboarded the Safaliba from the photograph, adding digital photos from the visit with the community person and adding English to create photocopied and stapled little Safaliba-English bilingual books, usually only 8 pages long. Figure 6 is a photo of the cover of a little book produced from the voices of children who visited a Safaliba Imam with Teacher Samua.

Figure 6. Safaliba-English bilingual cover of an 8-page little book from children's language and produced by Teacher Samua the Safaliba activists and allies.

One book was created for each child. Approximately one week later, each child in Teacher Samua's class and all the other classes up through Primary Six in Samua's school and a second school received their own copy of the little book. Additional schools occasionally also received little books. With all of the students having their own little book in hand, Teacher Samua led the class in choral read aloud sessions as he ran his finger under the words and had the children do the same. Children enthusiastically chimed in, and these events were great fun. Each day for a week, Teacher Samua also asked the children to draw and illustrate different themes from the little book of the week, as well as produce their own writings in invented spelling about each theme they drew. Teacher Samua, and sometimes a paraeducator, would move around the Primary One classroom and ask children to share aloud what they had written. Then the teacher or the paraeducator would write on the paper what that should look like in the Safaliba alphabet, modeling for each child how to hold a pencil, where to start a letter and finish it, and how to spell each word. Figure 7 shows Teacher Samua modeling writing what a student said they wrote in invented spelling. It also shows another photo of children drawing and writing about a theme from one of the little books that has their words in it and photos of one of their fieldtrips on foot during the Safaliba literacy program at their school.

Figure 7. Teacher Samua modeling writing what a student had written in invented spelling. Other students drawing and writing Safaliba in Teacher Samua's Primary One classroom.

These more structured and rule-governed aspects of language and the material practices of writing with a pencil or pen were also taught to the whole group at different times in each lesson, particularly when introducing letter-sound correspondences. But even in these more structured and rule-governed activities around writing skills (e.g., holding a pencil, starting and ending a letter), Teacher Samua was keen on bringing forward student input and student voices.

This transformed the classroom into a less predictable, open, and creative space, where children were asked to suggest words that began with different letter sounds. Since children were also learning English from Teacher Samua, they sometimes suggested English words that began with the same sound and letter as a Safaliba word. Teacher Samua enthusiastically wrote the English words on the chalkboard alongside the Safaliba words, which was a form of translanguaging, as it promoted the free use of language from the full repertoire of student language shared aloud and was relevant to sound-letter correspondences and practices. In many ways, this approach incorporated an organic, child-centered, developmental, and holistic understanding of learning that fit well with Safaliba cultural practices that were fluid and porous and close to the materiality of the earth, seasonal change, the production of food from the land, its storage during dry season, and human interactions among the Safaliba.

Teacher Samua also provided opportunities for each child to discuss their drawings with each other. The evident engagement in these discussions was palpable and natural. Its palpability was embodied in the faces of these children, in their excited smiles and their fluid Safaliba talk. In a sense, school was decolonized at these moments and took on a new life. School was shedding its postcolonial positionings as Teacher Samua transformed it into a Safaliba school. The postcolonial Ghanaian leadership had mandated Gonja, which was little known by the children on the Safaliba tribal lands, and it was Teacher Samua, a Safaliba, who set meaningful meaning making in motion.

In such acts, the institution of schooling sheds its postcolonial trappings that otherwise distanced Safaliba children from themselves and from bridges to an international language, such as English. Teacher Samua, with the support of other teacher activists, allies, and his community leadership, as well as parents, was able to do this with his characteristic care, respect, and trust for his language, for Safaliba children, for his community, and for its culture (Sherris, 2017, 2019, 2020a, b).

Safaliba literacy lessons also included traditional storytelling and singing (Figure 8). Teacher Samua would tell a story and conclude with a song. Sometimes a volunteer paraeducator or a guest visiting the school would tell a traditional story. The children often knew when to participate in the story, which was not true when they were taught in Gonja and English. These were also transformative, as they drew on new ways to integrate schooling into Safaliba culture.

Figure 8. Teacher activist Samua preparing to tell a story to his Primary One class.

Teacher Samua also facilitated structured and rule-governed practices in his classroom. These included spelling dictations, sound-letter matching games, and guessing games, all often with affordances for students to self- and peer-correct their writing with answer keys on the chalkboard. There were also rule-governed structured phonemic awareness group activities and alphabet tracing in the air to practice where to start an alphabet letter and where to end it. Students practiced writing letters of the alphabet (Figure 9) and small words in their notebooks during Safaliba lessons. Once a week, usually on Friday, Primary Six students joined Teacher Samua's Primary One classroom and led small groups of children in small group read aloud activities in Safaliba with the little book of the week. They themselves used the little books to improve their English.

Figure 9. Primary One students practicing writing letters of the Safaliba alphabet

Te zaŋsera naŋ asɛbe biye! Chɛ sɛberaa!
We learn the alphabet! We write!

Clearly, the heavy lifting within and across the Safaliba language and literacy project increases the number of languages an individual can read. Prior to the work of Safaliba community activists, there was neither an orthography of the language nor dedicated teachers to bring it to children and adults. Now, with both an orthography and little books created of and for the Safaliba with digital photos, a few laptops, and a photocopy machine, there is an increase in the number of *languages* an individual can read and write and an increase in the number of *individuals* who can read and write. Teacher activists teach Safaliba reading and writing adults and children. The production and reproduction of Safaliba reading and writing attracts the attention of the academy. Such attention potentially reduces or mediates marginalizing social forces in society, such as the wholesale adoption of Gonja as the only language of early schooling on Safaliba tribal lands. This raises the linguistic capital among all Safaliba and the academy as it increasingly decolonizes the institution of schooling -- 'Safalibanizing' it, if you will. Moreover, the processes of producing and reproducing Safaliba through writing and reading it, affirm, respect, and welcome potential family, clan, and community involvement in institutions and schooling (e.g., through Safaliba storytelling; talk about the community, country, livelihood, and vocations from the little books).

This project presents an evidentiary trail of grassroots language and literacy development that, while small scale, exemplifies an ecolinguistically sustainable path for additional Ghanaian languages in multilingual contexts, as they too will one day disrupt the discourse of repression by postcolonial erasure.

Conclusion

The two projects are very different. The large project in The Gambia has in place state mechanisms that are leveraged, whereas the small project in Ghana leveraged its community aspirations. The Gambia project is top-down; the Safaliba project is bottom-up. However, in both projects we demonstrate that the four goals are at play, although linguistic capital will take time to bear fruit. As far as next steps, in the Safaliba Project, scaling it up would be possibly of interest across additional unrecognized languages in the surrounding areas and beyond. In The Gambia project, deepening the roots within communities might be a next step. Scaling up and deepening roots would mediate imbalances in power leveraged in top-down and bottom-up processes. In both projects, developing workshops for writers and promoting and supporting family literacy might be encouraged.

16. The Challenges and Relevance of Tone Didactics

Venance TOKPA
Université Félix Houphouët Boigny

The challenge of a form of development that takes into account the socio-cultural and linguistic diversities inherent in each individual seems to be a challenge that governments must overcome in today's world. In this perspective, several reforms, including the introduction of mother tongues into education systems for teaching/learning, have been undertaken by public authorities, as the positive effects of using mother tongues at the beginning of schooling are now well established. This global innovation is a vast project on which several countries, including some in Africa, have embarked. However, African languages, languages with an oral tradition, have been undergoing changes for some years now: particularly given the beginning of a codification that allows them to pass from oral to written languages.

In Côte d'Ivoire, most languages are the subject of scientific studies by experts or interested individuals. At the institutional level, there is the Institute of Applied Linguistics (ILA), created by decree No. 66-375 of September 8th, 1966, mandated by Article 68 of the law of August 18th, 1977, to "manage as best as possible the effective use of national languages in the education system of Côte d'Ivoire and, in particular, to work towards the promotion of these languages by raising them to the rank of languages of instruction, both at the formal and non-formal levels" (Vahoua, 2017). In this perspective, the Integrated School Project (ISP) for the pilot phase of bilingual education occurs in the primary cycle.

Unfortunately, the research that has been done has been unable to provide a response to many questions on this subject, especially the question of tone within certain African languages known as tonal languages. Tone is the variation in pitch and melody that affects a syllable of a word in a tonal language. In fact, for the teaching of these languages, according to Tokpa (2019):

> If there is unanimity about taking consonants and vowels into account, taking tones into account on the other hand forms a separation between partners of the educational system. Indeed, some specialists think that the systematic consideration of tones in didactics is only one perspective in the minds of some researchers, contrary to the view that the speakers of these languages have on how their languages function.

The present work is a way forward for effective and efficient didactics of Ivorian languages, and therefore of African languages, through a case study of the tones of Toura, a Mande language from the Western region of Côte d'Ivoire, spoken in the Tonkpi region, in the Department of Biankouman. This main objective produces secondary objectives, specifically:

- To show the importance of tones in African languages and teaching/learning them.
- To highlight the obstacles that must be overcome for a better mastery and consideration of tones in the teaching of African languages.

The central question underlying this work is: why and how should tones be taken into account in the teaching of African languages? Our reflection will be articulated around three axes: we will first present the theoretical framework and working methodology, then we will present the advantages and importance that tones can have in languages and in their teaching before describing some problems that need to be solved for a successful integration of African mother tongues into the educational system.

1. Theoretical framework and working methodology

1.1- Theoretical framework

Our approach is in line with the auto-segmental theory developed by Leben (1971, 1973) and Goldsmith (1976) during their work on the tonal systems of African languages. This theory assumes an approach in which the tonal level benefits from a certain autonomy with respect to the segmental level. We will present the advantages of this theory, describe its principles and notation, and then establish a link between self-segmental phonology and lexical phonology.

1.2- Working methodology

The methodology used during our surveys consisted of observing classroom sessions in schools enrolled in the Integrated School Project (ISP) and in literacy centers, examining teaching manuals and interviewing decision-makers and field actors. This methodology enabled us to collect written and oral data consisting of video and audio recordings as well as photographs. We used Dictaphone recorders, still cameras and regular cameras to collect the various data.

1.2.1- Written data

Written data was collected from administrative documents (laws, decrees, excerpts from ministerial council communications, orders, circulars, and memos), scientific documents (books, articles, extracts from conferences, extensive survey sheets, in paper or digital form), and educational documents (textbooks, teacher guides, lesson plans).

1.2.2- Oral data

One aspect of the oral data consisted of interviews with local administrative authorities. These included conversations with the secretary general, the project manager of the Regional Directorate of National Education and Literacy (DRENA) of Man, the inspector of primary education in Biankouma, teachers from PEI schools in Canta-Blossè and Gnégbeyalé (the two directors, three teachers and one preschool teacher), and two literacy trainers. The other aspect was comprised of testimonies from the beneficiaries, i.e., the pupils/learners, the parents of the pupils and the chiefs of the two villages.

These interviews allowed us to reveal the organizational chart, the functionality, the mode of financing and the different perspectives of the integrated school project. Then, the participative observation sessions and the analysis of the pedagogical documents allowed us to identify the progression and the units subjected to teaching/learning in order to identify the linguistic facts taught.

2. The relevance of tones in didactics

Tones are, alongside intonation, one of the most used suprasegmental phenomena in the natural languages of the Niger-Congo language family, especially those south of the Sahara. The map below demonstrates this:

Figure 1: Map of African Tonal Languages

Tones contain several values that should be taken into account in the didactics of languages that use them.

2.1- The distinctive value of tones
Aside from a few languages such as those of the Western Atlantic group (Wolof, Pulaar, Seereer), African languages are tonal languages. This means that two words written with the same consonants and vowels can be different words with different meanings, which will then be read and understood in different ways, simply because they carry different tones. Therefore, tone plays a

distinctive role. This distinctive value is realized on two levels. Thus, two distinctive values emerge, specifically inherent value and typological value. We identify inherent, distinctive value as the ability that tonal languages possess and make use of for the purpose of distinguishing between two words with the same sound units (phonemes) combined in the same pattern, owing their difference only to a tone. In the languages analyzed in this study, Toura has four punctual tones: the high (H), low (B), mid-high (Mh) and mid-low (Mb) tone. By way of illustration, the following segmental sequences of Toura: /sɔɔ/; /ɓaa/; /gele/; / kele/ can have the following tonal patterns in (1):

(1)

Word (structure)	Tonal Structure	Meaning
	Mb-Mb	snail
	H-H	sheet (f) of raffia
/sɔɔ/	B-H	price; cost
	Mh-Mb	insult
	B-B	tree (m) sp.
/gele/	Mb-Mb	basin
	B-B	charm
	H-H	interior
/kele/	Mb-Mb	bark; shell
	H-H	roller; boot

The distinctive value of the tone is demonstrated at the lexical level (discrimination of words into minimal pairs). At the grammatical level, tone is also used to mark differences in tense and/or aspect.

Tone also serves to distinguish the aspect of statements, as the following akyé examples in (2) show:

(2)
a. ò dà
/3sg/paste+acc/
"He's on the lookout"
b. ó dà
/3sg/paste+inacc/
"He will be on the lookout"

In example (2.a), the low tone of /o/ expresses the completed action while the high tone of /o/ in example (2.b) expresses an uncompleted action.

It is clear from the above examples that a forgotten or incorrectly transcribed tone can render the statement uninterpretable. This feature of tones is considered an inherent distinction because it exploits the relevant oppositions within a single language variant.

The typological distinction, on the other hand, makes it possible to distinguish different types of speakers of the same language. For identical segmental structures, two neighboring languages will each opt for their own tonal structure. Thus, the difference in tonal patterns makes it possible to distinguish between two variants of the same language. When tones are absent, this creates some confusion or ambiguity between two speakers of the same language.

2.2- The tripod

In a tonal language, the tongue is like an African hearth composed of three stones (tripod).

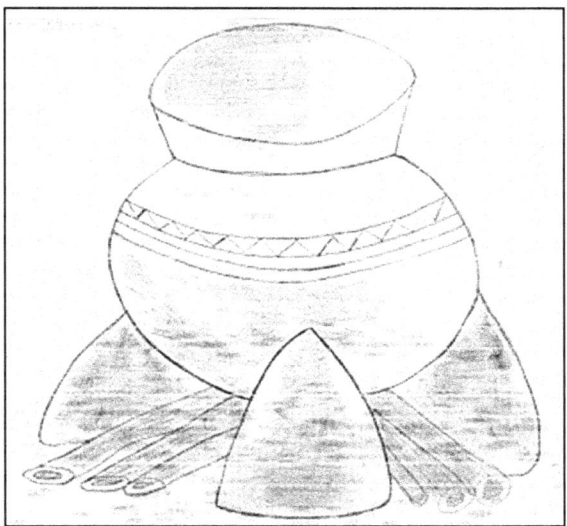

Figure 2: African focus (Tripod)

It is composed of consonants, vowels, and tones. Without one of the stones, the pot would fall to the ground. Without tones, the language is incomprehensible. These words are homographs in spelling. This is to say, they are written in the same way. Their consonants and vowels are identical, and only their tones distinguish them. How are speakers able to recognize which word it is? How do you know which tone to use? If the word is not put in a precise context, it is impossible.

2.3- Facilitating the reading and understanding of texts

In tonal languages, there is not, as in atonal languages (without tones) like French, only one /a/, one /i/, or one /o/, but, depending on whether the language uses two, three or four or more tones, there will be two, three or four or more /a/, /i/, or /o/. In the simplest case of Toura, which makes use of four tones (high, low, mid-high, and mid-low), one would have four /a/: low, high, mid-high, and mid-low; four /i/: low, high, mid-high, and mid-low. It so happens that, at present, the alphabets of tonal languages do not retain the tones but list out the letters as they are in atonal languages. On this basis, it is rare that countries make use of tone notation once the word, comprised of both consonants and vowels, is written, while all others believe that with the help of context, reading can be done without tone. Tone notation once the word, consonants, and vowels, is written assumes that the word is known to the writer, the word having been dictated to or expressed by him. This is not the case when the word is to be read after having been written without its tones. In this case, it is not possible to read without being provided the context, which, once known, will lead to the identification of meaning, allowing for the words to be identified, read, and pronounced. However, contextual knowledge is not available to every observer of a text and potential reader. Thus, tone marking greatly enhances text comprehension and makes it easier for learners to read texts.

3- The challenges of tone didactics

3.1- Establishment of a standard spelling of tones

One of the first challenges in the consideration of tones in didactics is the need for a standard and rather simple system of tone marking which would take into account the state of knowledge of the tonal system of languages, allowing the designation of all relevant tonal oppositions. This notation would be used in dictionaries, grammars, language manuals, and academic publications of texts. It would be a system that considers both lexical and grammatical tones. For textbooks and syllabaries do not present grammatical tones, and yet the functional output of tones in the languages where they are demonstrated is tilted towards grammar rather than lexicon.

3.2- The creation of neologisms related to tones

The availability of scientific terms required for teaching is one of the major constraints on the generalization of teaching in African languages. A language is an instrument of communication between speakers, in the sense that it shows an ability to express the realities belonging to that space and to assume communication between speakers. However, as soon as new realities such as "tone" are introduced into this space, the language surfaces because of the novelty of these realities, unable to express these realities and therefore unable to take charge of the communication that should eventually integrate them. This is the case when a language that has never assumed this function is instituted as a language of instruction. In order to become an instrument of communication, the language will need to be enriched and adapted to these new fields, including linguistics, mathematics, and life sciences. Thus, the neological action assisting in the creation of new words must, in the field of tones, define new meanings/different senses and gestures to identify tones. Start from the perception of tone among Africans: How do Africans perceive tones? We choose "Haut" (high) and "Bas" (low) in French, but in fact these are metaphors - there is nothing physically 'high' in a high tone. In other languages we speak of "high / low", "male / female", "thin / fat." The same goes for the hand gestures used by teachers to describe tones. In French, we raise our hand to show a high tone, but will this gesture be appropriate for Toura?

3.3- Teaching lexical and grammatical tones

Most textbooks and syllabaries for teaching local languages do not present grammatical tones. Yet in these languages, the functional output of tones is tilted towards grammar rather than lexicon. There is therefore a need to emphasize the teaching of grammatical tones, in addition to lexical tones, especially during grammar lessons - to take grammatical tones into account and distinguish them from lexical tones in teaching. In utterances, tones can change; this change obviously supports meaning. The changes that a tone can undergo are part of the grammar of the language. And mastering the writing of Toura requires observing the internal structure of words, as well as considering the changes that they can undergo in statements. It goes without saying that special attention must be paid to the tonal changes that words undergo within a statement.

In addition, the tones should be presented in relation to each other. It is also important to propose exercises that are conceived in regard to the principle of commutation and that lead, as much as possible, to study the tones by minimal pairs, allowing us to make comparisons (ex: high tone vs. low tone; mid-high tone vs. mid-low tone).

As far as the actual teaching of tones is concerned, we suggest starting with the presentation of syllables. Each syllable will be presented and read with the different tones of the language. Then, the combinations of different syllables with different tonal patterns will be made. Care will be taken to find syllables that coincide with the lexis of the language, avoiding artificial syllables and lexies. In this way, the learner will perceive and note the differences.

Conclusion

In summary, the development of spelling rules must obey a number of crucial elements. It is true that a certain convention is needed, and it is also true that the spelling system must seek a certain economy, but this should not lead to the easy way out by elaborating upon illogical and fanciful rules. Tones, which are still little understood nor mastered by the non-linguists, are intrinsic elements of tonal languages such African languages. They assume both lexical and grammatical functions. Their importance manifests itself at various levels, notably in the reading and understanding of texts, and they have many distinctive values. Not teaching them can seriously hinder the fulfillment of these roles and lead to difficulties in reading, understanding, and interpretation. Of course, the point here is not to oppose vowels and consonants to tones, but rather to highlight the importance of the latter in an approach to education, teaching in African languages.

Consequently, for better integration and use of African languages in education, it is necessary to promote tones by setting a standard orthography that includes both lexical and grammatical tones in teaching and to define neologisms and gestures to better reflect the phenomenon of tones at the risk of undermining learning. This is one of the requirements for the coherent implementation of education policies. It is also one of the aspects on which scientists and other actors in the African education system should base themselves in order to define effective and efficient didactics of African languages, especially if we consider that education in national languages should be an essential component of lifelong learning.

17. Fulfulde-French bilingual education: Advantages and solutions to the difficulties encountered

Djibrila TETEREOU
University of Kara

Pastoral populations, because of their mobility, are unable to educate their children in formal education schools, which is not suitable for their lifestyle. Therefore, non-formal education programs adapted to their mobility are designed and implemented by Non-Governmental Organizations (NGOs) and associations that have control over them and benefit from the support and accompaniment of technical and financial partners. Unfortunately, when implementing these programs, the emphasis is not laid on balanced bilingualism. Learners of these educational centers do not have sufficient literary skills in both Fulfulde and French languages. Indeed, they are not exposed to both languages throughout the learning process; either because the importance of bilingualism is obscured, or because of the difficulties encountered by teachers, the difficulties related to the acquisition of skills by learners in the two languages, or because of the principles established by the pedagogical approaches used. That is why my paper, on the one hand, seeks to highlight the importance of bilingual Fulfulde-French education for pastoralists and, on the other hand, suggests solutions to absorb the difficulties encountered.

1. Advantages of Fulfulde-French bilingual education

The advantages of French-Fulfulde bilingual education are identified thanks to an interview I had with learners from pastoral populations' education centers in Togo. Learners interviewed affirm that:

> Jannde ɗemngal amen fulfulde no walla men. Men paama jannde no hoyiri. Ammaa fulfulde tam heyataa. No haani men jannginnee faransiire du, sabu ley sarwiisiiji fu faransiiri kaaletee. Talki kaɓɓodiiɗi e luusagol fu faransiire mbinndiraa. Ɓe men koɗanta wawtu luusagol nanataa haala amen, menen du men nanataa haala maɓɓe. Faransiiri nden tam woni haala accuka men mbaawa men kaalda e maɓɓe. (Diallo Hamidou). Teaching in our mother tongue, Fulfulde, allows us to easily acquire the content of the program of education. But Fulfulde alone is not enough. We also need to be educated in French because French is the one which is used in all services. All documents related to transhumance are written in French. The populations who welcome us during the transhumance do not understand our mother tongue; we, too, do not understand theirs. So French is the lingua franca between us.

It is then obvious that learners have a certain desire to learn the two languages, Fulfulde and French, given the communication challenges they face in their everyday life. Monolingual education does not allow them to have skills that can ensure good communication in the administrative services or with the host communities during the transhumance. Another learner interviewed speaks of a lack of communicative autonomy when reading and writing skills are not developed in both Fulfulde and French languages.

> Soni men jannginaama fulfulde tam, men mbaawataa jeytude ko'e amen sabu wakkati mun sey men gollida e nantinooɓe soni men kaaldee e faransiire. Koni nantinooɓe ɓen wakkati fu jammoto men tam. Faa hannden du soni men jannginaama faransiire tam, men mbaawataa fiirtude finaatawa amen faa men keɓa annde kuuɓuɗe ɗe jannginooɓe kokkata men men ɓeyditoroo ley golle amen. Ndelle faa men jeyta ko'e amen banngal jannde e binndi, ko ɓuri nafude men non men jannginee fulfulde e faransiire. (Dicko Oumarou). If we only learn Fulfulde, we will not have a communicative autonomy because in this case, we will always have to ask for the help of interpreters although, they most of the times cause us troubles. If we only learn French, it will be difficult for us to

express our endogenous knowledge and to value it in relation to the scientific knowledge that our teachers give us. So, for us to be autonomous in terms of written and oral communication, we must be taught in our mother tongue, Fulfulde and in French.

It is then evident that the learners themselves are aware of the need for bilingual education in their mother tongue and in French. For breeders, monolingual education, whether done in their mother tongue Fulfulde or in French, does not ensure their communicative autonomy. Both languages are necessarily required. Teachers of the education centers also emphasize that learners are so interested in bilingual learning. One of them puts that:

Gilla wakkati ɓeydanngol marooɓe hakillo ko haɓɓodii nafaa jannde, so wi'aama ike jannde fulfulde e faransiire non, mono fu no yiɗi wara jannga. Ammaa so wi'aama ike fulfulde tam non, ɗum nanngataa hakillo maɓɓe sanne. Wakkati gom du janngooɓe no y'ama kam: meetiri ɗume wadi go no on janngina men fulfulde tam? On nji'ataa ike rafi bawka jannde e binndi faransiire du no tampina men? (Noaga Monimi).

Since the social mobilization, if we tell them that the teaching will be done in Fulfulde and in French, everyone is very motivated. But if we tell them that the teaching is done only in Fulfulde, they're not motivated enough. Sometimes, some learners come to me and ask me the question: teacher, why are you teaching us only in Fulfulde? You are not aware that we face several problems because we haven't an oral and written command of French?

Therefore, dual-language education in Fulfulde and French motivates learners. Not promoting dual-language education for African people in general and pastoral populations in particular, both in the mother tongue and in French or English, is, therefore, a real mistake. French, which is the official language of certain so-called French-speaking countries, is the one through which scientific and technical knowledge of the modern world is learned. It is, therefore, the language by which those people have access to globalization. For characterized by a multiplicity of local languages from one area to another, French plays the role of lingua franca for them. African languages, which are the first canals of socialization of individuals, however, remain essential in the acquisition of any type of knowledge. The mother tongue is the one through which learners can truly express endogenous knowledge. Taking the mother tongue into account in the education process is very necessary for the social, political, and economic well-being of learners. But monolingual education in the mother tongue cannot satisfy learners because, in general, in Africa, mother tongues are almost absent in administrative services and documents. For quality education, "only multilingual education can meet the demands of participation globally and nationally, and the specific needs of culturally and linguistically distinguished communities" (UNESCO, 2003: 18). Therefore, the educational process must involve a bilingual mother tongue-official language perspective.

2. Difficulties encountered in Fulfulde-French bilingual education

This section intends to highlight the difficulties that a teacher should expect in a Fulfulde-French bilingual education center.

The database analyzed in this essay is collected in literacy centers where the French language was introduced in the second year of the education process of learners in Togo. The corpus consists of recordings of oral expression sessions in French as well as written essays of learners in French. These data made it possible to identify the difficulties experienced by learners from a phonetic, spelling, grammatical and lexical point of view.

2.1 Difficulties due to the differentiated forms of writing between Fulfulde and French

The difficulty in acquiring spelling transcription in both languages is linked not only to the disparity of alphabetic letters but also to the forms of writing. Even though there are letters common to both languages, each of them has specific ones. In terms of spelling, while cursive writing is common in French, script writing remains the only one valid in Fulfulde.

[1]

Fulfulde	b	d	f	h	j	p	k
French	*b*	*d*	*f*	*h*	*j*	*p*	*k*

Facing this situation, the learner who acquires the form of writing in Fulfulde ignores the same letters written in French and vice versa. He must invest himself again in learning to recognize the same letters which he nevertheless reads and writes in one of the two languages.

2.2 Lexicographical difficulties

Homonymy and paronymy are also sources of confusion in learning French. Learners find it difficult to distinguish between homonymous and paronymous words, both spelling and semantically. In reading, they try to read homonymous words differently (verre ; ver ; vert ; vers) while the paronymous words are confused with each other.

2.3 Difficulties due to the pronunciation of sounds specific to French

The fact that Fulfulde and French have differentiated phonetic and phonological structures has an impact on the learning of French by Fulfulde speakers. The finding is more striking among adult learners in literacy centers. Indeed, for an adult, to learn French is to embark on a painful adventure due to the difficulties experienced in the pronunciation of sounds specific to French, to the point where some find themselves ridiculous. Even for those with higher education, the correct pronunciation of these sounds is not obvious. However, with repetitive exercises, they determine how to manage to train their phonatory organs. To avoid these difficulties, speakers resort to neighboring sounds familiar to them in the native language, as presented in the example below.

[2] (see Kantchoa and Tetereou, 2017: 92)
Fulfulde term of origin gloss
Biro byro "office"
Bu:**zi** buʒi "candle"
Masi:ni maʃin "machine"

When speaking French, Fulfulde speakers sometimes substitute the sounds [y], [ʒ] and [ʃ] respectively by [i], [z] and [s], which are present in Fulfulde and articulately close to those of French.

2.4 Letters pronounced differently depending on the context of their appearance and the hairpieces

Letters that are pronounced differently in different contexts, hairpieces letters as well as graphic groups that can be read in a single sound cause difficulties in learning French.

[3]
- **x** is pronounced [s] in "six"; [gz] in "exact"; [z] in "sixième" and [ks] in "texte" (Aritiba and Takassi, 2010:43)
- **ch** is pronounced [k] in "chorus", "psychology" and [ʃ] in "sing"

In the case of several letters for a single sound as well as hairpieces, beyond the confusion, learners tend to pronounce all the letters as in Fulfulde.

[4]
- **aux**; **eau** and **au** are pronounced in a single sound [o]
- **est**; **es**; **-ais**; **-ait**; **-aix** are pronounced [ɛ]
- vin**gt**, poi**ds**, doi**gt**, cor**ps** have hairpieces.

2.5 Lexical difficulties

Cases of linguistic interference are identified at the lexical level. Learners transpose directly into French the meaning of some Fulfulde words, while sometimes this transposition does not result in correct sentences in French.

[5]
- "Boire la cigarette" instead of "fumer de la cigarette".
- "Avoir la tête dure" instead of "être insolent"

For the first case, learners say fluently in French "il boit la cigarette" instead of "il fume de la cigarette". This is a case of interference due to the fact that in fulfulde they say:

Oɗo yara sigaari "he smokes"
He / drink-iacc/ cigarette
He drinks the cigarette

In the second case, the interference is explained by the fact that the learners say in their mother tongue:

Suka o na woodi hoore yornde "this child is insolent. "
Child / part / have / head / hardness +poss/
This child has a hard head.

2.6 Grammatical difficulties

Grammatical difficulties are generally related to respecting the syntactic order of words, especially in the use of pronouns.

[6]

"J'ai dit lui de venir" instead of "Je lui ai demandé de venir".

This interference is due to the fact that in the mother tongue, learners say:

Mi batii mo ike o wara "I asked him to come"
I/ say-acc./ he/ that/ he/ come
I told him to come

[7]

"Le maître n'a pas vu moi" instead of "le maître ne m'a pas vu".

This wording is explained by the fact that the speakers say in Fulfulde:

Jannginoowo yi'ay kam "the teacher did not see me"

Teacher / see-negative / me
The teacher did not see me.

The difficulties experienced in Fulfulde-French bilingual education are mainly due to the phonetic-phonological, orthographic, grammatical, lexicographical and lexical structures differentiated between Fulfulde and French.

The phonetic-phonological difficulties are linked to the fact that French has specific sounds that do not exist in Fulfulde. So, when it comes to pronouncing these sounds specific to French, the learner has to subject his phonatory organs to a test which sometimes, in order to be successful, requires repetitive exercises.

The alternation of spelling forms from one language to another is a source of spelling difficulties.

Lexical difficulties are dependent on the disparate perceptions of the world by each culture. Indeed, each people sees the world as its language allows it to see and understand it. So, learning French presupposes moving from one culture to another in order to be able to properly use lexical structures.

At the grammatical level, the differentiated syntactic order in the use, especially of pronouns, is the source of the confusion.

In terms of orthographic systems, in Fulfulde, the letters are in the script, while in French, cursive writing is the most commonly used. In terms of spelling rules, "in Fulfulde, any letter that is written is pronounced separately and distinctly. In French, several letters can be combined to make one sound" (in Fulfulde, any letter that is written is pronounced separately and distinctly. In French, several letters can be combined to give a single sound) Diallo et al. (2009: 19). In Fulfulde, vowels made long as well as consonants whose pronunciation is marked by hardening are graphically doubled, while in French, doubling a letter has no impact on pronunciation.

3. Solutions to the difficulties encountered in Fulfulde-French bilingual education

To remedy the difficulties encountered by learners in a Fulfulde-French bilingual learning's program, it is necessary to review the training of any dual-language education program's teachers. Thus, for Félix Nicodème Bikoi (2013: 407-408), the skills expected of a teacher at the end of training are: "the mastery of the discipline and its epistemology, the mastery of the didactics of the discipline, the mastery of the pedagogy of the discipline, the mastery of the learning theories and student's psychology, the use of ICT in social practice". Those skills must be relevant to the acquisition of a good oral and written command of both languages by the learners.

N°	Sounds	Fulfulde spelling		French spelling	
		Symbols	examples	Symbols	examples
1	[a]	a	maral "breeding	a; â	image "image"; baton "stick"
2	[e]	e	**erewol** "paper	é; and; -ai; -ez; er; -ed	étable "stable"; les moutons et les boeufs "oxen and sheep"; je viendrai "I will come"; vous mangez "you eat"; voter "to vote"; pied "foot"
3	[ɛ]	e	yitere "eye	e; è; ê; -ei; est; es; -es; -ait; -aît, -ais; ait	lettre "letter"; père "father"; tête "head"; teigne "moth"; il est venu "he came"; tu es bon "you are good"; lait "milk"; jamais "never"; il connaît "he knows"; il jouait "he was playing"; tes boeufs "your oxen"
4	[i]	i	ndiyam "water	i; y	lire "reading"; lycée "high school"
5	[o]	o	ommbude "close"	o, -au; water; ô; au; -eaux	tomate "tomato"; faute "fault"; taureau "bull"; role "role"
6	[ɔ]	o	kosam "milk	o	collecte "collection"; école "school"
7	[u]	u	lewru "month/moon	or; where; -out; -oût; -oû; -oup	cou "neck"; l'un ou l'autre "either"; tout "any"; coup "blow"; coût "cost"
8	[a :]	aa	**laawol** "path	-	
9	[e :]	ee	**Teetude** "remove "	-	

10	[ɛ :]	ee	ñegeere "wc	-	
11	[i :]	ii	y'iiy'am "blood"	-	
12	[o :]	oo	hootude "go home"	-	
13	[ɔ :]	oo	**hoore** "head	-	
14	[u :]	uu	**suumaade** "fasting	-	
15	[y]	-		u; eu	mur "wall"; j'ai eu mon BAC II "I got my BAC II"
16	[ø]	-		eu, eux; -eux . – eut ;	peu "little", eux-mêmes "themselves"; pluvieux "rainy"; il peut "he can"
17	[œ]	-		eu	peur "fear"; meurtre "murder"

18	[ə]	-		e	fermeté "firmness"
19	[ɛ̃]	-		-in, -aim, -ein ;	fin "end"; faim "hunger"; rein "kidney"
20	[ã]	-		an; am; en; -amp	tante "aunt"; tambour "drum"; en 2010 "in 2010"; champ "field"
21	[ɔ̃]	-		on; -on; ont	monde "world"; allons-y "let's go"; ils ont gagné "they've won"; ils viendront "they'll come"
22	[œ̃]	-		un; -unt	brun "brown"; défunt "deceased"
23	[ɥ]	-		oui; ouïe	je dis oui "I say yes!" le sens de l'ouïe " the sense of hearing"

Talking about the principle that language is above all, a communication tool before being written into account, oral production must be at the center of learning. Education must begin with the language of first socialization of the learner, Fulfulde. Once the mother tongue skills have been developed, the learner can use it to effectively learn French that should be introduced by the development of skills in oral expression before the passage to writing. French should not be taught like a mother tongue to learners who have Fulfulde as their mother tongue. If the combination of oral and writing in Fulfulde's teaching is possible, this should not be the case for French. The Fulfulde is already spoken at home, writing skills will only materialize what they already say. That is why start teaching French (that some learners speak for the first time in class) by oral expression is quite imperative, in order to avoid tedious learning to the learner.

For the learner to acquire reading-writing skills concomitantly in both languages during the educational process, it is necessary to start from phonetics and sounds. Teaching the language starting with phonetics allows rapid acquisition, the correct pronunciation of words and the resolution of pronunciation difficulties of certain sounds.

A reconciliation between the two languages makes it possible to recover the differences and the similarities of sounds and spelling symbols.

For a good acquisition of oral and written skills in both languages, the teacher can use the tables below to organize the reading-writing sessions.

The learner can then acquire the reading-writing skills of Fulfulde and French starting from 23 vocalic sounds. Then, what about consonants?

The Fulfulde language, all dialects considered, has 27 consonants. Moreover, "the four consonants q, z, v and sh can be found in some dialects. The consonants q and z are borrowed from Arabic, while v and sh are variants of w and c respectively" (the four consonants q, z, v and sh can be found in certain dialects. The consonants q and z are borrowed from Arabic, while v and sh are variants of w and c, respectively) KA et al. (2012: 7).

N°	sounds	Fulfulde Spelling		French spelling	
		Symbols	Examples	Symbols	Examples
1	[b]	b	baali "sheep	b	bâton "stick"
2	[c]	c	ceede "silver	tch	match "match"
3	[d]	d	diidol "line	d	donner "to give"
4	[f]	f	**fowru** "hyena	f; ph	faible "weak"; phrase "sentence"
5	[g]	g	**gorko** " man "	g	garçon "boy"
6	[h]	h	hayre " caillou	h [23]	hache "axe"; hero "hero"; habitude "habit"
7	[ɟ]	j	**jalo** "hoe	dj	**Djibouti**
8	[k]	k	**kosam** "milk	k; c; ch	kapokier "kapokier"; calcul "calculation"; psychologie "psychology»
9	[l]	l	laɓi "knife"	l	labourer "plough"
10	[m]	m	miilo "thought"	m	mouton "sheep"
11	[n]	n	naange " sun "	n	nez "nose"
12	[ɲ]	ñ	**ñaaki** "bee	gn; -gne	igname "ignam"; montagne "mountain"
13	[p]	p	peewol "freshness	p	pauvreté "poverty"
14	[q]	q	qur'aana "koran	q	querelle "quarrel"; calque "layer"
15	[r]	r	rafoo "hunger"	r	rein "kidney"
16	[s]	s	**sowru** "chick	s; c; x	saluer "to greet"; placer

---

[23] In French, there is the "h muet" and the "h aspiré.

					"to place"; six "six"
17	[t]	t	tewu "meat	t; th-	television "television"; théâtre "theatre"
18	[w]	w	**wamnde** "mountain	w	william
19	[j]	y	**yayre** "clearing	y	loyer "rent"; octroyer "grant"
20	[']	'	na'i "oxen	-	
21	[ɓ]	ɓ	**ɓiɓɓe** "son"	-	
22	[ɗ]	ɗ	**ɗaɗol** "root"	-	
23	[mb]	mb	**mbaala** "sheep	-	
24	[nd]	nd	**ndiyam** "water	-	
25	[ng]	ng	**ngoonga** "truth	-	
26	[nɟ]	nj	**njaareendi** "sand	-	
27	[ŋ]	ŋ	ŋari "beauty"	-	
28	[y̌]	y̌	**y̌iiy̌am** "blood"	-	
29	[z]	z	**zakaat** "alms	z; x	zéro "zero"; sixième "sixth"
30	[v]	v	**vamnde** "mountain	v	Voter "to vote"
31	[sh]	sh	sheede "silver	-	
32	[ʃ]	-		ch; sch	Chant "sing"; schéma "pattern"
33	[ʒ]	-		j	je "I"
34	[gz]	-		x	exact "exact"
35	[ks]	-		x	texte "text"

Table 2: Support for teaching the reading and writing of consonants in Fulfulde and in French

The learner can then acquire the reading-writing skills of Fulfulde and French through 35 consonant sounds. From the table above, it appears the following:

- There are 21 consonant sounds common to Fulfulde and French: [b];[c];[d];[f];[g];[h];[ɟ];[k];[l];[m];[n];[ɲ];[p];[q];[r];[s];[t];[w];[j]; [z];[v];

- There are 10 sounds specific to the Fulfulde language: ['];
  [ɓ] ;[ɗ];[mb];[nd];[ng];[nɟ];[ŋ];[ƴ]; [sh];
- There are 4 sounds specific to the French: [ʃ]; [ʒ]; [gz] et [ks].

At the level of vowels:

- The two languages have in common 7 vowel sounds: [a]; [e]; [ɛ]; [i]; [o] and [ɔ]; their long correspondents are graphically materialized in Fulfulde;
- 9 vowels are specific to French: [y]; [ø]; [œ]; [ə]; [ɛ̃]; [ã]; [ɔ̃]; [œ̃] and [ɥ].

There are orthographically identical letters in both languages, but which are pronounced differently:

- The letter "c" is pronounced [c] in Fulfulde and [s] or [k] in French.
- The letter "j" is pronounced; [ɟ] in Fulfulde and [ʒ] in French.

According to my proposal that I have presented through the two tables above, teaching reading and writing in Fulfulde and French can be done through 23 vowel sounds and 35 consonant sounds with their respective spelling symbols in each language.

Conclusion

To summarize, the need for bilingual Fulfulde-French education for the Fulani's pastoral populations is very necessary. Only considering the two languages throughout the educational process can ensure a certain communicative autonomy for learners in education and training centers for pastoral populations. The difficulties associated with bilingual Fulfulde-French education are phonetic, spelling, lexical and grammatical. To overcome these difficulties, I propose the learning of French through the skills developed in Fulfulde language. The teachers must also rely on 23 vocalic sounds and 35 consonantal sounds to help learners acquire reading and writing skills in the two languages, Fulfulde and French.

Conclusion

Ayé Clarisse HAGER-M'BOUA and Fabrice JAUMONT

Language is a fundamental aspect of human interaction and communication, and it plays a crucial role in shaping our social world and our sense of identity. It is not just a set of words, but the medium through which we express our thoughts, ideas, emotions, and experiences, and the tool we use to connect with others, understand and be understood, and share and learn. Language defines us and connects us to our culture, history, and background. It is a reflection of our unique experiences and perspectives, and it is the key to understanding and appreciating the diversity of human cultures. It is the glue that binds us together, and it is the tool that allows us to transcend our individual selves and become part of a larger community. As many of this book's authors discussed, language is an essential part of one's identity – not only because of its ability to restructure our personalities and the way we think, but also because it has the power to connect us with others. It is the foundation of our human social world and its importance cannot be overstated.

In Africa's multilingual environment, the importance of the native or first language in child development cannot be overstated. As the continent is home to a diverse range of languages and cultures, the acquisition of a native language is a crucial social competence that is made possible by the biological substrates of the human being. The innate ability to learn language is a biological characteristic of human beings, and the native or first language plays a crucial role in the development of the innate faculty of language in individuals.

Our authors have further demonstrated that the native or first language is a key factor in the development of a child's cognitive style and their perception of the world. The native language is the main means of communication through which individuals organize their thoughts and understand the world around them. This highlights the importance of the native language or mother tongue in child development, particularly in multilingual environments such as Africa. The use of the native language enables children to understand and interpret the world around them in a way that is unique to their community and culture.

Furthermore, the way in which human beings perceive the world is not only based on biological substrates but also on behavioral manifestations and socio-cultural environments. The historical and cultural knowledge and know-how of different communities shape the way in which individuals understand and interpret the world around them. This further emphasizes the link between our thoughts and the use of our native language. It also shows the importance of native or first language in child development in Africa's multilingual environment, where it is essential for children to have access to their native language in order to fully understand and engage with their cultural and societal context.

Education programs, language policies, and the widespread view of multilingualism all play a crucial role in shaping the multilingual identities of students. These factors have been guided by previously unexamined assumptions for decades and have greatly influenced the development of bilingual education programs. However, with the advancements in research and knowledge on multilingualism, there is now an opportunity to re-evaluate and re-conceptualize the way we approach and think about multilingualism. This shift in perspective can lead to the creation of new and innovative programs that support the multilingual identities of students, as well as the reform of existing programs that may not adequately support multilingual students. Furthermore, this approach can be adapted and implemented in Africa and other regions where multilingualism is prevalent. By considering the unique linguistic and cultural backgrounds of students, we can create more inclusive and empowering educational environments that promote multilingualism as a valuable asset rather than a hindrance. As Professor Diagne explained, what is happening in Senegal is representative of the difficult linguistic situation that African nations face. The status of national languages such as Wolof and Pular in school systems, for example, is still unequal vis-à-vis the status of

French or English, a situation that remains at the heart of current debates, as it is linked to students' academic failure and identity issues, as well as to the economic development of the country.

The fight against poverty through the improvement of education in developing countries has become a pressing global issue. According to the UNESCO Institute for Statistics and the Global Education Monitoring Report, a staggering 420 million people could potentially be lifted out of poverty through access to secondary education. However, the reality is that many countries in Sub-Saharan Africa are facing significant obstacles in achieving this goal, particularly in ensuring that all girls and boys have access to high-quality education and are able to complete their secondary education. The lack of literacy skills among students is a major contributor to this problem, as children who are unable to read or write are often forced to drop out of school.

To address this issue and improve the education systems in African countries, it is essential to establish clear and effective standards for quality education and to focus on early childhood development. Additionally, the use of the children's mother tongue as a medium of instruction has been found to be a crucial factor in improving literacy rates and ensuring successful learning outcomes. By implementing these strategies, we can work towards ensuring that all children in Sub-Saharan Africa have access to a high-quality education and are able to lift themselves and their families out of poverty.

Schooling in French-speaking sub-Saharan Africa, for instance, has made significant strides since the early 2000s. However, the quality of education remains poor with more than 50% of children not having the basic skills expected at the end of primary school. One of the major contributing factors to this issue is the use of French as the language of instruction, despite many students and teachers having low proficiency in the language. This hinders the success of early learning and the pursuit of higher education. Studies have shown that the introduction of mother tongues in the first years of primary school can help establish a stronger foundation for literacy, highlighting the need to develop bilingual education programs in

French-speaking Africa. This approach not only addresses the linguistic barriers faced by students and teachers, but also helps to preserve and promote the diverse cultural heritage of the region.

Supporting the construction and continuous development of literacy in the mother tongue of children is of critical importance as it serves as the foundation for acquiring other languages and for overall cognitive development. Through the personal and professional experiences of our authors, we delved into the significance of cultural subtleties and how they can make a difference in approaches to language teaching. Our authors emphasize that bilingual programs should be primarily based on the experiences and knowledge that children acquire through their mother tongue in their first years of life. This approach not only helps children to better understand and retain information, but it also allows them to maintain their cultural identity and promote multilingualism. Furthermore, it is essential for educators to understand the linguistic and cultural background of the children, and to adapt their teaching methods accordingly, to ensure that their students receive the most effective and meaningful education.

The importance of African languages in the quest for linguistic integration and development throughout the African continent cannot be overstated. Decision-makers at the national and continental level, including practitioners, educators, linguists, sociologists, and other stakeholders, have emphasized the need for African languages to be given equal footing with international languages such as English, Portuguese, Arabic and French in terms of linguistic integration and sustainable development. The authors of this book have also emphasized the need for resources and efforts to be directed towards the promotion and development of African languages, so that they can be used in a wide range of domains within society, particularly in education as scholarly languages. This is crucial for the well-being of all individuals and communities on the African continent.

As we have learned in these chapters, a bilingual revolution for Africa would involve a comprehensive approach to promoting the use and value of multiple languages throughout the continent. This could take the form of various initiatives and policies, such as:

- Implementing bilingual education programs in schools, which would give students the opportunity to learn and become proficient in multiple languages, including their mother tongues and other national or regional languages.
- Encouraging the use of multiple languages in government and business settings, which would foster a more inclusive and diverse society. This could include providing translation and interpretation services in public services, and promoting multilingualism in job interviews and job requirements.
- Recognizing and valuing the diverse linguistic heritage of Africa, which would help to preserve and promote the use of different languages. This could include supporting research and documentation of endangered languages, and promoting the use of local languages in media and literature.

To achieve a bilingual revolution, there must be a significant investment in language education and resources. This could include training teachers in multiple languages, providing resources for students and teachers, and increasing the number of language classes offered in schools. Furthermore, fostering a sense of community and promoting understanding among different groups can be achieved by encouraging language exchange and multilingualism. This could include language exchange programs or language clubs, or promoting social and cultural events where different languages are spoken. It is worth noting that achieving this kind of revolution would require a significant shift in societal attitudes towards language and a commitment to investing in language education and resources. Additionally, there may be challenges in achieving this revolution due to factors such as linguistic diversity and limited resources for language education.

A bilingual revolution in Africa would bring numerous benefits to the continent. One of the most significant advantages would be the economic opportunities that come with being proficient in multiple languages. This includes better job prospects, greater access to international markets, and a boost in tourism. By promoting the use and value of multiple languages, we can create a more inclusive and diverse society. This would foster understanding and respect among different groups, while also promoting social and cultural cohesion. Additionally, valuing the diverse linguistic heritage of Africa can help to preserve endangered languages and promote the use of local languages in media and literature.

Bilingual education can also have a positive impact on students' educational outcomes. This includes improved cognitive development, increased problem-solving skills, and better academic performance. Being proficient in multiple languages can improve communication and understanding among different groups and individuals, promoting peace and stability in the region. This can also enhance the ability of individuals and communities to engage with the global community in areas such as business, education, and cultural exchange. Furthermore, bilingualism can improve cognitive development, such as better memory, attention, and problem-solving skills, as well as cognitive flexibility, which is the ability to switch between different languages, concepts and tasks efficiently. Multilingualism can also expose individuals to different cultures and ways of thinking, promoting greater understanding and appreciation of diversity.

African nations that possess a high degree of linguistic diversity and a large number of endangered languages would greatly benefit from a bilingual revolution. Countries such as Nigeria, Cameroon, Ethiopia, South Africa and Senegal, which are among the most linguistically diverse nations in Africa, would see significant benefits from promoting the use and value of multiple languages. These initiatives would not only preserve endangered languages and promote the use of local languages in education and media, but also foster social and cultural cohesion within these countries. Additionally, this approach would create more inclusive and empowering educational environments that recognize the unique linguistic and cultural backgrounds of students. A bilingual revolution in Africa would not only promote multilingualism as a valuable asset, but also improve literacy rates of young people aged 15 and older (in 2017, Côte d'Ivoire had a literacy rate of 43.90%, Guinea-Bissau had a rate of 45.58%, and Mauritania had a rate of 45.50%), as well as education outcomes and economic opportunities for many individuals and communities.

In conclusion, language is an essential aspect of human identity and a crucial tool for human interaction and communication. It connects us to our culture, history, and background, and it is the medium through which we express our thoughts, ideas, emotions, and experiences. Education programs, language policies, and the widespread view of multilingualism all play a crucial role in shaping the multilingual identities of students. With advancements in research and knowledge on multilingualism, there is now an opportunity to re-evaluate and re-conceptualize the way we approach and think about multilingualism. This shift in perspective can lead to the creation of new and innovative programs that support the multilingual identities of students, as well as the reform of existing programs that may not adequately support multilingual students. In Africa and other regions where multilingualism is prevalent, this approach can be adapted and implemented to promote multilingualism as a valuable asset rather than a hindrance. Furthermore, the use of the children's mother tongue as a medium of instruction is crucial for improving literacy rates and ensuring successful education outcomes. Addressing the issue of poverty through the improvement of education in developing countries is a pressing global issue and requires clear and effective standards for quality education, as defined by the targets of SDG 4 with a focus on early childhood development, and the use of the mother tongue to improve literacy rates in native and second languages in African countries.

About the authors

Maria J. Aaron, PhD is Consultant of Obolo Language and Bible Translation for the Obolo Bilingual Education Centre (OBEC) in Nigeria, a model school for bilingual education. She is also since 2019 a language and education specialist with SIL Africa, liaising with other NGOs and Government for the promotion of the use of African languages in education. She has lived for many years in Obolo (Nigeria).

Djeneba Deby Bagayoko is an Italian-born Maninka and Bamana African from Mali and Senegal, a Black language researcher and comparative African linguist. In her work, she bridges the gap between the diaspora and the continent of Africa by showing how characteristics present in Bamanankan, Wolof, and Esan have been retained in their diasporan counterpart: Ebonics.

Thomas Bearth is a linguist specialized in African languages. He is the coordinator of the essay, which was written in collaboration with other educational actors. He introduced the alphabet to the world of the Toura people in the mountainous region of Man (Côte d'Ivoire) as part of a PhD in General Linguistics at the University of Geneva and later as a researcher and Scientific Coordinator of the LAGSUS project (Language, Gender and Sustainability), commissioned by the Volkswagen Foundation.

Pierre de Galbert is a visiting Assistant Professor at Brown University in the Education Department. His research is focused on language in education policies, and specifically on identifying factors to support systems (re)introducing non-dominant languages (NDLs) in the formal education system. He is particularly interested in the multi-dimensional set of factors that influence both the policy decisions regarding African languages and their implementation.

Mbacké Diagne is Director of Research at the Centre de Linguistique Appliquée de Dakar at the Cheikh Anta Diop University (UCAD) of Senegal and Head of the Laboratory of English and African Linguistics and Grammar. He has published extensively on the description of African languages, language policy and planning, and language didactics in multilingual contexts.

Carole Fleuret is a full professor in the Faculty of Education at the University of Ottawa. Her research focuses on second language didactics, multiliteracies and multilingualism. Her research focuses on second language didactics, multi-literacies repertoires and multilingualism. She conducts studies on the appropriation of writing (spelling development) and on the socio-cognitive and cultural components involved in the socialization of writing among minority populations from an intercultural perspective in Canada and internationally.

Ama Edith Flora M'Baye holds a master's degree in Language and Communication Sciences from the Université Alassane Ouattara (UAO), in Bouaké, Côte d'Ivoire. As a young African, her wish is to see African languages evolve and contribute to the education of young Africans. According to Miss M'Baye, using local languages in addition to French in the education system of Côte d'Ivoire is the best thing to do for a quality education.

Cornelius Wambi Gulere is Senior Lecturer at Uganda Christian University in the Department of Languages and Literature. He received his Ph.D. in Literature from Makerere University in 2016. His current research interests include riddles, riddling and collective knowledge creation, aesthetic documentation, and authentic translation. His recent publications include 20 Lusoga-English children's stories with African Storybook Project.

Ayé Clarisse Hager-M'Boua is Assistant Professor at the Université Alassane Ouattara (UAO) in Bouaké, Côte d'Ivoire. She is a member of the Laboratoire des Sciences du Langage Appliquées aux Langues Locales (LASLALL) and a Developing Country Fellow of the International Society for the Study of Behavioural

Development (ISSBD). She promotes bilingual education in the education system of Côte d'Ivoire: simultaneous use of the local language (or mother tongue) and French to better acquire French.

Fabrice Jaumont is a scholar-practitioner, award-winning author, non-profit leader, and education advisor based in New York. He is President of the Center for the Advancement of Languages, Education, and Communities, a nonprofit publishing organization based in New York and Paris. He has published seven books on bilingualism and education, philanthropy, and higher education, including *The Bilingual Revolution: The Future of Education is in Two Languages*.

Ahou Pascaline Kouamé is in the fourth year of her PhD in the Department of Language and Communication Sciences at the Université Alassane Ouattara (UAO). Her Master's thesis focuses on the linguistic identity of bicultural children: children whose parents are from different ethnicities. In her dissertation, she explains how bicultural children deal with family bilingualism in their identity choices.

Félicien Masanga Maisha holds a PhD in Anthropology (University of Florida). He is a languages teacher and translator (Swahili & English). He is a research coordinator for the emerging pathogens Institute (EPI/UF) in Goma and affiliated with the Department of sociology at the University of Goma.

Koliswa Moropa is the Head of the Language Unit 5-year strategic project called "*Transformation - building capacity for South African languages*" within the Department of Tuition Support and Facilitation of Learning. The project is responsible for monitoring the implementation of the Unisa language policy, and Moropa's responsibility is to ensure that all academic departments play an important role in the achievement of multilingual education and the development of official South African languages as languages of teaching and learning, scholarship, and research. She serves as a member of the advisory committee that assists the national Department of Sport, Arts and Culture in establishing the South African Language Practitioners' Council as per the 2014 *South African Language Practitioners' Council Act*.

Tony V. Muzau is a Master student, Applied Linguistics, at the University of Bonn (Germany). He is interested in Linguistics of Congolese languages, most notably Lingala, Kikongo and Kisonde. He has professional experience as a teacher in primary, secondary and higher education, and as a translator and interpreter for English, French and Lingala.

Julia Ndibnu-Messina Ethe is a Professor at the University of Yaoundé I, a member of the IFADEM expert group and an associate researcher at CERDOTOLA. She is also a Visiting Professor at the Francophone Mobility Chair in Ottawa (Canada). Her research focuses on language didactics and ICT. She is a sociolinguist, applied to situations of multilingualism, and is the author of several articles and book chapters.

Daniel N. Obah is a Professional Accountant, Financial Consultant, Life Coach, and an Inspirational Author/Speaker who derives joy in impacting knowledge, promoting value reorientation, peace in Africa through his Organization named: Value Reorientation and Developmental Initiative AFRICA (VARDIAFRICA). He is the author of two books.

Joy K. Peyton, PhD is a Senior Fellow at the Center for Applied Linguistics (CAL) in Washington, DC. She has been working on issues of heritage language and mother tongue education for over 30 years. She was a founding member of the Alliance for the Advancement of Heritage Languages, hosted at CAL in Washington, and is now President of the Coalition for Community-Based Heritage Language Schools.

Ari Sherris is an Associate Professor of Bilingual Education at Texas A&M University - Kingsville. During the 2015-2016 academic year, he was a Fulbright Scholar at the University of Education, Winneba (Ghana). His ethnographic work documents situated practice in grassroots policy initiatives and school-based activism among the Safaliba in rural Ghana. He also explores applications of task-based language teaching in the pedagogy of revitalization.

Feziwe Shoba joined the Department of Linguistics and Modern Languages at Unisa as a researcher in the project *African languages in Teaching and Learning* from 2013 to 2017. She is now employed as a Language Specialist in the Language Unit 5-year strategic project called "*Transformation - building capacity for South African languages*" within the Department of Tuition Support and Facilitation of Learning. The project is responsible for monitoring the implementation of the Unisa language policy, and promotion of multilingualism within the institution. She serves as a facilitator in the Community Engagement project called, *Skills training for Editors and Translators*.

Michelle L. Solorio earned a PhD. in Education policy with a concentration in international comparative education from Michigan State University in 2020. Her dissertation looked at the intersection between language policy and use in education and the implications for peace and conflict in Côte d'Ivoire. She has collected data in French and Bamanankan (Bambara or Dioula) in urban Côte d'Ivoire.

Djibrila Tetereou is a PhD student at the University of Kara (Togo) in the Department of Language Sciences. Since 2014, he is an Educator of pastoral populations in dual-language (Fulfulde / French).

Venance Tokpa is a PhD student at the Department of Language Sciences of the Université Félix Houphouët Boigny (UFHB), Abidjan, Côte d'Ivoire. His work focuses on the analysis of tones and the description of African languages (languages with tones), particularly Ivorian languages. He shows the importance that tone can have in African languages and in their teaching, in order to set up an effective and efficient didactic system.

Agnès Ndiaye Tounkara is a French-Senegalese woman living in the United States of America. She is now the coordinator of the French Heritage Language Program (FHLP), an educational program of the FACE Foundation, which helps French-speaking immigrants and young Americans of French origin to preserve their linguistic and cultural heritage and to make French an asset.

Brenda A. Wawire is an Associate research scientist in the Education and Youth Empowerment research unit at the African Population and Health Research Center (APHRC) in Nairobi, Kenya. Her research interests include literacy acquisition across languages, second language acquisition, language of instruction policy, curriculum design, and reading teacher training as well as best practices for teaching multilingual learners.

References

Aaron, M. J. (1998). A way to improve literacy in primary education in nigeria. *Notes on Literacy*, 24 (2), 1-57.

Abd-Kadir, J., & Hardman, F. (2007). The discourse of whole class teaching: A comparative study of Kenyan and Nigerian primary English lessons. *Language and Education, 21*(1), 1–15.

Abiria, D. M., Early, M., & Kendrick, M. (2013). Multilingual pedagogical practices in a policy-constrained context: A Northern Ugandan case study. *TESOL Quarterly*, 47, 567–590.

Ackers, J., & Hardman, F. (2001). Classroom interaction in Kenyan primary schools. *Compare: A Journal of Comparative and International Education, 31*, 245–261.

Adetuyi-Olu-Francis, O., & Opara, C. (2018). Life-long education for sustainable economy in Africa: The role of French language education. *Journal of Teaching and Education, 08*(02), 403–412.

Afiesimama, A. F. (1991). *Linguistic Complexity in Rivers State: Implications for Language Use in Primary Education.* (PhD), University of Port Harcourt.

African Union. (2015). *Agenda 2063: The Africa We Want.* African Union Commission.

Albaugh, E. A. (2014). State-building and multilingual education in Africa. New York, N.Y.: *Cambridge University Press*.

Amadi, E. A. (2012). Parents' and teachers' preferred medium of instruction in primary schools in Enugu, Nigeria. *Educational Research and Reviews*, 7(28), 632.

Ancarno, C. Bouy, B., & Jeng, M. (forthcoming). Challenges for Gambian primary schools aiming to enhance literacy through the use of national languages. In E. Erling, J. Clegg, C. Rubagumya, & C. Reilly (Eds.), *Multilingual learning in Sub-Saharan Africa: Assessment, ideologies and policies.* (Vol. 2). Routledge.

Andersen, R. W. (1978). An implicational model for second language research. *Language Learning, 28*(2), 221–282.

Aritiba, A. S. et Takassi, I. (2010). *Linguistique et acquisition des compétences en Français.* Université de Lomé.

August, D., & Shanahan, T. (2006). *Developing Literacy in Second-Language Learners: Report of the National Literacy Panel on Language-Minority Children and Youth.* Mahwah, NJ: Lawrence Erlbaum Associates.

Awedoba, A. K. (2009). Attitudes towards instruction in the local language-a case study of the perspectives of the 'small' stakeholder. *Institute of African Studies Research Review,* 2009 (9), 35-64.

Baba-Moussa, A. R., Glanz, C., & De Grauwe, A.(2014). *Élaboration du cadre normatif dans une approche sectorielle de l'éducation en République démocratique du Congo : enjeux, défis et perspectives.* Institut de l'UNESCO pour l'apprentissage tout au long de la vie.

Baker, C. (2011). *Foundations of Bilingual Education and Bilingualism,* 3rd ed. Clevedon. Multilingual Matters.

Bakhtin, M. (1981). *The Dialogic Imagination: Four Essays* (C. Emerson & M. Holquist, Trans.). Austin: University of Texas Press.

Bamgbose, A. (2009). Foreword. In B. Brock-Utne & I. Skattum (Eds.), *Languages and Education in Africa: A Comparative and Transdisciplinary Analysis* (pp. 13–14). Oxford, England: Symposium Books.

Banque Mondiale, (2019). *Ending Learning Poverty: What Will It Take?* World Bank, Washington, DC.

Baya, J. (s.d.) La politique de l'école obligatoire pour tous en Côte d'Ivoire : l'apport du Projet Ecole Intégrée (PEI) dans la région du Tonkpi. In: Bearth, T. & Diallo, D. *African Multilingualism and the Agenda 2030.* Berlin: Lit Verlag.

Bearth, T. & Diallo, D. (éd.) (2021). *African Multilingualism and the Agenda 2030. Multilinguisme Africain et l'Agenda 2030.* Berlin : Lit Verlag.

Bearth, T. et Fan, D. (2006). The local language - a neglected resource for sustainable development. In: Ernest W.B. Hess-Lüttich (ed.). *Eco-Semiotics.* Umwelt-und Entwicklungskommunikation. Tübingen Basel: Francke. p. 273 - 293.

Bearth, T. (2013). Language and sustainability. In Rose Marie Beck (ed.). *The Role of Languages for Development in Africa Micro and Macro*

Perspectives. Frankfurter Afrikanistische Blatter. Cologne. Rudiger Koppe.

Berens, M. S., Kovelman, I., & Petitto, L. A. (2013). Should bilingual children learn reading in two languages at the same time or in sequence?. *Bilingual research journal, 36*(1), 35–60.

Bitjaa Kody, Z.- D. (2004). *La dynamique des langues camerounaises en contact avec le français.* Thèse de doctorat de 3e cycle, Université de Yaoundé I.

Bikoi, F. N. (2013). Pour un changement de paradigme dans la formation à l'enseignement concomitant du français et des langues partenaires. Dans Nglasso-Mwatha, M. (dir.). *Le français et les langues partenaires : convivialité et compétitivité.* (p.403-410). Presses universitaires de Bordeaux.

Borel., & al. (2009). Enjeux d'une didactique plurilingue : entre représentations et pratiques courantes. *Bulletin suisse de linguistique appliquée.* N° 89. p. 217 - 238, Centre de linguistique appliquée, Université de Neuchâtel.

Bourdieu, P. (1972). *Esquisse d'une théorie de la pratique.* Paris, France : Droz.

Bourdieu, P. (1977). The economics of linguistic exchanges. *Social Science Information, 16*(6), 645-668.

Bourdieu, P. (1983). *Language and Symbolic Power.* Cambridge: Harvard University Press.

Braslavsky, C. (1999). Bilinguisme ou plurilinguisme. Les droits de l'homme et les langues étrangères. *Revue internationale d'éducation de Sèvres,* (24), 59-65.

Brock-Utne, B. (2001). Education for all: In whose language? *Oxford Review of Education, 27*(1), 115–134.

Brou-Diallo, C. (2011). Le projet école intégrée (PEI), un embryon de l'enseignement du français langue seconde (FLS) en Côte d'Ivoire. *Revue Électronique Internationale de Sciences du Langage Sudlangues, 15,* 40-51.

Bunyi, G. (2001). Language and education inequalities in Kenya. In M. Heller &M. Martin-Jones (Eds.), *Voices of Authority: Education and Linguistic Difference* (pp.77–100). Westport, CT: Ablex.

Bunyi, G. (2008). Constructing elites in Kenya: Implications for classroom language practices in Africa. In M. Martin-Jones, A. M.

Mejıa, & N. H. Hornberger (Eds.), *Encyclopedia of Language and Education: Vol. 3, Discourse, and Education* (2nd ed., pp. 147–157). Dordrecht, Netherlands: Springer.

Canagarajah, S. (2011). Translanguaging in the classroom: Emerging issues for research and pedagogy. *Applied Linguistics Review*, 2 (2011), 1-28.

Candelier, M. (2008). Approches plurielles, didactiques du plurilinguisme : le même et l'autre. *Recherches en didactique des langues et des cultures : les Cahiers de l'Acedle* [numéro thématique : L'Alsace au cœur du plurilinguisme], 5, 65-90.

Cardinal, L. (1994). Ruptures et fragmentations de l'identité francophone en milieu minoritaire ; un bilan critique. Sociologie et sociétés, 26(1), 71-86.

Cardinal, L. (2012). L'identité en débat : repères et perspectives pour l'étude du Canada français. *International Journal of Canadian Studies*, (45-46), 55-68.

Castellotti, V., Coste, D., et Duverger, J. (2008). Propositions pour une éducation au plurilinguisme en contexte scolaire. France : Association pour le Développement de l'Enseignement Bi/plurilingue (ADEB).

Castellotti, V., & Moore, D. (2010). Valoriser, mobiliser et développer les répertoires plurilingues et pluriculturels pour une meilleure intégration scolaire. Strasbourg : Division des Politiques linguistiques. Direction de l'Education et des langues, DGIV. Conseil de l'Europe.

Cavanagh, M., Cammarata, L., et Blain, S. (2016). Enseigner en milieu francophone minoritaire canadien : synthèse des connaissances sur les défis et leurs implications pour la formation des enseignants. *Revue canadienne de l'éducation*, 39(4), 1-32.

Cenoz, J., & Gorter, D. (2013). Towards a multilingual approach in English language teaching: Softening the boundaries between languages. *TESOL Quarterly*, 47, 591–599.

Chumbow, B. S. (2005). The language question and national development in Africa. *African intellectuals: Rethinking Politics, Language, Gender and Development, 165192.*

Cincotta-Segi, A. (2011). Talking in, talking around and talking about the L2: Three literacy teaching responses to L2 medium of instruction in the Lao PDR. *Compare: A Journal of Comparative and International Education, 41*(2), 195–209.

Cissé, M. (n.d.). *La francophonie dans l'approche des politiques éducatives et linguistiques en Afrique occidentale*, Université Cheick Anta Diop, Dakar.

Cleghorn, A. (1992). Primary level science in Kenya: Constructing meaning through English and indigenous languages. *International Journal of Qualitative Studies in Education*, 5, 311–323.

Coleman, H. (2013). *The English language in Francophone West Africa* British Council.

Corinne A. Seals & Joy Kreeft Peyton (2016): Heritage language education: valuing the languages, literacies, and cultural competencies of immigrant youth, *Current Issues in Language Planning.*

Coste, D., Moore, D., & Zarate, G. (1997). *Compétence plurilingue et pluriculturelle. Vers un Cadre Européen commun de référence pour l'enseignement et l'apprentissage des langues vivantes.* Strasbourg, France : Editions du Conseil de l'Europe.

Coste, D. (1994). L'enseignement bilingue dans tous ses états. *Études de linguistique appliquée, 96*, 9.

Creese, A., & Blackledge, A. (2010). Translanguaging in the bilingual classroom: A pedagogy for learning and teaching? *The Modern Language Journal, 94*(1), 103-115.

Cummins, J. (1979). Linguistic interdependence and the educational development of bilingual children. *Review of Educational Research, 49*(2), 222-251.

Cummins, J. (1980). The Cross-Lingual Dimensions of Language Proficiency: Implications for Bilingual Education and the Optimal Age Issue. *TESOL Quarterly, 14* (2).

Cummins, J. (2000). *Language, Power and Pedagogy*. Bristol: Multilingual Matters.

Cummins, J. (2008). BICS and CALP: Empirical and theoretical status of the distinction. *Encyclopedia of language and education, 2*(2), 71-83.

Cummins, J. (2016). Reflections on Cummins (1980), the cross-lingual dimensions of language proficiency: implications for bilingual education and the optimal age issue. *TESOL Quarterly*.

Cuq, J.-P. (2003). *Dictionnaire de didactique du français langue étrangère et seconde*. Paris : CLE International.

Dagenais, D. et Moore, D., (2008). Représentations des littératies plurilingues, de l'immersion en français et des dynamiques identitaires chez des parents en chinois. *Revue canadienne des langues vivantes*, n° 65 (1), p. 11-32.

Dagenais, D., (2012). Littératies multimodales et perspectives critiques. Recherches en didactique des langues et des cultures. *Les Cahiers de l'ACEDLE*, 9(2), p. 1546.

Dagenais, D. (2020). Explorations du plurilinguisme et de la multimodalité dans l'enseignement des littératies en contextes minoritaires. Dans. J. Thibeault et C. Fleuret (Dir.) *Didactique du français en contextes minoritaires : entre normes scolaires et plurilinguismes*, (p.35-55). Presses de l'Université d'Ottawa.

Daff, M., & Akissi Boutin, B. (2010). L'intercompréhension au cœur des processus d'apprentissage bilingue et tremplin pour une didactique plurilingue à visée convergente et intégrée en Afrique. *Revue du Réseau des Observatoires du Français Contemporain en Afrique Noire*, (13), 351-359.

Davidson, M. (2013). *Books that Children Can Read: Decodable Books and Book Leveling*. Washington, DC: U. S. Agency for International Development (USAID).

De Galbert, P. G. (2021). Language-in-education policies: an analytical framework applied to Kenya and Uganda. In C. Benson & K. Kosonen (Eds.), *Language Issues in Comparative Education II* (pp. 276–300). Brill Sense.

Delpit, L. (1998). What should teachers do ? Ebonics and culturally responsive instruction. In Perry T. and Delpit L., *The Real Ebonics Debate. Power, Language, and the Education of African-American Children* (p. 17). Boston : Beacon Press.

Dhillon, J., & Wanjiru, J. (2013). Challenges and strategies for teachers and learners of English as a second language: The case of an urban primary school in Kenya. *International Journal of English Linguistics*, *3*(2), 14-24.

Diallo, I. et al. (2009). *Bi-Grammaire Fulfulde-Français*. Organisation internationale de la francophonie.

Djité, P. G. (2008). The sociolinguistics of development in Africa. *Multilingual Matters: Vol. 139*. Multilingual Matters.

Doumbia, A. T. (2000). L'enseignement du bambara selon la pédagogie convergente au Mali : théorie et pratiques. *Nordic Journal of African Studies* 9-3. (p 98-107).

Dubeck, M. M., Jukes, M. C., & Okello, G. (2012). Early primary literacy instruction in Kenya. *Comparative Education Review*, *56*(1), 48-68.

Dubeck, M. M., & Gove, A. (2015). The early grade reading assessment (EGRA): Its theoretical foundation, purpose, and limitations. *International Journal of Educational Development, 40,* 315-322.

Eberhard, D. M., Simons, G. F., & Fennig, C. D. (2019). Languages of Uganda. *Ethnologue*. (Twenty-second edition). SIL International.

Eberhard, D. M., Simons, G. F., & Fennig, C. D. (Eds.). (2021). Languages of the World. *Ethnologue* (Twenty-fourth edition). SIL International.

Egwujioha, L. C., Nebo, C. N. Aloh, L., & Offorma, G. (2021). The politics of French language education at the basic education level in Nigeria. *Nigerian Journal of Curriculum Studies*, *27*(4), 92–101.

Evans, R., & Cleghorn, A. (2014). Parental perceptions: a case study of school choice amidst language waves. *South African Journal of Education*, 34, 1-19.

Fairclough, M., & Beaudrie, S. (2016). *Innovative Strategies for Heritage Language Teaching. A practical guide for the classroom*. Georgetown University Press.

Farné, R. (2003). *Buona maestra TV. La RAI e l'educazione da "Non è mai troppo tardi" a "Quark"*. Rome : Carocci.

Faso, B. (2009). *Profils et conditions de travail des enseignants des écoles bilingues et classiques.* Ouagadougou, Laboratoire citoyennetés.

Fathman, A. (1975). Language background, age and the order of acquisition of English structures. In H. C. Dulay & M. K. Burt

(Eds.), *New Directions in Second Language Learning, Teaching and Bilingual Education* (75th ed., pp. 33–43). TESOL.

Fehrler, S., & Michaelowa, K. (2009). *Education Marginalization in Sub-Saharan Africa*. Zürich: Institut für Politikwissenschaft.

Fichtner, S. (2017). *Enseigner autrement en Afrique. La formation à la pédagogie active et participative en République Démocratique du Congo.* HAL. alshs-02536426

Fishman, J. A. (Ed.). (2001). *Can Threatened Languages Be Saved? Reversing Language Shift, Revisited.* Clevedon, UK: Multilingual Matters.

Fleuret, C. et Auger, N. (2019). Translanguaging, recours aux langues et aux cultures de la classe autour de la littérature de jeunesse pour des publics allophones d'Ottawa (Canada) et de Montpellier (France): opportunités et défis pour la classe. *Cahiers de l'ILOB*, 10, 107-136.

Fleuret, C. (2020). Apprenants, langues et contextes : quelles configurations pour l'apprentissage du français de scolarisation en contexte minoritaire ? Dans. J. Thibeault et C. Fleuret (Dir.) *Didactique du français en contextes minoritaires : entre normes scolaires et plurilinguismes* (p.11-30). Presses de l'Université d'Ottawa.

Floccia et *al.* (2018), *Vocabulary of 2-Years-Olds Learning English and an Additional Language: Norms and Effects of Linguistic Distance*. Society for Research in Child Development. USA.

Fon, N. N. A. (2019). Official bilingualism in Cameroon: an endangered policy? *African Studies Quarterly*, *18*(2), 55–66.

Gajo, L. (2009). Politiques éducatives et enjeux socio-didactiques : l'enseignement bilingue francophone et ses modèles. *Glottopol–revue de sociolinguistique en ligne*, *13*, 14-27.

Garcıa, O. (2009). *Bilingual education in the 21st century: A global perspective*. Malden, MA: Wiley-Blackwell.

Ghana. *Ghana's Constitution of 1992 with Amendments through 1996.*

Githiora, C. (2018). Sheng: the expanding domains of an urban youth vernacular. *Journal of African Cultural Studies*, *30*(2), 105-120.

Global Education Monitoring Report team. (2019). *Beyond Commitments: How countries implement SDG 4*. Paris, France. UNESCO.

Goldsmith, J. (1976). *Autosegmental and Metrical Phonology*. Oxford: Blackwell.

Goswami, U. (2015). Cambridge primary review. *A report for the Cambridge Primary Review Trust.*

Goswami, U. (2015). Children's cognitive development and learning, Research reports: CPRT Research Survey 3 (new series), Cambridge (UK): *The Cambridge Primary Review.*

Gove, A., & Wetterberg, A. (2011). *The Early Grade Reading Assessment: Applications and Interventions to Improve Basic Literacy.* Research Triangle Institute. RTI Press.

Grin, F. (1990). The economic approach to minority languages. *Journal of Multilingual and Multicultural Development*, 11(1-2), 153-173.

Grosjean, F. (1993). *Le bilinguisme et le biculturalisme : essai de définition. In : Bilinguisme et biculturalisme : Théories et pratiques professionnelles.* Institut de Linguistique de l'Université de Neuchâtel, Suisse. p. 13 - 41.

Grosjean, F. (2008). *Studying Bilinguals*. Oxford: Oxford University Press.

Grosjean, F. (2018). « Être bilingue aujourd'hui ». *Revue Française de Linguistique Appliquée* (RFLA). N°2. Vol. XXIII. p. 7 – 14

Hager-M'Boua, A. C. (2019). Bilinguisme et performativité scolaire : vers un modèle d'apprentissage standardisé abidji / français. In : *Les Cahiers de l'ACAREF.* Vol. 1. N°2. p. 09 - 38.

Hager-M'Boua, A. C. (2020). La langue : indice d'intégration des immigrés de 2ème et 3ème génération en Suisse. In : L'Harmattan. *Jeux et Enjeux de la Catégorisation : Entre dénomination, discours social et développement.* p. 131 - 151.

Hager-M'Boua, A. C. (2021). Compétences bilingues comme clé d'une éducation de qualité tournée vers la globalisation. In : SANKOFA, *Revue ivoirienne des Arts et de la Culture*. N° 20. CRAC INSAAC, Abidjan, Côte d'Ivoire. p. 170 - 188.

Hager-M'Boua, A. C. (2022). Langues ivoiriennes et développement durable en Côte d'Ivoire. Les lignes de Bouaké-la-neuve, *Revue électronique des sciences humaines de l'Université Alassane Ouattara, Bouaké*, Côte d'Ivoire. p. 188 - 210.

Hager-M'Boua, A. C. (2022). Education bilingue dans le système éducatif de Côte d'Ivoire - enjeux de l'enseignement en langue maternelle et perspectives d'avenir. In : *Études africaines en Suisse* (EAS), Berlin : LIT-Verlag, p. 133 - 176.

Heller, M., & Martin-Jones, M. (2001). *Voices of Authority: Education and Linguistic Difference.* Westport, CT: Ablex.

Heller, M. (2005). Language and Identity. In U. Ammon, N. Dittmar, K. Mattheier & P. Trudgill (Ed.), *Vol. 2: An International Handbook of the Science of Language and Society* (pp. 1582-1586). Berlin: De Gruyter Mouton.

Heugh, K. (1999). Language, development, and reconstructing education in South Africa. *International Journal of Educational Development.* vol. 19/4-5. p. 301 - 313.

Hinrichs, L. (2006). *Codeswitching on the Web.* Amsterdam: John Benjamins.

Hymes, D. (1980). What is ethnography? In D. Hymes (Ed.), *Language in Education: Ethnolinguistic Essays* (pp. 88–103). Washington, DC: Center for Applied Linguistics.

Irele, M. (2018). Nigeria: 120 French Businesses Exist in Nigeria – Ambassador. *AllAfrica Premium.* 2018, January 8.

Iveković, R. (2007). Langue coloniale, langue globale, langue locale. *Rue Descartes*, (4), 26-36.

James, M. (2021). « Qui chantera la chanson de MSF ? » : politique de la « proximité » et pratique de l'humanitaire dans l'Est de la République démocratique du Congo. *Violences extrêmes. Enquêter, secourir, juger : Syrie, Rwanda, République démocratique du Congo,* 179.

Jasinska, K. K., Hager-M'Boua, A. C., Amon, A., Guëï, S., Kakou, C., Koffi, S., Séri, A. (2017c). *Promoting Literacy Development in Children in Rural Cocoa Producing Communities.*

Jaumont, F. (2017). *The Bilingual Revolution: The Future of Education is in Two Languages.* New York, TBR Books.

Jaumont, F. (2022). *Conversations on Bilingualism.* New York, TBR Books.

Ka, F. S. et al. (2012). Orthographe standard et unifié pour la langue Pulaar/Fulfulde. *Casas Monograph* n°246.

Kadima-Tshimanga, B. (1982). La société sous le vocabulaire : blancs, noirs et évolués dans l'ancien Congo belge. *Mots*, n°5, octobre 1982.

Kantchoa, L. et Tetereou, D. (2017). Les emprunts du fulfulde du Togo au français et à l'anglais : une analyse de leur intégration aux plans phonologique, morphologique et sémantique (p. 87-99). *Cahiers ivoiriens de recherche linguistique* n°41.

Keita A. (2001). La non-notation des tons en transcription orthographique du dioula du Burkina : quelques points de réflexion. *Mandenkan* 37, 33-47

Kembo-Sure, E., & Ogechi, O. N. (2016). Literacy through a foreign language and children's rights to education: An examination of Kenya's medium of instruction policy. *Nordic Journal of African Studies, 25* (1), 92–106.

Kiramba, L. K. (2016a*). Communicative practices in a bi-/multilingual, rural, fourth grade classroom in Kenya* (Unpublished doctoral dissertation). University of Illinois at Urbana-Champaign.

Kiramba, L. K. (2016b). Heteroglossic practices in a multilingual science classroom. International *Journal of Bilingual Education and Bilingualism*, 1–14.

Kiramba, L. K. (2017a). Multilingual literacies: Invisible representation of literacy in a rural classroom. *Journal of Adolescent and Adult Literacy, 61,* 267–277.

Kiramba, L. K. (2017b). Translanguaging in the writing of emergent multilinguals. International *Multilingual Research Journal, 11*(2), 115–130.

Kouamé Pascaline A. (2017). *La question de l'identité linguistique de l'enfant biculturel à Bouaké*. Mémoire de Master. Université Alassane Ouattara, Bouaké, Côte d'Ivoire.

Kwon, E.-Y. (2005). The "natural order" of morpheme acquisition: A historical survey and discussion of three putative determinants. *Teachers College, Columbia University Working Papers in TESOL & Applied Linguistics, 5*(1), 1–21.

Lahire, B., (2001), *L'Homme pluriel. Les ressorts de l'action.* Armand Colin.

Lahire, B., (2008), *La raison scolaire. École et pratiques d'écriture, entre savoir et pouvoir.* Presses universitaires de Rennes.

Landry, R., Allard, R., et Deveau, K. (2010). École et autonomie culturelle : étude pancanadienne en milieu scolaire francophone minoritaire. *Nouvelles perspectives canadiennes*. Ottawa - Ontario : Patrimoine canadien.

Larouche, L. (2018). *Pratiques déclarées d'enseignants de l'intermédiaire en contexte minoritaire et pluriethnique relativement à l'enseignement de la grammaire* [Thèse de maîtrise publiée, Université d'Ottawa].

Lavoie, C. (2009). *Education bilingue et développement humain durable au Burkina Faso*. Thèse.

Leben, W. (1971). Suprasegmental and segmental representation of tone. *Studies in African Linguistics Supplement 2*.183-200.

Leben, W. (1973). *Suprasegmental phonology*. Cambridge, Massachusetts: MIT. PhD dissertation.

Leclerc, J. (2013). Sénégal. In *L'aménagement linguistique dans le monde*. CEFAN, Université Laval.

Leconte, F. (2015). Une éducation bilingue français/langues africaines ? Absence institutionnelle et comportements contrastés des familles. *Éducation bilingue en France. Politiques linguistiques, modèles et pratiques*. Lambert-Lucas.

Lewis, M.P., Simons, G.F., & Fennig, C.D. (Eds.) (2016). *Ethnologue: Languages of Ghana*. Nineteenth edition. Dallas, TX: SIL International.

Lipsky, M. (1969). *Toward a Theory of Street-Level Bureaucracy*. Institute for Research on Poverty, University of Wisconsin.

Lo Bianco, J., & Peyton, J. K. (Eds.) (2013). Vitality of heritage languages in the United States. *Special issue of the Heritage Language Journal*, 10 (3).

Lory, M-P. et Prasad, G. (2020). Instaurer un espace de collaboration linguistique et culturelle dans les écoles de l'Ontario. Dans. J. Thibeault et C. Fleuret (Dir.) *Didactique du français en contextes minoritaires : entre normes scolaires et plurilinguismes* (p.35-55). Presses de l'Université d'Ottawa, (p81-99).

M'Batika, A. (2015). République Démocratique du Congo : Système éducatif. *Numéro thématique*.

M'Baye Flora. A. (2019*). La problématique de l'acquisition des connaissances dans l'environnement diglossique des Centre d'Action

Communautaire pour l'Enfance (CACE) d'Olienou. Mémoire de Master. Université Alassane Ouattara, Bouaké, Côte d'Ivoire.

Magnan, M.-O., & Pilote, A. (2007). Multiculturalisme et francophonie(s). Enjeux pour l'école de la minorité linguistique. *Glottopol*, 9, 80-82.

Makalela, L. (2015). Moving out of linguistic boxes: The effects of translanguaging strategies for multilingual classrooms. *Language and Education*, 29 (3), 200-217.

Makita, J. C. M. (2013). La politique linguistique de la RD Congo à l'épreuve du terrain : de l'effort de promotion des langues nationales au surgissement de l'entrelangue. *Synergies Afrique des Grands Lacs*, (2), 45-61.

Malcom X. (1964). *Importance of Women's Education*.

Martin-Jones, M., & Jones, K. (2000). Introduction: Multilingual literacies. In M. Martin-Jones & K. Jones (Eds.), *Multilingual literacies: Reading and writing different worlds* (pp. 1–15). Amsterdam, Netherlands: John Benjamins.

Maurice, G. (1980). *Le bon usage, grammaire française avec des remarques sur la langue française d'aujourd'hui*. Duculot.

Mazrui, A. A., & Mazrui, A. M. (1995). *Swahili state and society: The political economy of an African language*. East African Publishers.

Mazrui, A. M. (2002). The English language in African education: Dependency and decolonization. *Language policies in education: Critical issues*, 267-282.

McGlynn, C., & Martin, P. (2009). 'No vernacular': Tensions in language choice in a sexual health lesson in The Gambia. *International Journal of Bilingual Education and Bilingualism*, *12*(2), 137-155.

Meier, I. (1983a). Comment écrire les tons de manière simple et satisfaisante : un apport de la linguistique à un problème d'alphabétisation. In J. Nicole (Ed..) *Etudes Linguistiques préliminaires dans quelque langue du Togo*. (p 243-259). Lomé. SIL.

Menken, K. & Ofelia García. (2010). *Negotiating Language Policies in Schools: Educators as Policymakers*. New York: Routledge.

Merritt, M., Cleghorn, A., Abagi, J., & Bunyi, G. (1992). Socialising multilingualism: Determinants of codeswitching in Kenyan primary classrooms. *Journal of Multilingual and Multicultural Development, 13*(1–2), 103–121.

Métangmo-Tatou, L. (2019). *Pour une linguistique du développement. Essai d'épistémologie sur l'émergence d'un nouveau paradigme en sciences du langage.* Québec : Éditions science et bien commun.

Ministère de l'Éducation de l'Ontario. (2004). *Politique d'aménagement linguistique de l'Ontario.*

Ministère de l'Éducation de l'Ontario (2009). *Une approche culturelle de l'enseignement pour l'appropriation de la culture dans les écoles de langue française de l'Ontario pour l'appropriation de la culture dans les écoles de langue française de l'Ontario.*

Ministry of Education, Science and Technology (MoEST), Republic of Kenya. (2014). *Basic education statistical booklet.* Nairobi: Ministry of Education, Science and Technology.

Montes-Alcalá, C. (2007). *Blogging in two languages: Code-switching in bilingual blogs.* In Selected Proceedings of the Third Workshop on Spanish Sociolinguistics (pp. 162-170). Somerville, MA: Cascadilla Proceedings Project.

Moore, D., (2006), *Plurilinguisme et école.* Didier.

Moore, D. et Sabatier, C., (2014). Les approches plurielles et les livres plurilingues. De nouvelles ouvertures pour l'entrée dans l'écrit et pour favoriser le lien famille-école en milieu multilingue et multiculturel. *Nouveaux Cahiers de la Recherche en Éducation,* n° 17 (2) 32-65.

Moore, D. & Gajo, L. (2009): Introduction – French voices on multilingualism and pluriculturalism: theory, significance and perspectives, *International Journal of Multilingualism,* 6:2, 137-153

Murakami, A., & Alexopoulou, T. (2016). L1 influence on the acquisition order of English grammatical morphemes: A learner corpus study. *Studies in Second Language Acquisition, 38*(3), 365–401.

Muroya, A. (2019). L1 Transfer in L2 acquisition of English verbal morphology by Japanese young, instructed learners. *Languages, 4* (1), 1.

Muthwii, M. J. (2004). Language of instruction: A qualitative analysis of the perceptions of parents, pupils and teachers among the Kalenjin in Kenya. *Language Culture and Curriculum, 17*(1), 15-32.

Mutiga, J. (2013). Effects of language spread on a people's phenomenology: The case of Sheng'in Kenya. *Journal of Language, Technology & Entrepreneurship in Africa*, 4(1), 1-15.

Myataza, K. A. (2021). Losing my language. (Chakanetsa, K., Interviewer) *The Comb.* BBC.

N'Guessan, J. K. (2007). Le français : langue coloniale ou langue ivoirienne ? *Hérodote*, (3), 69-85. Ouane, A., & Glanz, C. (2010). *Pourquoi et comment l'Afrique doit investir dans les langues africaines et l'enseignement multilingue : note de sensibilisation et d'orientation étayée par les faits et fondée sur la pratique.* Institut de l'UNESCO pour l'apprentissage tout au long de la vie.

Namyalo, S., & Nakayiza, J. (2014). Dilemmas in implementing language rights in multilingual Uganda. *Current Issues in Language Planning*, 1–16.

Ndao, F. (2016). Au nom du savoir et de la démocratie, enseignons dans les langues africaines ! *Le Monde Afrique.*

Ndibnu-Messina Ethe, J. (20120). *Recherche d'une méthodologie pour l'enseignement de la culture nationale dans les écoles primaires en milieu plurilingue camerounais.* Thèse de doctorat. Université de Yaoundé I.

Ngumu, P. C. (1985). *Identité culturelle et art musical. L'identité culturelle Camerounaise.* Actes du Colloque de la deuxième semaine culturelle nationale. Yaoundé : ministère de la Culture.

Njiale, P. M. (2009). Entre héritage et globalisation : l'urgence d'une réforme de l'école au Cameroun., *Revue internationale d'éducation de Sèvres* : Colloque 2009 : Un seul monde, une seule école ? Les modèles scolaires à l'épreuve de la mondialisation.

Noyau, C. (2016). Transferts linguistiques et transferts de connaissances à l'école bilingue, recherches de terrain dans quelques pays subsahariens. Dans *Les approches bi-plurilingues d'enseignement-apprentissage : autour du programme Ecole et langues nationales en Afrique (ELAN)*, B. Maurer (coord.). Paris : Editions des Archives Contemporaines, coll. PLID, pp. 55-82.

Nzomo, P., Ajiferuke, I., Vaughan, L., & McKenzie, P. (2016). Multilingual information retrieval & use: Perceptions and practices amongst bi/multilingual academic users. *The Journal of Academic Librarianship*, 42(5), 495-502.

Ochs, E. et Schieffelin, B., (1987), *Language Socialization across Cultures*. Cambridge, United Kingdom: University Press.

Ogechi, N. O. (2005). On lexicalization in Sheng. *Nordic Journal of African Studies*, *14* (3), 22-22.

Orellana, M. F., & Reynolds, J. F. (2008). Cultural modeling: Leveraging bilingual skills for school paraphrasing tasks. *Reading Research Quarterly*, *43* (1), 48-65.

Organisation Internationale de la Francophonie (OIF) : *La langue française dans le monde* - Édition 2018.

Organisation Internationale de la Francophonie (OIF) : *La langue française dans le monde* - Gallimard, Édition 2022.

Ouane, A., Glaz., C., UNESCO Institute for Lifelong Learning, Association for the Development of Education in Africa (2010). *Why and how Africa should invest in African lnaguages and multilingual education : An evidence- and practice-based policy advocacy brief.* Hamburg : UNESCO Institute for Lifelong Learning.

Pacific, Y. K. T. (2015). Foreign Direct Investment in Anglophone and Francophone African Countries. *International Journal of Academic Research in Business and Social Sciences*, *5* (12), 39–57.

PASEC. (2020). Qualité des systèmes éducatifs en Afrique subsaharienne francophone : Performances et environnement de l'enseignement-apprentissage au primaire. In *Population pyramids of the world from 1950 to 2100*. Dakar, Sénégal : Programme d'Analyse des Systèmes Éducatifs de la CONFEMEN.

Piper, B., & Miksic, E. (2011). Mother tongue and reading: Using early grade reading assessments to investigate language-of-instruction policy in East Africa. *The early grade reading assessment: Application and intervention to improve basic literacy*, 139-182.

Piper, B., Zuilkowski, S. S., Kwayumba, D., & Oyanga, A. (2018). Examining the secondary effects of mother-tongue literacy instruction in Kenya: Impacts on student learning in English, Kiswahili, and mathematics. *International Journal of Educational Development*, *59*, 110-127.

Pontefract, C., & Hardman, F. (2005). The discourse of classroom interaction in Kenyan primary schools. *Comparative Education*, 41, 87–106

Prah, P. K. (2013). No country can make progress on the basis of a borrowed language. (A. Mitchell, Interviewer). *eLearning Africa*.

Reddick, C., & Chopra, V. (2021). Language considerations in refugee education: Languages for opportunity, connection, and roots. *Language and Education*.

Republic of Kenya. (2015). *The Basic Education Regulations*, 2015. Kenya Gazette Supplement No. 57, Legislative Supplement No. 21, pp. 421-426.

Republic of The Gambia (2011). *Report on Early Grade Reading ability assessment.* Ministry of Basic and Secondary Education. In-Service Education and Training Unit.

Republic of Uganda. (2005). *Constitution of the Republic of Uganda*.

République de Côte d'Ivoire, Assemblée Nationale. (1977). *Loi n° 77-584 du 18 août 1977 portant réforme de l'enseignement*.

République de Côte d'Ivoire, ministère de l'Enseignement Supérieur (MES). (1966). *Décret N° 66-375 du 8 septembre 1966 portant création de l'Institut de Linguistique Appliquée* (ILA).

Richards, J. C., Platt, J., & Platt, H. (1992). *Longman Dictionary of Language Teaching and Applied Linguistics* (Second Edition). Longman Group UK Limited.

Riches, C., & Genesee, F. (2006). Literacy: Crosslinguistic and Crossmodal Issues. In F. Genesee, K. Lindholm-Leary, W. M. Saunders, & D. Christian (Eds.), *Educating English language learners: A synthesis of research evidence* (pp. 64-108). Cambridge University Press.

Rispail, M. (2006). Le français en situation de plurilinguisme : un défi pour l'avenir de notre discipline ? Pour une socio-didactique des langues et des contacts de langues. *La lettre de l'AIRDF, 38* (1), 5-12.

Roberts, D. (2011a). Autosegmental and pedagogical considerations in preparation for a tone orthography experiment. *Journal of West African Languages*, 38. 2, (p 87-106).

Rosekrans, K., Sherris, A., & Chatry-Komarek, M. (2012). Education reform for the expansion of mother-tongue education in Ghana. *International Review of Education, 58* (5), 593-618.

Rubio-Marín, R. (2003). Language rights: Exploring the competing rationales. *Language rights and political theory, 52*, 73-76.

Schaefer, P. (2008a). Safaliba syntax in principles and parameters theory. (Academic Seminar Week: Proceedings of the 2005 and 2006 Seminars). *GILLBT Working Papers, 2*, 27–41.

Schaefer, P. (2008b). 'Focus' markers: Theory and application to Safaliba. (Academic Seminar Week: Proceedings of the 2005 and 2006 Seminars). *GILLBT Working Papers,2,* 45–55.

Schaefer, P. (2008c). Safaliba pronoun forms and participant reference. (Academic Seminar Week: Proceedings of the 2005 and 2006 Seminars). *GILLBT Working Papers, 2,* 76–79.

Schaefer, P. (2009). *Narrative storyline marking in Safaliba: Determining the meaning and discourse function of a typologically-suspect pronoun set.* Dissertation, University of Texas at Arlington.

Schaefer, P. (2015). Hot eyes, white stomachs: Emotions and character qualities in Safaliba metaphor. In E. Piirainen and R. Sherris (Eds.), *Language endangerment: Disappearing metaphors and shifting conceptualization* (pp. 91–110). Amsterdam: John Benjamins.

Schaefer, P., & Schaefer, J. (2003). Collected field reports on the phonology of Safaliba. *Collected Language Notes*, 25. Legon, Ghana: Institute of African Studies, University of Ghana.

Schaefer, P., & Schaefer, J. (2004). Verbal and nominal structures in Safaliba. Studies in the languages of the Volta Basin II. In M. E. Kropp Dakubu & E. K. Osam (Eds.), *Languages of the Volta Basin II* (pp. 183–201). Legon, Ghana: Department of Linguistics, University of Ghana.

Scott, V. M., & DeLaFuente, M. J. (2008). What's the problem? L2 learners' use of the L1 during consciousness-raising, form-focused tasks. *The Modern Language Journal, 92*(1), 100–113.

Sebba, M. (2012). Researching and theorizing multilingual texts. strategies for multilingual classrooms. *Language and Education, 29*, 200–217.

Sebba, M., Mahootian, S., & Jonsson, C. (Eds.). (2012). *Language mixing and code-switching in writing: Approaches to mixed-language written discourse.* Routledge.

Senghor, A. R. (2003). L'héritage colonial et les langues en Afrique francophone. *Revue internationale d'éducation de Sèvres*, (33), 77-85.

Shatz, I. (2017). Native language influence during second language acquisition: A large-scale learner corpus analysis. In *Proceedings of the Pacific Second Language Research Forum (PacSLRF 2016)* (pp. 175–188).

Sherris, A. (2017). Talk to Text Safaliba literacy activism: Grassroots Ghanaian educational language policy. *Writing & Pedagogy*, 9(1), 163-195.

Sherris, A. (2019). Early childhood Safaliba literacy in Ghana. In A. Sherris & J. K. Peyton (Eds.), *Teaching writing to children in Indigenous languages: Instructional practices from global contexts* (pp. 70–88). Routledge.

Sherris, A. (2020a). Safaliba community language awareness: "Safaleba—A dageya ka o bebee!" ["Safaliba—it is important for it to exist!"], *Language Awareness, 29*(3-4), pp. 304-319.

Sherris, A. (2020b). Situated Safaliba practices in school literacies that resist dominant discourses in Ghana. In A. Sherris & S. Penfield (Eds.), *Rejecting the marginalized status of minority languages: Educational projects pushing back against language endangerment* (pp. 135-151). Bristol, UK: Multilingual Matters.

Sherris, A., & Peyton, J. K. (2019). *Teaching writing to children in Indigenous languages: Instructional practices from global contexts.* New York and London. Routledge.

Sherris, A., Schaefer, P., Aworo, M. S. (2019). The paradox of translanguaging in Safaliba: A rural indigenous Ghanaian language. In A. Sherris & E. Adami (Eds.), *Making signs, translanguaging ethnographies: Exploring urban, rural and educational spaces* (pp. 152-169). Bristol, UK: Multilingual Matters.

Sherris, A., & Yakubu, K. (anticipated publication 2022). Drumming, storytelling, and writing: Indigenous Safaliba sign making in rural Ghana. In R. Horowitz (Ed.), *The Routledge handbook of international research on writing.* New York: Routledge.

Silue, J. (2010). L'alphabétisation en langues nationales et le développement durable. Dans *EDUCI/ROCARE*. Africa education development issues N°2. (p.111-132). Spécial JRECI 2006 & 2009.

Sibomana, E. (2018). Unpeeling the Language Policy and Planning Onion in Rwanda: Layer Roles. *International Journal of Social Sciences and Humanities, 2*(2), 99–114.

Simons, G. F., & Fennig, C. D. (Eds.). (2018). *Ethnologue: Languages of the world, Twenty-first edition.* Dallas, Texas: SIL International.

Slabakova, R. (2018). The native language: problem or solution on the way to L2 acquisition? *Language Teaching Research*, 1–32.

Solorio, M.L. (2020a). *Language wars? Language of instruction and the Ivorian post-conflict transition.* Doctoral dissertation, Michigan State University. ProQuest.

Solorio, M. (2020b). Refugees, immigrants, and language in Ivorian education. *Global Education Review, 7*(4), 93-107.

Sonck, G. (2005). Language of instruction and instructed languages in Mauritius. *Journal of Multilingual and Multicultural Development, 26,* 37 - 51.

Ssentanda, M. E. (2014). The challenges of teaching reading in uganda: curriculum guidelines and language policy viewed from the classroom. *Apples – Journal of Applied Language Studies.* Vol. 8, 2, 1– 22

Statistique Canada. (2019). *Données démolinguistiques. Recensement 2016* (par province).

Street, B., (2003). What's "new" in New Literacy Studies? Critical approaches to literacy in theory and practice », *Current Issues in Comparative Education*, n° 5, (2), p. 77-91.

Stumpf, R. (1979). *La Politique linguistique au Cameroun de 1884 à 1960. Comparaison entre les administrations allemande, française et britannique et du rôle joué par les sociétés missionnaires.* Berne : Peter Lang.

Tabi-Manga, J. (2000). *Les Politiques linguistiques du Cameroun.* Paris : Karthala.

Tadadjeu, M. (1982). *Propositions pour l'enseignement des langues camerounaises.* Yaoundé : Centre de recherches et d'études anthropologiques.

Taylor, S. K., & Snoddon, K. (2013). Multilingualism in TESOL: Promising controversies. *Tesol Quarterly*, 439-445.

Tembe, J., & Norton, B. (2008). Promoting local languages in Ugandan primary schools: The community as stakeholder. *Canadian Modern Language Review, 65* (1), 33–60.

Tokpa, V. (2019). Esquisse pour une didactique du ton : cas du toura. *Revue du LTML (Laboratoire de Théories et de Méthodes linguistiques) no°16,* décembre 2019, pp 57-72.

Toulemonde, M. (2021). COP26 : où vont les financements climatiques en Afrique ? *Jeune Afrique,* novembre 2021.

Trudell, B. (2016). Language choice and education quality in Eastern and Southern Africa: A review. *Comparative Education, 52* (3), 281-293.

Trudell, B. (2016). *The impact of language policy and practice on children's learning: Evidence from Eastern and Southern Africa.* UNICEF ESARO, Basic Education and Gender Equality (BEGE) Section.

Umukoro, G. M. (2015). Where there is no second language: the problems faced by international tourists during the Calabar Christmas festival. *International Journal of Humanities and Cultural Studies (IJHCS), 2* (2), 499–519.

Umukoro, G. M., & Ohanyere, L. (2020). "French is not my Language": Reactions by Foreign Language Learners in Africa. *Lwati: A Journal of Contemporary Research, 17* (2), 122–142. UNDP. (2021). *Latest Human Development Index Ranking: From the 2020 Human Development Report.* UNDP.

UNESCO Institute for Statistics. (2021). *Literacy.*

UNESCO. (2003). *L'éducation dans un monde multilingue.* Paris.

USAID and EQUALL. (2012). *Education quality for all: Final report.* USAID/Ghana Cooperative Agreement.

USAID and Ghana Partnership for Learning. (2015). *Learning annual performance report, 4th quarter* (FHI 360).

USAID and Ghana Partnership for Learning. (2017). *Year three quarterly performance report,* (FHI 360).

Vahou, Kakou M. (2018). *L'insécurité linguistique chez des élèves en Côte d'Ivoire.* Paris : L'Harmattan.

Vahoua, A. Kallet. (2017). Le projet école intégrée (PEI) en Côte d'Ivoire : quel bilan après plus d'une décennie de fonctionnement ? *Revue Ivoirienne des Sciences du Langage et de la Communication,* n° 11/2, pp.282-298.

Valdés, G. (2001). Heritage language students: Profiles and possibilities. In J. K. Peyton, D. A. Ranard, & S. McGinnis (Eds.),

Heritage languages in America: Preserving a national resource (pp. 37-77). Washington, DC and McHenry, IL: CAL and Delta Systems.

Van-Overbeke M. (1972). *Introduction au problème du bilinguisme. Langues et Cultures.* Paris/Bruxelles. Fernand Nathan. Editions Labor.

Vogel, S., & García, O. (2017). Translanguaging. In G. Noblit & L. Moll (Eds.), *Oxford Research Encyclopedia of Education*. Oxford, Oxford University Press.

Vuzo, M. (2018). Towards achieving the sustainable development goals: Revisiting language of instruction in Tanzanian secondary schools. *International Review of Education, 64* (6), 803-822.

Walther, R. (2007). *Vocational Training in the Informal Sector or How to Stimulate.* Paris: Agence Française de Développement.

Wei, L. (2011). Moment analysis and translanguaging space: Discursive construction of identities by multilingual Chinese youth in Britain. *Journal of Pragmatics, 43* (5), 1222-1235.

Wei, L. (2011). Multilinguality, multimodality, & multicompetence: Code- and modeswitching by minority ethnic children in complementary schools. *The Modern Language Journal 95* (3): 370–383.

White, B. W. (2008). *Rumba Rules.* Duke University Press.

Williams, C. (2002). *A Language Gained: A Study of Language Immersion at 11–16 Years of age.* Bangor, UK: School of Education, University of Wales

World Bank. (2021). *Loud and Clear: Effective Language of Instruction Policies for Learning.*

Xiberras, V. (1992). *Analyse du concept d'intellectuel à travers la figure sociale de l'" évolué" du Congo belge, 1945-1960.* Mémoire. École des gradués de l'université Laval.

Yohannes, M. A. G. (2009). Implications of the use of mother tongues versus English as languages of instruction for academic achievement in Ethiopia. In B. Brock-Utne & I. Skattum (Eds.), *Languages and education in Africa: A comparative and transdisciplinary analysis* (pp. 189–200). Oxford, England: Symposium Books.

Index

Abidji, 33, 34, 35
Abron, 28
academic language, 99, 140
academic performance, 5, 243
academic success, 6, 13, 73, 76, 78, 95, 181
accents, 18, 19, 186, 188
Addis Ababa, 153
ADLAS, 44
administrators, iv, 101, 194, 197
advocacy, 6, 115, 116, 118, 119, 120, 121, 266
Adzopé, 33
African languages, 5, iii, 6, 8, 21, 37, 43, 47, 50, 51, 54, 55, 58, 60, 63, 66, 68, 70, 82, 85, 93, 101, 102, 112, 132, 133, 135, 136, 137, 141, 142, 144, 145, 146, 147, 148, 149, 151, 152, 153, 154, 156, 161, 164, 169, 214, 215, 217, 221, 222, 223, 227, 241, 245, 246, 247, 249
African Population and Health Research Center, 92, 250
African Union, 153, 251
Afrikaans, 132, 136, 137, 140, 142, 144
Agenda 2063, 153, 251
Akan, 202
Akuapem Twi, 202
alphabet, 32, 53, 54, 65, 181, 183, 185, 186, 209, 211, 212, 245

Amharic, 58
ANACLAC, 63
anglophone, 8
antonyms, 33, 35
Arabic, 152, 234, 241
ARED, 43
Aruba, 58
Asante Twi, 202
assimilationist, 68
Atié, 33
Bamako, 52, 53
Bamana, 52, 53, 245
Bamanankan, 52, 53, 245, 249
Bambara, 13, 52, 249
Bantu, 65, 157, 160
Baoulé, 182
Basa, 69, 71
Baselites, 66, 68
Basoga, 129
Belgian colonial administration, 169, 171
beliefs, 95, 117, 122, 123, 124, 125
benefits, 5, 9, 19, 20, 29, 30, 38, 51, 57, 86, 112, 118, 119, 120, 121, 130, 139, 162, 183, 215, 242, 243
Beni, 175
Benin, 30, 155
Berlin Conference, 151
Beti, 69
bi/multilingual programs, 6, 7
Biankouma, 182, 183, 189, 216
Bible, 63, 65, 66, 103, 204, 245

biculturalism, 24, 26, 27, 66, 70, 71
Biculturalism, 69, 78
Bilingual Christian University, 175
bilingual education, v, 3, 6, 9, 40, 44, 84, 86, 98, 132, 214, 240
bilingual pedagogy, 98
bilingual revolution, 7, 40, 41, 42, 46, 47, 123, 241, 242, 243
Bilingual Revolution, i, ii, iii, 1, 2, 3, 59, 247, 260, 288
bilingualism, iv, 6, 14, 17, 19, 24, 25, 26, 27, 28, 29, 30, 31, 40, 41, 42, 44, 46, 47, 63, 66, 67, 70, 71, 78, 95, 97, 152, 170, 171, 173, 175, 224, 243, 247
Bilingualism, 5, 23, 25, 28, 29, 40, 93, 170, 180, 252, 258, 260, 261, 263, 287
biliteracy, 7
Birifor, 203
Boston, 15, 256
Brafé, 79, 80, 82, 83, 87
British Columbia, 64
British Council, 155, 162, 163, 255
Bron, 28
Bukavu, 175, 177
Bulu, 65, 66
bureaucracy, 123, 262
Burkina Faso, 30, 54, 57, 88, 155, 180, 262
Cameroon, iv, 36, 63, 64, 67, 68, 69, 70, 71, 76, 77, 78, 152, 243, 258

Canada, 7, 29, 36, 63, 71, 72, 75, 78, 246, 248, 254, 258, 270
Canadian Charter of Rights and Freedoms, 72, 73
Canta-Blossè, 216
capacity building, 6, 24
Carde Law of 1921, 68
case studies, i, ii, iv, 30, 123, 289
Catholic, 73
Center for Applied Linguistics, v, 7, 193, 248, 260, 272
Center for the Advancement of Languages, Education, and Communities, 4, 7, 8, 247, 287, 289
Cheikh Anta Diop University, 246
Choruba, 203
Ciluba, 160
classroom, 5, 6, iii, 2, 8, 13, 14, 17, 18, 19, 21, 37, 67, 76, 78, 81, 82, 83, 84, 85, 86, 87, 88, 89, 90, 93, 94, 96, 97, 100, 101, 110, 122, 123, 124, 125, 130, 181, 192, 207, 209, 210, 211, 216, 253, 254, 255, 257, 261, 266, 270
code-mixing, 93
code-switching, ii, 97, 268
codified language, 32
cognitive abilities, 5, 29, 31, 32
colonial ideology, 172
colonial languages, ii, 5
colonial legacies, 1, 2, 95
colonial legacy, 101
colonial powers, 19, 151

colonialism, iv, 49, 151, 202
colonization, 25, 169, 171, 173
communication, 3, 23, 26, 30, 32, 38, 39, 40, 43, 64, 65, 75, 92, 93, 95, 100, 102, 105, 107, 108, 109, 111, 134, 135, 139, 148, 151, 154, 158, 173, 179, 184, 197, 221, 225, 226, 234, 238, 243, 244
community, 2, 4, 6, 8, 9, 14, 15, 19, 20, 25, 27, 31, 39, 43, 44, 50, 53, 56, 73, 75, 82, 83, 84, 85, 86, 89, 90, 92, 93, 96, 97, 101, 102, 103, 117, 122, 124, 125, 126, 128, 130, 150, 169, 170, 172, 174, 179, 193, 194, 195, 197, 202, 204, 206, 207, 211, 212, 213, 225, 227, 238, 239, 241, 242, 243, 269, 270, 287, 289, 290
competence, 17, 21, 25, 39, 40, 183, 238
comprehension, 15, 24, 26, 32, 33, 36, 76, 85, 86, 110, 128, 178, 181, 195, 197, 220
Congo, 92, 152, 172, 175, 217, 252, 258, 260, 261, 262, 263, 272
Côte d'Ivoire, iv, 7, 8, 23, 24, 25, 26, 28, 29, 30, 31, 33, 34, 36, 54, 246, 247, 252, 253, 259, 260, 261, 263, 267, 271
Côte d'Ivoire, 5, 8, 23, 25, 31, 33, 79, 80, 82, 83, 84, 88, 90, 155, 161, 180, 186, 187, 188, 214, 215, 245, 246, 249
Cours Elémentaire 1, 33
Cours Moyen 1, 33
Cours Préparatoire, 33, 126
Covid-19 pandemic, 1

CP, 36, 44, 45, 46, 182, 184
Creole, 58, 156
cultural diversity, 6, 69, 289
cultural heritage, 5, 13, 15, 102, 241, 249, 289
cultural values, 27
culture, ii, 2, 3, 5, 14, 16, 19, 26, 27, 30, 31, 37, 58, 64, 65, 66, 67, 71, 73, 74, 75, 77, 78, 79, 80, 85, 86, 91, 95, 115, 120, 122, 152, 153, 163, 199, 203, 205, 211, 230, 238, 239, 244, 264, 265
Curaçao, 58
curricula, v, 1, 3, 102, 122, 130, 155, 157, 158, 163
Cushitic, 92
Daara, 45
Dagaare, 202, 203
Dagbani, 202
Dakar, 44, 246, 255, 266
Dangme, 202
Dar es Salaam, 178
decolonization, 1, 263
Deg, 203
Democracy, 57
Democratic Republic of Congo, 6, 8, 152, 155, 159, 160, 161, 162, 163, 169, 170, 171, 173, 174, 175, 176, 177, 178, 179, 247, 169
development, i, ii, v, 2, 5, 6, 21, 23, 27, 37, 38, 55, 58, 59, 67, 70, 75, 78, 86, 87, 94, 100, 101, 115, 117, 120, 122, 123, 128, 130, 132, 133, 134, 137, 138, 139, 140, 141, 144, 145, 147, 148, 149, 150, 152, 160, 164, 184, 185, 186, 194, 195, 196, 197, 199, 200, 205, 206, 213, 214, 222, 234, 238, 239, 240, 241,

243, 244, 246, 247, 254, 255, 257, 259, 260
Dhuluo, 92
Diourbel, 45
Directorate of Language Services, 134, 142
discursive practices, 76
Djoula, 54
Djula, 83, 84, 89
Douala, 64
DRC, *See* Democratic Republic of Congo
Duala, 65, 66, 67, 69, 71
dual-language, 226
Dual-Language Learning, 7, 32
Dutch, 58
Early Grade Reading Assessment, 35, 194, 259
Ebonics, 50, 51, 245, 256
economic growth, iii, 6, 58, 100, 153
economic prosperity, 95
education, 4, 5, 6, i, ii, iii, iv, v, 7, 1, 2, 3, 5, 6, 7, 8, 9, 14, 15, 16, 19, 21, 23, 24, 25, 26, 27, 28, 29, 31, 32, 37, 38, 39, 40, 41, 42, 43, 45, 46, 48, 49, 50, 51, 53, 55, 57, 59, 63, 64, 66, 67, 70, 71, 72, 73, 79, 82, 83, 84, 86, 87, 88, 90, 91, 92, 93, 95, 97, 98, 101, 102, 103, 104, 105, 106, 107, 108, 109, 112, 115, 116, 118, 119, 120, 121, 122, 123, 125, 126, 127, 128, 130, 132, 133, 135, 137, 140, 141, 147, 148, 149, 150, 151, 152, 153, 154, 156, 158, 159, 161, 163, 164, 165, 169, 170, 171, 172, 173, 174, 175, 176, 177, 178, 179, 182, 183, 184, 185, 186, 188, 189, 194, 199, 200, 202, 203, 214, 216, 223, 224, 225, 226, 227, 228, 230, 231, 237, 239, 240, 241, 242, 243, 244, 245, 246, 247, 248, 249, 251, 252, 253, 254, 255, 258, 260, 261, 263, 264, 266, 267, 270, 271, 272, 287, 289, 290
education systems, ii, iii, 2, 5, 21, 29, 37, 38, 46, 64, 71, 150, 214, 240
ELAN, i, 21, 42, 71, 265
Elibou, 33
EMiLe, 44
empowering, ii, 4, 6, 239, 243, 289, 290
empowerment, 8, 6, 60
endogenous knowledge, 1, 226, 227
endogenous values, 65
England, 67, 252, 272
English, i, 3, 5, 8, 9, 13, 14, 15, 16, 17, 19, 24, 28, 29, 30, 31, 36, 50, 52, 58, 59, 63, 65, 66, 67, 68, 69, 70, 72, 78, 92, 95, 97, 100, 102, 103, 104, 105, 106, 107, 108, 109, 110, 111, 112, 119, 122, 125, 128, 129, 132, 134, 135, 137, 140, 142, 144, 150, 151, 152, 153, 154, 156, 157, 158, 159, 160, 161, 162, 163, 164, 165, 169, 170, 171, 174, 175, 176, 177, 178, 179, 185, 194, 195, 196, 197, 198, 202, 205, 206, 207, 208, 210,

211, 212, 226, 240, 241, 246, 248, 251, 254, 255, 256, 257, 258, 263, 264, 266, 267, 272, 287
EPSA, 46
equal opportunities, 78
equitability, 97, 101
equity, 6, 8, 9, 97, 100, 289
ESVS, 43, 46
Ethiopia, 57, 243, 272
ethnic minorities, 64
ethnolinguistic, 72, 77, 91, 202
Europe, 16, 17, 41, 254, 255
European languages, 50, 51, 52, 53, 57, 66, 104, 125, 151, 152, 161, 169
evaluation, 43, 44, 100, 108, 126, 176
Ewe, 22, 202
Ewondo, 71
expansion of access, 6
Fante, 202
Fatick, 44, 45
first language, ii, 5, 32, 37, 39, 40, 65, 75, 125, 140, 151, 156, 159, 238, 239
fluency, 17, 30
fragmentation, 151
France, 14, 21, 51, 67, 68, 153, 253, 254, 255, 258, 262
Franco-British mandates, 67
francophone, 7, 13, 14, 15, 16, 19, 20, 21, 31, 35, 73, 74, 75, 151, 152, 153, 154, 156, 158, 159, 161, 162, 163, 165, 254, 258, 262, 266, 268
Francophone, 7, 14, 19, 64, 73, 74, 75, 152, 155, 162, 248, 255, 266
free choice, 70
freedom of education, 70
French, 5, 6, i, iii, 3, 5, 7, 9, 13, 14, 15, 16, 17, 19, 20, 21, 23, 24, 25, 26, 29, 31, 32, 33, 34, 35, 36, 37, 39, 40, 42, 43, 44, 46, 47, 51, 52, 55, 57, 63, 65, 66, 67, 68, 69, 70, 72, 73, 74, 75, 76, 78, 79, 80, 81, 82, 83, 84, 85, 86, 87, 88, 89, 91, 102, 122, 126, 127, 150, 151, 152, 153, 154, 155, 156, 157, 158, 159, 160, 161, 162, 163, 164, 165, 169, 170, 171, 172, 173, 174, 175, 177, 178, 181, 183, 185, 186, 187, 191, 192, 220, 221, 224, 225, 226, 227, 228, 229, 230, 231, 232, 234, 235, 236, 237, 240, 241, 246, 247, 248, 249, 251, 257, 260, 264, 271, 287, 288
Fulani, 22, 53, 237
Fulɓe, 53
Fulfulde, 6, 9, 224, 225, 226, 227, 228, 229, 230, 231, 232, 234, 235, 236, 237, 249, 260
funding, 44, 45, 149, 153, 164, 165, 201
future generations, 3, 4, 48
Ga, 202
Gao, 52
Georgia, 20
German, 66, 67, 185
Germany, 66, 185, 248
Ghana, 6, 8, 31, 50, 154, 193, 202, 203, 204, 206, 213, 248, 258, 262, 267, 268, 269, 271
Ghomala, 71
Gĩkũyũ, 59
global citizenship, 95
Global Partnership for Education, 193
globalization, 28, 75, 226

Gnégbeyalé, 216
Goma, 175, 177
Gonja, 202, 203, 205, 210, 211, 213
governance, 38, 39, 67, 119
government, 15, 38, 40, 42, 44, 52, 66, 69, 72, 73, 79, 89, 93, 108, 123, 126, 137, 182, 185, 199, 202, 203, 205, 206, 242
grammar skills, 45
Great Britain, 77
Grosjean, François, 24, 25, 26, 27, 259
Guinea, 13, 30, 52, 54, 155, 243
Guinea Conakry, 30, 54
Guinea-Bissau, 243
Haiti, 13
Hausa, 53, 54
heritage language, 16, 17, 19
heritage languages, 5, 7, 16, 17, 63, 262
Hewlett Foundation, 44
history, 287
human development, iii, 170
identity, ii, 2, 5, 14, 18, 19, 26, 28, 69, 75, 90, 95, 97, 99, 202, 238, 240, 241, 244, 247
IFEF, 43, 71
immersion programs, 7
immigrants, 7, 15, 16, 64, 76, 182, 249, 270
implementation, 23, 38, 39, 43, 44, 46, 63, 95, 96, 125, 128, 132, 133, 134, 135, 140, 141, 142, 144, 147, 149, 161, 165, 184, 223, 245, 247, 249
inclusiveness, iii, 97, 101
inclusivity, 6, 9, 98, 100

Independence, 70
indigenous languages, iii, 5, 8, 39, 78, 93, 97, 101, 132, 140, 173, 255
Institute of Applied Linguistics, 214
integration, 6, iii, v, 6, 8, 13, 14, 18, 39, 50, 53, 59, 63, 67, 71, 76, 78, 98, 151, 153, 154, 165, 169, 170, 178, 215, 223, 241
intercultural education, 67
International Organization of La Francophonie, *See* OIF
isiNdebele, 132, 135, 136, 147
isiXhosa, 132, 135, 136, 140, 147
isiZulu, 132, 135, 136, 142, 144, 147
Italian, 31, 51, 52, 55, 58, 186, 245
Italy, 51, 52, 55, 58
Ivorian French, 25
Ivory Coast, 13, *See* Côte d'Ivoire
Japan, 51, 58
Japanese, 51, 264
Jola-Fonyi, 196, 197
Joola, 42
Jula, 54, 203
Kaffrine, 45
Kamara, 203
Kamerun, 66, 67
Kampala, 175
Kanuri, 54
Kaolack, 44, 45
Karon, 196, 197
Kasem, 202
Kayes, 52
Kédougou, 43

Kenya, iv, 8, 51, 59, 92, 93, 95, 96, 97, 98, 99, 100, 101, 250, 253, 255, 256, 257, 261, 264, 265, 266, 267
Kidal, 52
Kihunde, 177
Kikongo, 160, 174, 248
Kikuyu, 59, 92
Kinande, 177
Kinshasa, 171, 174, 177
Kirega, 177
Kisangani, 161, 177
Kiswahili, 59, 92, 95, 98, 160, 161, 266
Kmhmu, 124
knowledge production, 96
Kongo, 22
Koroboro, 52
Koulango, 28
Kyambogo, 130
L1, 23, 24, 27, 32, 33, 34, 35, 36, 40, 42, 44, 46, 94, 156, 157, 158, 160, 165, 196, 264, 268
L2, 23, 24, 27, 32, 33, 34, 35, 36, 40, 42, 44, 46, 94, 196, 255, 264, 268, 270
language acquisition, 5, 35, 86, 150, 151, 156, 159, 162, 250, 269
language ideologies, i
language of evangelization, 66
language of instruction, 23, 31, 66, 79, 86, 88, 92, 94, 95, 97, 98, 99, 129, 151, 154, 156, 158, 159, 171, 174, 179, 221, 240, 250, 272
language of schooling, 33, 76, 78
language policies, 93, 140
language proficiency, 96, 151, 153, 154, 162, 165
language repertoire, 99
language-rationalization, 93
languages, 287, *See* Language, *See* Language
Languages, 287
Lao, 124, 255
Laos, 124
League of Nations, 67, 68
lexicon, 32, 33, 34, 35, 92, 221
Lingala, 151, 156, 157, 160, 174, 248
lingua franca, 28, 53, 54, 56, 67, 125, 160, 225, 227
linguistic amalgamation, 25
linguistic awareness, 76
linguistic communities, 290
linguistic diversity, i, 41, 122, 125, 134, 242, 243
linguistic ecosystem, 47
linguistic heritage, 7, 9, 21, 51, 181, 242, 243
linguistic heterogeneity, 26
linguistic human rights, 97
linguistic insecurity, 8, 14, 18, 76, 182, 183
linguistic integration, 6, 241
linguistic minorities, 77
linguistic skills, 6, 15, 97, 122, 123, 125, 126, 127, 174
literacy, 8, 9, 23, 24, 56, 68, 94, 95, 102, 109, 110, 112, 123, 126, 131, 193, 194, 195, 197, 199, 203, 204, 209, 211, 212, 213, 216, 227, 228, 240, 241, 243, 244, 250, 251, 255, 257, 259, 261, 266, 269, 270
Lobiri, 203
Louga, 45
Lubumbashi, 161
Luganda, 125, 129
Lusoga, 123, 126, 128, 129, 131, 246
Maine, 15, 20

Makerere, 130, 175, 246
Makerere University, 175, 246
Mali, 30, 51, 52, 53, 57, 155, 245, 257
Malinké, 22, 54
Mandate Act, 67
Mandinka, 42, 43, 196, 197
Maninka, 52, 54, 245
Maninkakan, 196, 197
Manjak, 196
Mashi, 177
Matam, 45
mathematics, 43, 45, 46, 91, 221, 266
Mauritania, 155, 243
Mauritius, 152, 163, 270
medium, 2, 8, 26, 28, 30, 42, 44, 46, 79, 80, 81, 82, 85, 92, 93, 96, 97, 100, 101, 105, 108, 112, 116, 123, 126, 135, 153, 159, 165, 191, 238, 240, 244, 251, 255, 261
medium of instruction, 2, 8, 46, 79, 80, 81, 82, 85, 92, 93, 96, 97, 100, 112, 116, 123, 126, 135, 240, 244, 251, 255, 261
meta functions, 99
metalinguistic, 18, 32, 78
Miami, 15
Michigan, 20, 79, 249, 270
migration, 16, 116, 161
Ministry of Education, 40, 74, 87, 88, 91, 93, 130, 185, 264
minority, 1, 16, 20, 30, 38, 58, 63, 72, 73, 75, 81, 115, 246, 259, 269
minority language, 16
missionaries, 64, 65, 66, 68, 69, 70
missionary school, 172

mobility, 9, 45, 89, 116, 160, 224
models, i, iii, 6, 8, 21, 59, 69, 70, 97
MOHEBS, 41, 42, 43, 45, 46, 47
Mombasa, 178
Moncton, 30
monocultural education, 67
monolingual, i, v, 17, 18, 26, 28, 29, 30, 37, 39, 40, 142, 144, 170, 171, 173, 182, 226, 227
monolingualism, iv, 39, 93, 98
Montessori, Maria, 31
Moore, 54, 64, 77, 254, 255, 256, 264
Mooré, 182
moratorium, 68, 69
mother tongue, iii, 2, 3, 7, 8, 9, 15, 16, 23, 24, 27, 31, 32, 33, 34, 35, 36, 37, 39, 41, 44, 46, 49, 50, 51, 53, 56, 58, 68, 92, 95, 96, 102, 103, 104, 106, 107, 108, 109, 111, 112, 115, 118, 121, 137, 141, 142, 170, 183, 186, 192, 194, 195, 198, 200, 201, 205, 225, 226, 229, 230, 234, 239, 240, 241, 244, 247, 248
multiculturalism, 17, 66, 67, 69
multilingual education, iii, iv, 4, 37, 82, 88, 91, 115, 118, 120, 121, 227
multilingual families, 6, 289
Multilingual Literacies, 77
multilingualism, i, ii, iii, iv, 7, 8, 5, 6, 7, 13, 21, 43, 51, 56, 57, 59, 75, 78, 84, 96, 101,

133, 134, 137, 140, 141, 147, 149, 150, 161, 170, 193, 194, 239, 241, 242, 243, 244, 246, 248, 249, 263, 264, 289, 290
multiliteracy, 6, 77, 193
multiliterate repertoires, 77
Mungaka, 67
Mushi, 177
myths, 6
N'ko, 54
Nairobi, 175, 250, 264
NALAP, 206
Nande, 177
national languages, 2, 3, 9, 14, 18, 20, 21, 38, 40, 41, 42, 43, 45, 56, 58, 63, 66, 69, 71, 126, 160, 161, 174, 214, 223, 239, 251
National Languages, i, 42
national unity, 55, 70
native language, 6, ii, 5, 6, 16, 17, 25, 35, 36, 53, 58, 66, 74, 78, 82, 86, 89, 150, 173, 181, 182, 197, 199, 228, 238, 239, 244, 270
New York, 3, 4, ii, iii, 7, 13, 15, 19, 247, 251, 260, 263, 269, 288
Nguni, 135
Niger, 52, 92, 217
Nigeria, 50, 69, 102, 103, 104, 109, 111, 121, 153, 154, 163, 243, 245, 251, 257, 260
Nigerian Educational Board, 69
Nilotic, 92
N'ko, 54, 196, 197
North Kivu, 174
Nouchi, 25
numeracy, 23, 24, 94, 95
Nzema, 202

Obolo, 102, 103, 104, 105, 106, 107, 108, 109, 110, 111, 245
OIF, i, 20, 21, 42, 266
ONECS, 44
Ontario, 5, 7, 63, 71, 72, 73, 74, 75, 76, 262, 264
oral tradition, 76, 214
orthography, 36, 126, 128, 200, 204, 212, 223, 267
pan-African, 63, 71
Pan-Africanism, 153
PanSALB, 134, 145
parental involvement, 45
parents, iv, 8, 13, 20, 26, 39, 41, 49, 54, 57, 70, 72, 79, 80, 81, 82, 83, 84, 85, 86, 88, 90, 95, 97, 98, 107, 173, 175, 182, 183, 186, 199, 211, 216, 247, 256, 264, 290
Paris, 3, 247, 253, 256, 258, 265, 270, 271, 272
peace, i, 3, 117, 243, 248, 249
pedagogical practices, 8, 9, 74, 76, 96, 97, 98, 251
pedagogical training, 96, 163
PEI, 8, 23, 33, 34, 79, 83, 84, 85, 86, 87, 88, 91, 183, 186, 192, 216, 252, 253, 271, *See* Programme d'école intégr, *See* Programme d'école intégrée
Pël, 53
performance, 24, 33, 35, 39, 96, 109, 110, 176, 184, 271
Peul, 22, 53
Phoneme, 34
phonological awareness, 33, 34, 35
policies, ii, v, 2, 39, 63, 67, 71, 72, 73, 74, 78, 93, 95, 97, 98, 101, 122, 123, 125, 126, 129, 130, 131, 132, 133,

140, 147, 151, 154, 159, 161, 164, 165, 223, 239, 241, 244, 245, 251, 263
policy, iii, iv, 66, 68, 73, 81, 86, 87, 90, 92, 93, 95, 96, 97, 99, 100, 122, 123, 124, 125, 126, 127, 128, 129, 130, 131, 133, 134, 135, 140, 142, 144, 147, 149, 152, 154, 159, 162, 165, 201, 202, 203, 205, 245, 246, 247, 248, 249, 250, 251, 261, 266, 269, 270, 271
Portuguese, 5, 52, 58, 66, 102, 152, 241
poverty, 150, 152, 235, 240, 244
pre-colonial language, 93
Presbyterian, 68
preservation, 6, 7, 70
Programme d'Ecole Intégrée, 23, 33
PROPELCA, 71
Pulaar, 42, 43, 45, 52, 53, 56, 122, 126, 196, 197, 217, 260
quality, 5, i, ii, v, 6, 7, 8, 9, 21, 23, 24, 35, 37, 38, 39, 40, 41, 43, 46, 70, 102, 103, 109, 119, 135, 144, 145, 164, 175, 176, 227, 240, 244, 246, 271, 289
quality education, 8, 9, 23, 37, 38, 39, 119, 227, 240, 244, 246, 289
Quebec, 72
Reading For All Program, 45
reduction of inequalities, 6
reforms, 3, 92, 214
regional school, 68
Rufisque, 44
Rwanda, 152, 260, 269

Saafi, 44
Safaliba, 193, 202, 203, 204, 205, 206, 207, 208, 209, 210, 211, 212, 213, 248, 268, 269
Saint-Louis, 44
San Marino, 58
Sawa, 65, 66
school system, 72, 73, 130
schools, ii, iv, v, 3, 7, 8, 15, 19, 20, 23, 33, 34, 39, 41, 42, 43, 44, 45, 49, 50, 53, 55, 59, 64, 66, 67, 68, 69, 70, 71, 73, 74, 75, 79, 80, 83, 85, 86, 87, 92, 93, 94, 95, 96, 99, 101, 102, 103, 109, 110, 111, 112, 115, 121, 122, 125, 126, 127, 129, 130, 131, 153, 154, 159, 160, 161, 163, 164, 171, 172, 173, 174, 175, 176, 179, 194, 197, 199, 200, 201, 205, 206, 208, 216, 224, 242, 251, 266, 270, 272, 290
science, 45, 58, 96, 99, 132, 137, 138, 139, 152, 153, 255, 261, 264
SDG, 23, 24, 244, 258, 289, 290
secularism, 70
Seereer, 42, 43, 44, 45, 126
Segou, 52
Senegal, i, 13, 30, 37, 38, 39, 40, 42, 44, 45, 46, 47, 51, 54, 56, 57, 123, 126, 128, 130, 131, 155, 195, 239, 243, 245, 246
Senoufo, 55, 80
Sepedi, 132, 136, 142, 144
Serahule, 196, 197
Serer, 56, 196, 197

Sesotho, 50, 132, 136, 142, 147
Setswana, 132, 147
Seychelles, 152
Sheng, 92, 258, 265, 266
Sikasso, 52
Sikensi, 33
SIL, iv, 7, 44, 63, 245, 257, 262, 263, 270
siSwati, 132, 135, 136, 147
Siti, 203
social, 287
social justice, iii, 98
socialization, 77, 227, 234, 246
Somalia, 57
Soninke, 53
Sooninke, 42, 43
Sotho, 50, 144
South Africa, 6, ii, iv, 7, 50, 121, 132, 133, 137, 140, 142, 144, 145, 147, 148, 149, 243, 260
Spanish, 31, 150, 152, 159, 264, 288
standard language, 33, 169
strategy, 6, 19, 44, 71, 100
sub-Saharan Africa, 5, iii, 7, 25, 31, 37, 38, 39, 40, 41, 46, 64, 76, 240
Suriname, 58
sustainable development, i, 6, 23, 47, 150, 151, 152, 154, 241, 252, 272
Susu, 13
Swahili, 174, 177, 263
Swedish, 54
Switzerland, 35, 36, 58
synonym, 35
synonym test, 35
teacher training, iv, 44, 81, 82, 87, 122, 128, 130, 165, 250

teachers, 5, 6, iv, v, 8, 17, 18, 32, 45, 50, 53, 57, 70, 74, 75, 76, 79, 81, 82, 84, 87, 88, 90, 91, 95, 96, 97, 98, 99, 100, 101, 102, 103, 104, 105, 106, 108, 109, 110, 111, 118, 119, 122, 123, 124, 125, 126, 127, 128, 129, 130, 131, 149, 154, 163, 164, 170, 175, 180, 181, 188, 194, 195, 197, 199, 200, 201, 202, 205, 212, 216, 221, 224, 226, 231, 237, 240, 242, 251, 256, 264, 289, 290
terminology, 134, 137, 138, 139, 140, 141, 142, 144, 145, 146, 147, 148
textbooks, 2, 32, 45, 54, 81, 102, 103, 105, 111, 155, 157, 195, 197, 200, 216, 221
The French mandate, 68
the Gambia, 8, 194
The Gambia, 6, iv, 193, 194, 195, 196, 199, 213, 263, 267
The German protectorate, 66
the Netherlands, 58
the Vatican, 58
Thiès, 43
Togo, 9, 30, 155, 224, 227, 249, 261, 263
Tomutu, 52
Tonal Languages, 217
Tones, 217, 222
Toura, 180, 181, 182, 183, 185, 186, 187, 189, 191, 192, 215, 218, 220, 221, 222, 245
transformation, 1, 3, 101, 132, 137, 142, 148
translanguaging, 8, 18, 94, 98, 99, 100, 101, 210, 263, 269, 272

Translanguaging, 5, 8, 92, 94, 97, 98, 99, 254, 255, 258, 261, 272
Treaty of Versailles, 67
trilingualism, 71
Tshivenda, 132, 136, 147
Tumutu, 52
Turkey, 58
Tuscan, 55
UCBC, 175
Uganda, 122, 123, 125, 126, 128, 129, 130, 131, 246, 256, 257, 265, 267, 270
Uganda Christian University, 122, 246
UNESCO, 5, 7, 1, 3, 58, 116, 163, 164, 193, 227, 240, 252, 258, 265, 266, 271
unification, 53, 70
Unisa, 132, 133, 134, 135, 141, 144, 145, 148, 247, 249
United Nations, 1, 159, 170, 289
United States, 5, 7, 13, 14, 15, 16, 17, 19, 20, 31, 41, 249, 262
Université Alassane Ouattara, 246, 247, 259, 261, 263
Université Félix Houphouët Boigny, 214, 249
University of Cape Town, 141
University of Education, Winneba, 248
University of Geneva, 185, 245
University of Kara, 48, 224, 249
University of Ottawa, 63, 246
University of Stellenbosch, 140
University of Yaoundé I, 248
USA, 4, i, ii, iv, v, 258
USAID, 35, 256, 271
Vagla, 203
Vietnam, 58
village school, 68
Volkswagen Foundation, 185, 245
Waali, 203
Wisconsin, 20, 262
Wolof, 13, 22, 42, 43, 45, 50, 52, 53, 54, 56, 122, 126, 127, 196, 197, 217, 239, 245
World Bank, 184, 193, 201, 252, 272
World Vision Senegal, 44
Xitsonga, 132, 136
Yacouba, 182
Yakubu, 204, 269
Yaoundé, 63, 153, 248, 253, 265
Yengbèyalé, 180, 184, 185
Zambia, 36

About TBR Books

TBR Books is a program of the Center for the Advancement of Languages, Education, and Communities. We publish researchers and practitioners who seek to engage diverse communities on topics related to education, languages, cultural history, and social initiatives. We translate our books in a variety of languages to further expand our impact.

BOOKS IN ENGLISH

Bilingual Children: Families, Education, and Development by Ellen Bialystok

The Heart of an Artichoke by Linda Ashour and Claire Lerognon

French All Around us by Kathleen Stein-Smith and Fabrice Jaumont

Navigating Dual Immersion: A Teacher's Companion for the School Year and Beyond by Valerie Sun

Conversations on Bilingualism by Fabrice Jaumont

One Good Question: How to Ask Challenging Questions that Lead You to Real Solutions by Rhonda Broussard

Can We Agree to Disagree? by Sabine Landolt and Agathe Laurent

Salsa Dancing in Gym Shoes by Tammy Oberg de la Garza and Alyson Leah Lavigne

Beyond Gibraltar; The Other Shore; Mamma in her Village by Maristella de Panizza Lorch

The Clarks of Willsborough Point by Darcey Hale

The English Patchwork by Pedro Tozzi and Giovanna de Lima

Peshtigo 1871 by Charles Mercier

The Word of the Month by Ben Lévy, Jim Sheppard, Andrew Arnon

Two Centuries of French Education in New York: The Role of Schools in Cultural Diplomacy by Jane Flatau Ross

The Bilingual Revolution: The Future of Education is in Two Languages by Fabrice Jaumont

📖 BOOKS IN OTHER LANGUAGES

Deux siècles d'enseignement français à New York : le rôle des écoles dans la diplomatie culturelle by Jane Flatau Ross

Sénégalais de l'étranger by Maya Smith

Le projet Colibri : créer à partir de "rien" by Vickie Frémont

Pareils mais différents by Sabine Landolt and Agathe Laurent

Le don des langues by Kathleen Stein-Smith and Fabrice Jaumont

📖 BOOKS FOR CHILDREN (available in several languages)

Franglais Soup e by Adrienne Mei

Rainbows, Masks, and Ice Cream by Deana Sobel Lederman

Korean Super New Years with Grandma by Mary Chi-Whi Kim and Eunjoo Feaster

Math for All by Mark Hansen

Rose Alone by Sheila Decosse

Uncle Steve's Country Home; The Blue Dress; The Good, the Ugly, and the Great by Teboho Moja

Immunity Fun!; Respiratory Fun!; Digestive Fun! By Dounia Stewart-McMeel

Marimba by Christine Hélot, Patricia Velasco, Antun Kojton

Our books are available on our website and on all major online bookstores as paperback and e-book. Some of our books have been translated in over a dozen languages. For a listing of all books published by TBR Books, information on our series, or for our submission guidelines for authors, visit our website at:

www.tbr-books.org

About CALEC

The Center for the Advancement of Languages, Education, and Communities (CALEC) is a nonprofit organization focused on promoting multilingualism, empowering multilingual families, and fostering cross-cultural understanding. The Center's mission is in alignment with the United Nations' Sustainable Development Goals. Our mission is to establish language as a critical life skill, by developing and implementing bilingual education programs, promoting diversity, reducing inequality, and helping to provide quality education. Our programs seek to protect world cultural heritage and support teachers, authors, and families by providing the knowledge and resources to create vibrant multilingual communities.

The specific objectives and purpose of our organization are:

- To develop and implement education programs that promote multilingualism and cross-cultural understanding, and establish an inclusive and equitable quality education, including internship and leadership training. [SDG # 4, Quality Education]

- To publish and distribute resources, including research papers, books, and case studies that seek to empower and promote the social, economic, and political inclusion of all, with a focus on language education and cultural diversity, equity, and inclusion. [SDG # 10, Reduced Inequalities]

- To help build sustainable cities and communities and support teachers, authors, researchers, and families in the advancement of multilingualism and cross-cultural understanding through collaborative tools for linguistic communities. [SDG # 11, Sustainable Cities and Communities]
- To foster strong global partnerships and cooperation, and mobilize resources across borders, to participate in events and activities that promote language education through knowledge sharing and coaching, empowering parents, and teachers, and building multilingual societies. [SDG # 17, Partnerships for the Goals]

SOME GOOD REASONS TO SUPPORT US

Your donation helps:

- develop our publishing and translation activities so that more languages are represented.
- provide access to our online book platform to daycare centers, schools, and cultural centers in underserved areas.
- support local and sustainable action in favor of education and multilingualism.
- implement projects that advance dual-language education
- organize workshops for parents, conferences with large audiences, meet-the-author chats, and talks with experts in multilingualism.

DONATE ONLINE

For all your questions, contact our team by email at contact@calec.org or donate online on our website:

www.calec.org

www.ingramcontent.com/pod-product-compliance
Lightning Source LLC
Chambersburg PA
CBHW040302170426
43194CB00021B/2862